IMAGES
of America

BLECKLEY COUNTY

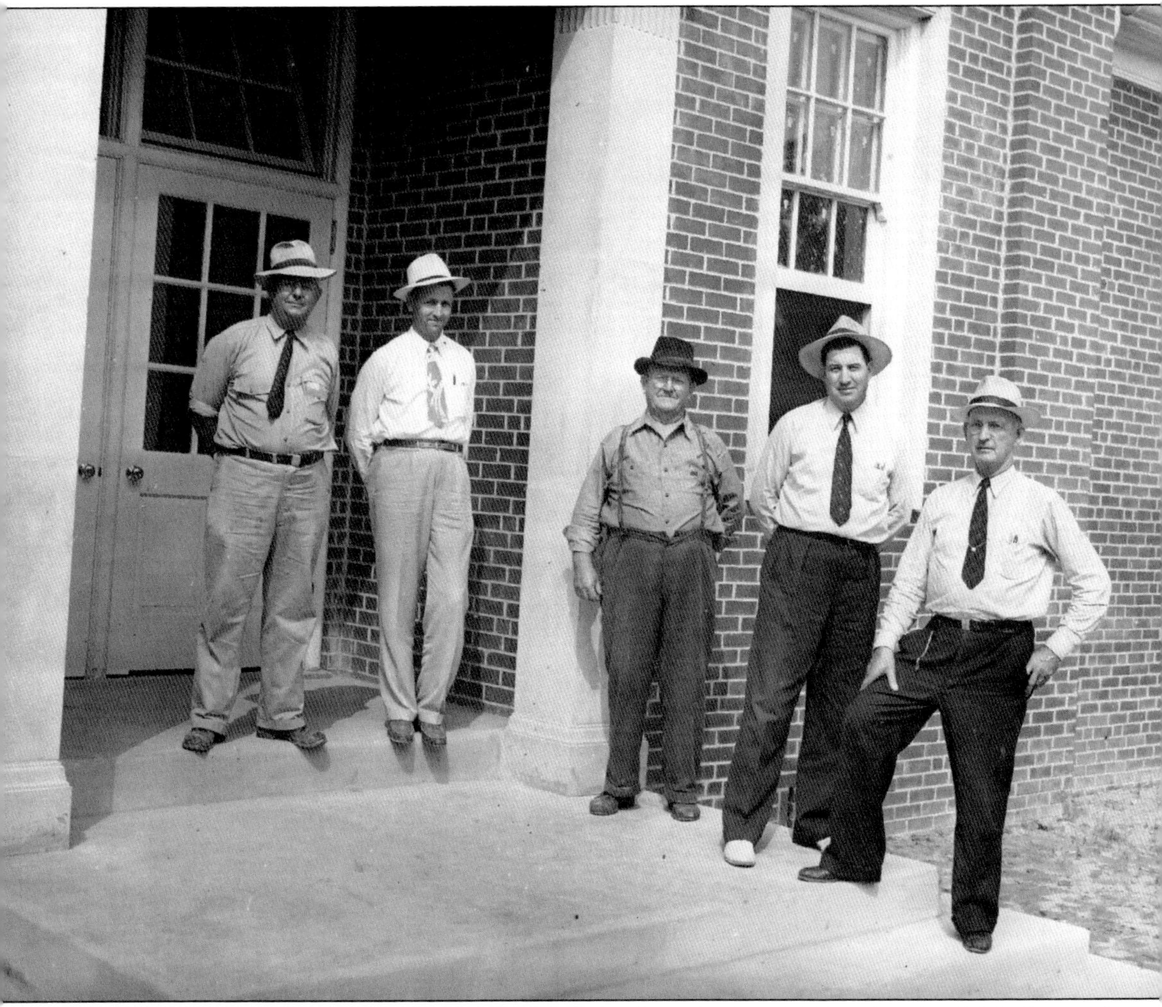

On the Cover: The Cochran Elementary School was built in 1940 under the WPA. Pictured, from left to right, are A. A. Yelvington (construction superintendent), Mr. Johnson (WPA official), J. E. "Bud Ed" Hinson (foreman), Mr. Ragan (WPA official), and I. A. "Gus" Poole (mayor of Cochran). Today this building is the Cochran Police Department. (Photograph by Clyde Hill. Courtesy of Anne Hill Porter and Layne Greene.)

IMAGES
of America

BLECKLEY COUNTY

William Lonnie Barlow

ARCADIA
PUBLISHING

ISBN 978-0-7385-8591-8

Published by Arcadia Publishing
Charleston SC, Chicago IL, Portsmouth NH, San Francisco CA

Printed in the United States of America

Library of Congress Control Number: 2009941998

For all general information contact Arcadia Publishing at:
Telephone 843-853-2070
Fax 843-853-0044
E-mail sales@arcadiapublishing.com
For customer service and orders:
Toll-Free 1-888-313-2665

Visit us on the Internet at www.arcadiapublishing.com

This book is dedicated to the churches of Bleckley County, from whom we have derived a "sweet, sweet spirit in this place" and from whom "we shall know that we have been redeemed when we shall leave this place." ("Sweet, Sweet Spirit" by Doris Akers. Courtesy of Manna Music, Inc.)

Contents

ACKNOWLEDGMENTS

Cochran has always been a community of sharing, compassionate people. During her years as a realtor, Jerri Tuck made pictures of all houses and businesses she listed for sale. When she closed Tuck Realty, she gave these to me, and they provide the basis of the "Homes" chapter of this book. Jack Lucas, principal of Bleckley County Schools, provided pictures of county schools, as well as most of the church pictures. Dr. Peyton Williams, State of Georgia assistant school superintendent, provided the Thompson Street School picture. Mattie Lee Baxley provided pictures of the John Mullis home and the Barkwell Thompson family. Deborah Ellis and Lola Harris Ellis helped in so many ways with pictures of the Cochran First United Methodist Church and First Baptist Church of Cochran. George A. Noah spent a lifetime photographing Cochran, and his wife, Bertha Noah, and daughter, Leanna Noah, made valuable contributions. Layne Greene and Anne Hill Porter provided photographs of her brother, Clyde Hill, who made interesting photographs of Cochran during his long life. Paul Robards, MLS, provided pictures of Middle Georgia College. Mary Anne Barlow was invaluable in proofreading the entire text. Others who helped with identification, technical information, and photographs are Barney W. Hendricks, Bennett Whipple, Marcia S. Manning, Jane and Robert Wynne, Lilla Lee Purser, James E. Adams, Linda D. Padgett, Charlie Elvis Butler, Carolyn H. Young, Faye Mullis, Joe Meadows, Kathryn D. Fisher (director, Cochran-Bleckley Chamber of Commerce), and James Davidson (Edgewater Media). To all of these, I express my thanks and sincere appreciation. Unless otherwise noted, the images in the book are from my collection.

INTRODUCTION

The building of the Macon and Brunswick Railroad resulted in the small rural town of Dykesboro being incorporated in 1868 as Cochran. With north/south rail traffic bringing resources and people to the new town, Cochran was able to develop by exporting agricultural crops of cotton and corn. Naval stores were exported by trail and ship. The need for lumber also increased the shipment of timber from vast virgin forests. When the east/west railroad connected Cochran with Dublin and Hawkinsville, further economic development allowed the shipment of goods, cotton, and timber by water along the Ocmulgee River and the Oconee River to coastal ports at Darien and Brunswick for shipment to New England and overseas to Liverpool. Cochran continued to grow and entered the 20th century with new homes, downtown sidewalks, running water, and telephone service. Education was always promoted by the City of Cochran and by the area churches. Ebeneezer Academy, founded in 1884, became Middle Georgia College in 1931 and is a unit of the University System of Georgia. In addition to the excellent local schools, Middle Georgia College promotes Cochran, Bleckley County, and the middle Georgia area as a learning center for students beyond high school.

Bleckley County was created by the State of Georgia in 1912; the jail and courthouse were built in 1913, and the county courthouse began operation on January 1, 1914. The local economy was good, and World War I brought a period of prosperity due to the need for food and fiber. The 1920s brought the devastation of the agricultural cotton economy due to the bowl weevil. The Great Depression brought loss of economic wealth and financial hardships, which were not relieved until 1941 when the Japanese attack on Pearl Harbor brought another national war effort for food and fiber. The rural economy of the state of Georgia was best suited to fill this need with cotton, corn, and timber, leaving Cochran almost daily to aid the war effort. The post–World War II era has been the greatest period of peace and prosperity for America in general and for Cochran and Bleckley County in particular.

Home, church, school, and government are the four institutions on which society is built. Home and church are created by God. Government and schools are instituted by men. All four are necessary for a group of people to live in a community, work together, marry, raise families, and enjoy what Thomas Jefferson called "the pursuit of happiness" in this life. In Cochran and Bleckley County, Georgia, these four have, for 160 years, provided a wonderful place to live, which is worthy of remembrance in the pages of this book.

One

Government

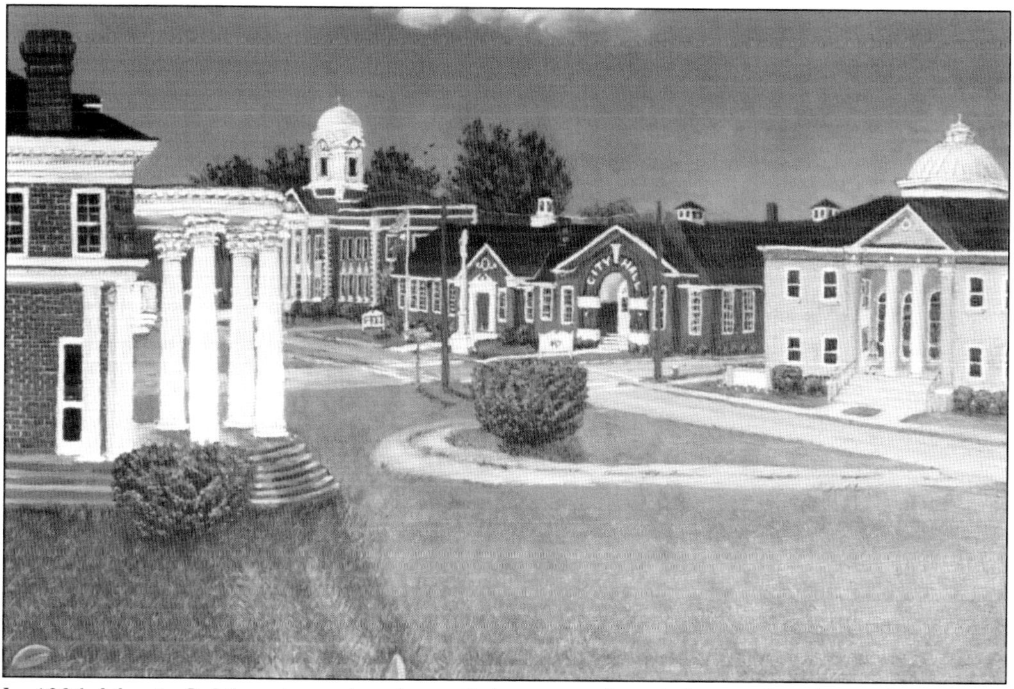

In 1996, Marcia S. Manning painted an oil depicting, from left to right, the Mullis-Howard home (built in 1910), the Bleckley County Courthouse (built in 1913), the Cochran Elementary School (1940–1964), the city hall and city auditorium (built in 1928), and First Baptist Church (built in 1917).

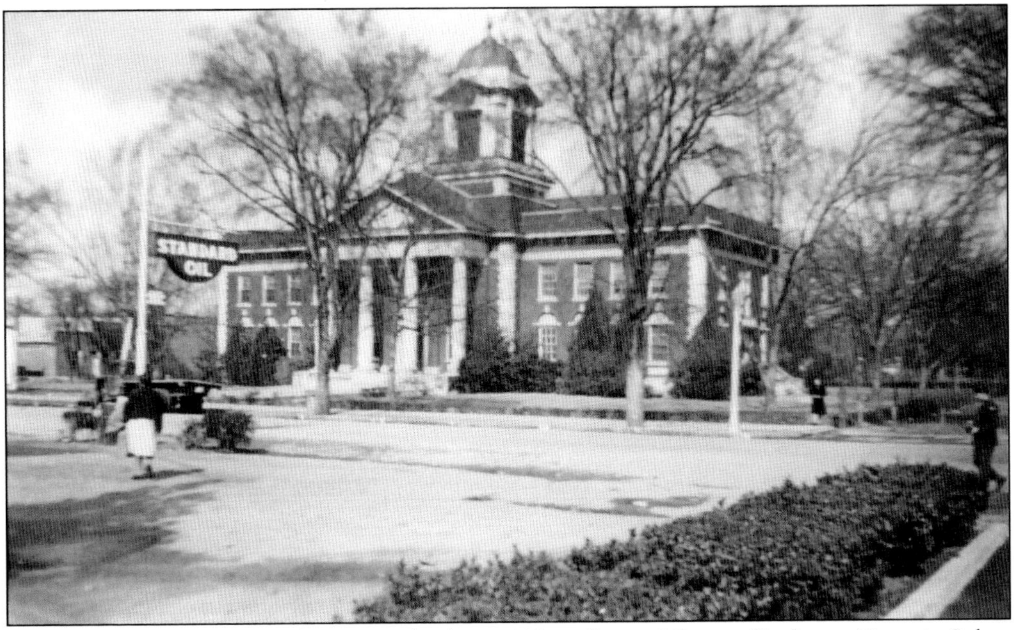

The Bleckley County Courthouse was built in 1913 on Second Street, Cochran, Georgia. It has continuously served Bleckley County to the present time. The photograph above, taken in 1941, shows the Toombs Kimborough Standard Oil service station sign across the street. (Courtesy of Cochran-Bleckley Chamber of Commerce, Kathryn Davis Fisher, director.)

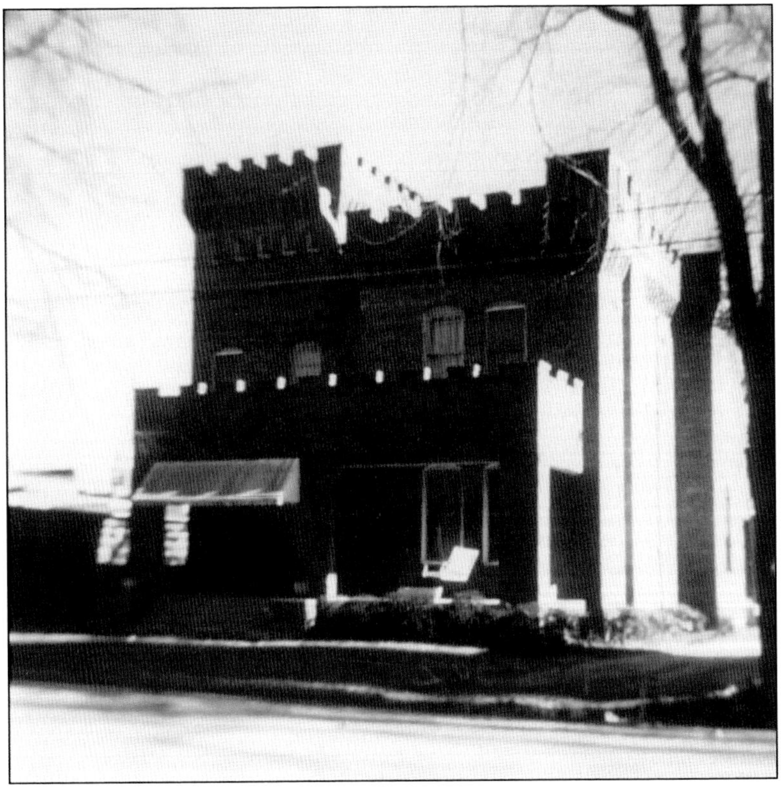
The Bleckley County Jail was built on Beech Street in Cochran in 1913. It was the home of the sheriff until the 1950s and housed all prisoners until 2007, when a new law enforcement center was built.

The original Cochran City Hall (1869–1928) was housed in this building on First Street (the present location of the State Farm Insurance office).

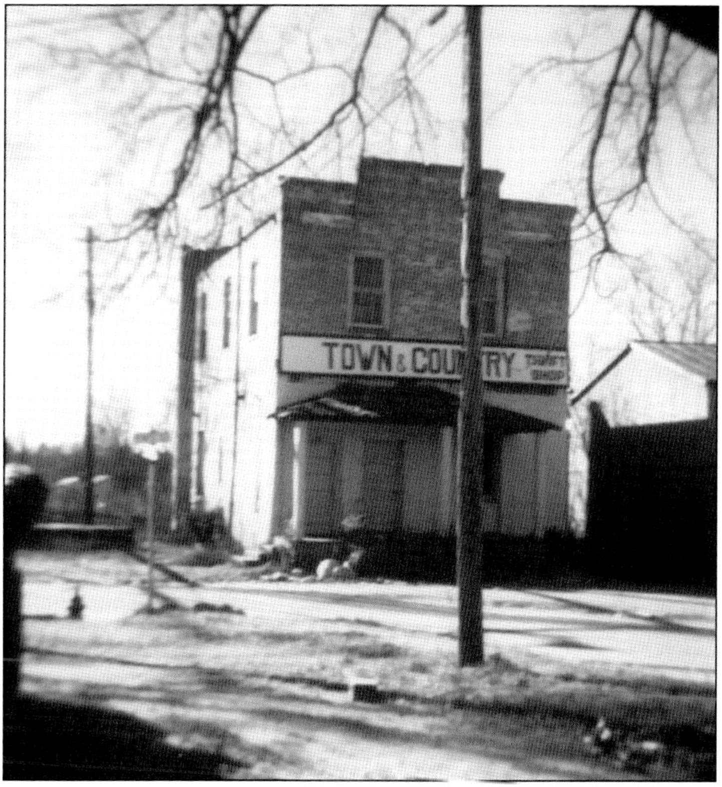

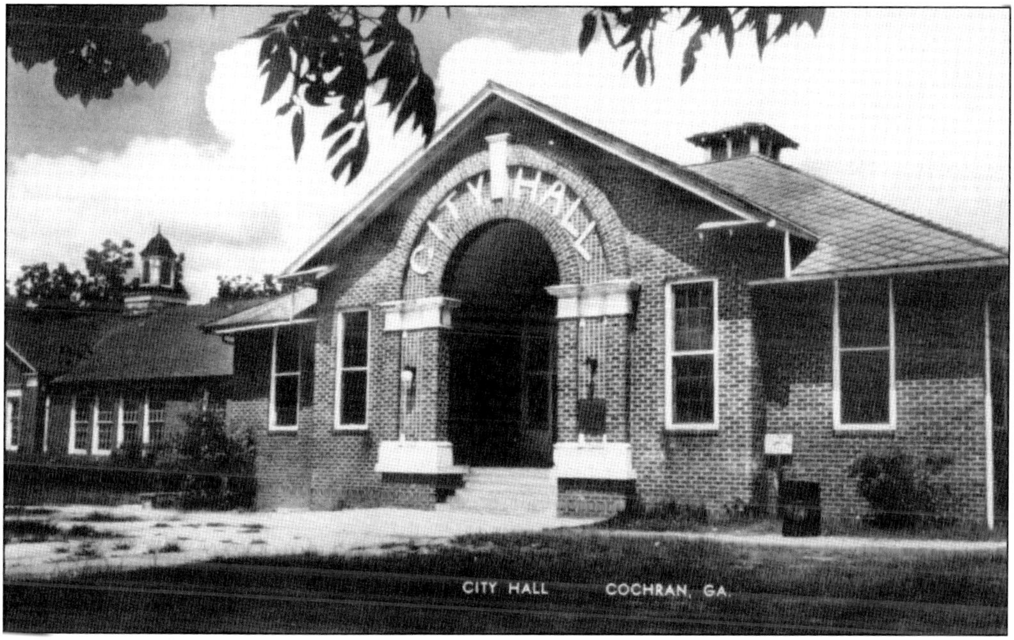

The second Cochran City Hall (1929–1964), on Second Street, was built together with the Cochran City Auditorium. It joined the Cochran High School in the rear. In 1940, Cochran Elementary School was added on Second Street. Today the old city hall portion is the Cochran-Bleckley Chamber of Commerce, and the school portion is the Cochran Police Department.

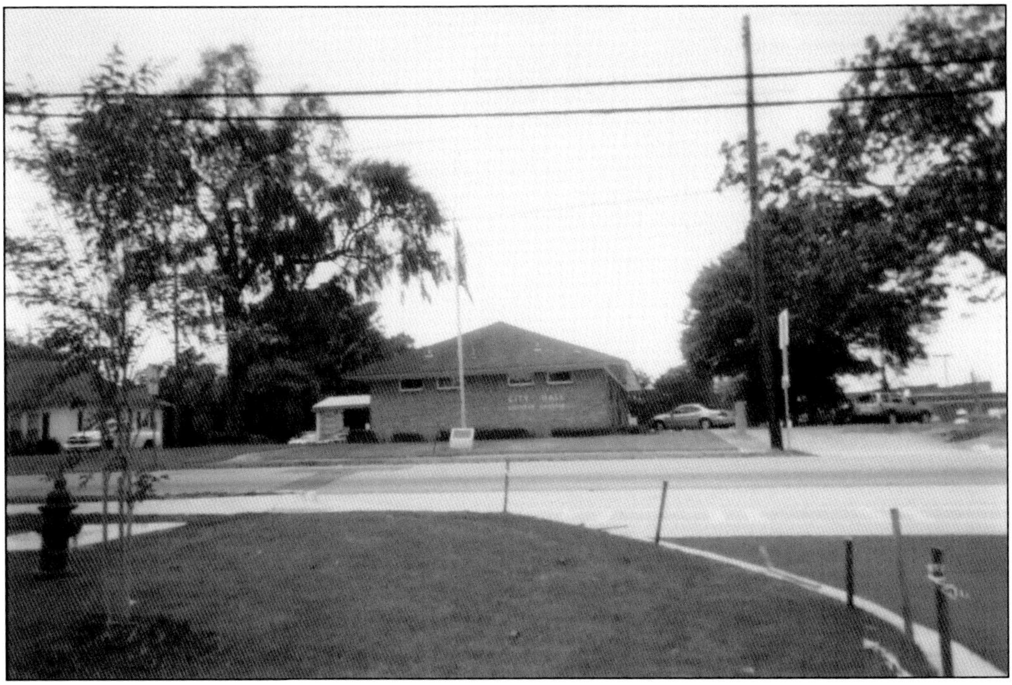

The present city hall building (constructed in 1964) on Dykes Street was originally built for a physician's office.

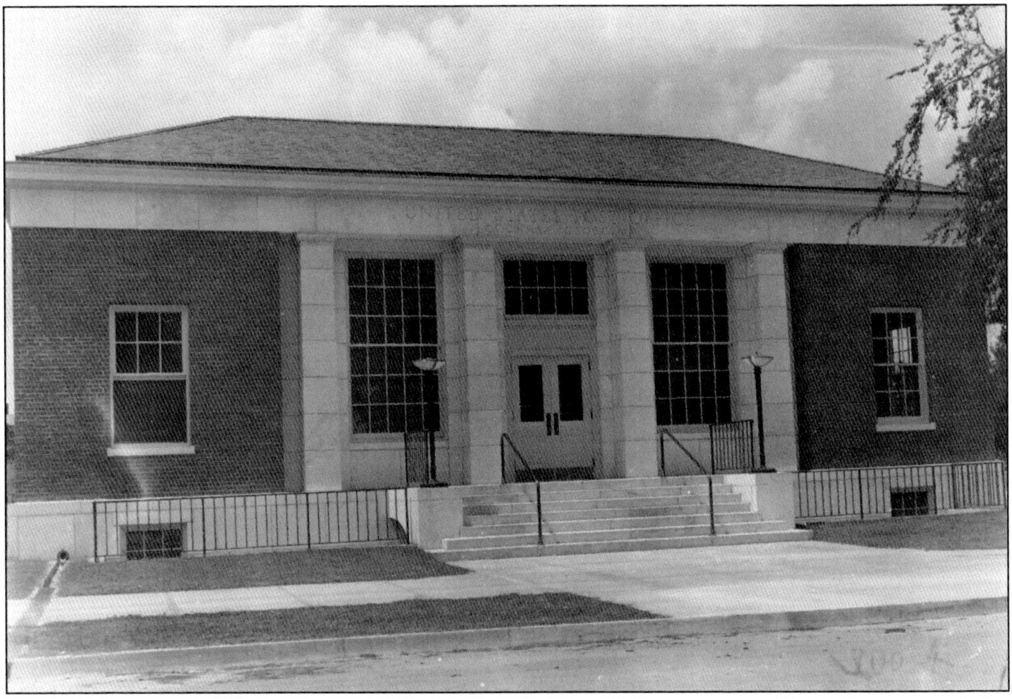

The Cochran Post Office on Second Street was built in 1937 at a cost of $75,000 as part of the local WPA programs. It is the only post office in Bleckley County, Georgia. (Photograph by Clyde Hill. Courtesy of Anne Hill Porter.)

Judge Arthur Cochran, the man for whom Cochran was named in 1868, was president of the Macon and Brunswick Railroad when the railroad track was laid in 1867 connecting middle Georgia with the Atlantic coast. (Courtesy of Emmett H. Hall, great-grandson of Judge Cochran.)

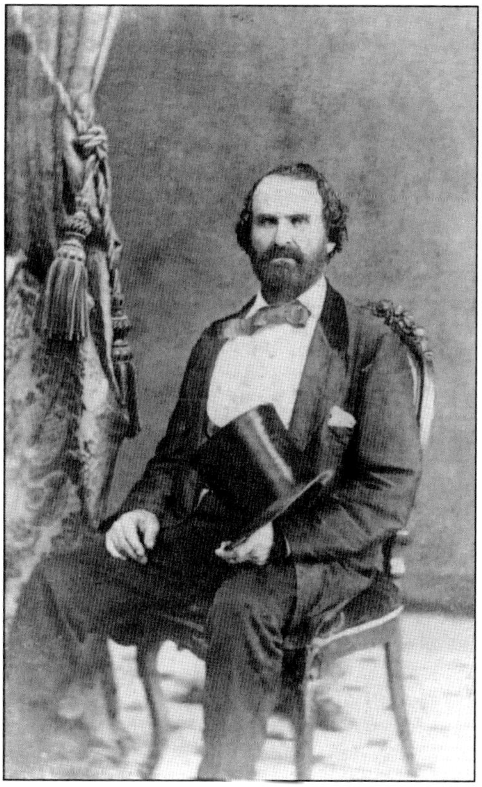

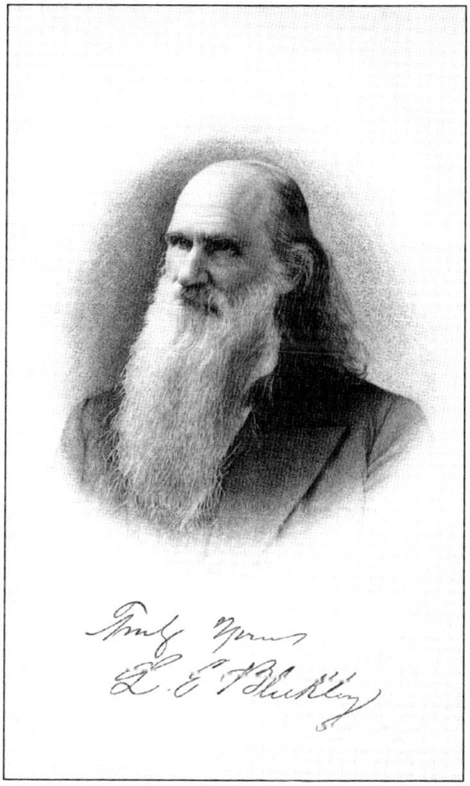

Judge Logan E. Bleckley, the man for whom Bleckley County was named in 1912, was the first chief justice of the Georgia Supreme Court. (Courtesy of State Bar of Georgia.)

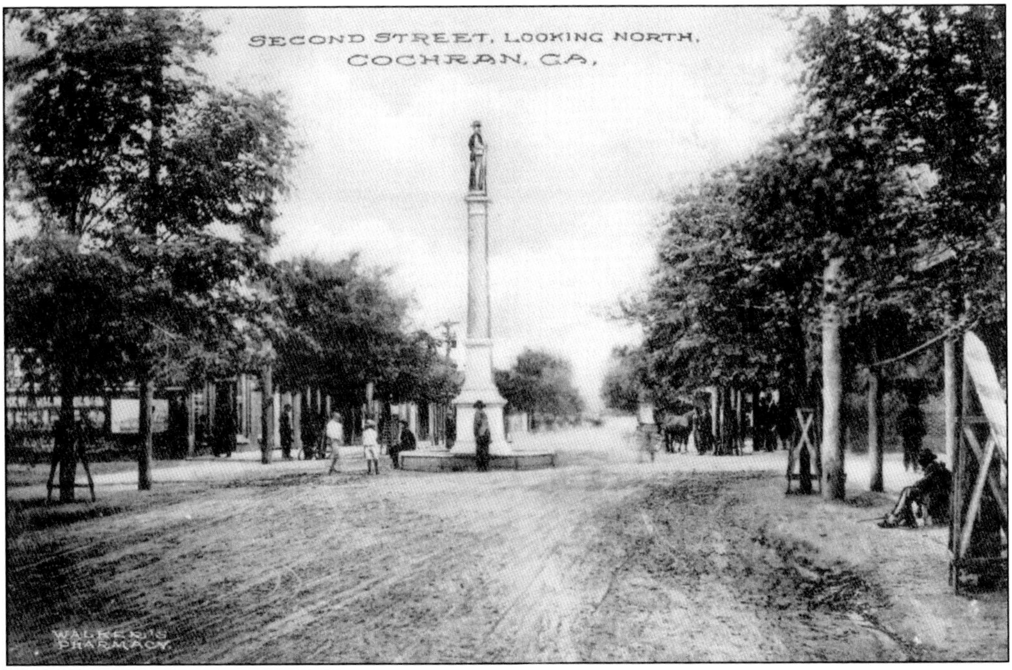

The downtown Confederate monument was erected at the intersection of Beech Street and Second Street in 1910 with the Confederate soldier facing north up Beech Street. The monument was moved in 1937 to the schoolyard across from the post office when Second Street was paved. (Courtesy of Mrs. Ralph W. Abney Jr. [Brenda].)

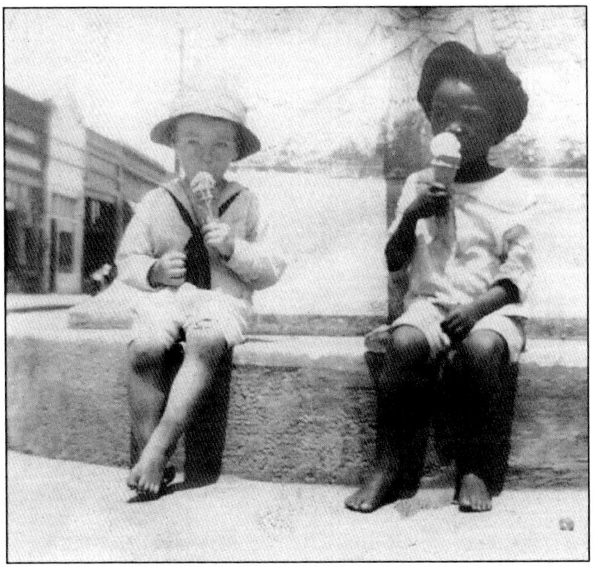

The original Confederate monument had a water supply pouring from cannons on each of four sides to water horses when wagons were a primary means of travel. There was a rail around the pool of water. Lee Howard Jr. (left) eats his chocolate ice cream cone while his friend, Joe Williams (right), eats his vanilla ice cream cone while sitting on the rail of Cochran's Confederate memorial in its original location at the intersection of Beech Street and Second Street, Cochran, Georgia, about 1925. The ice cream cones were purchased at McVay's Drugs nearby. (Courtesy of Virginia Harris Howard and Deborah L. Ellis.)

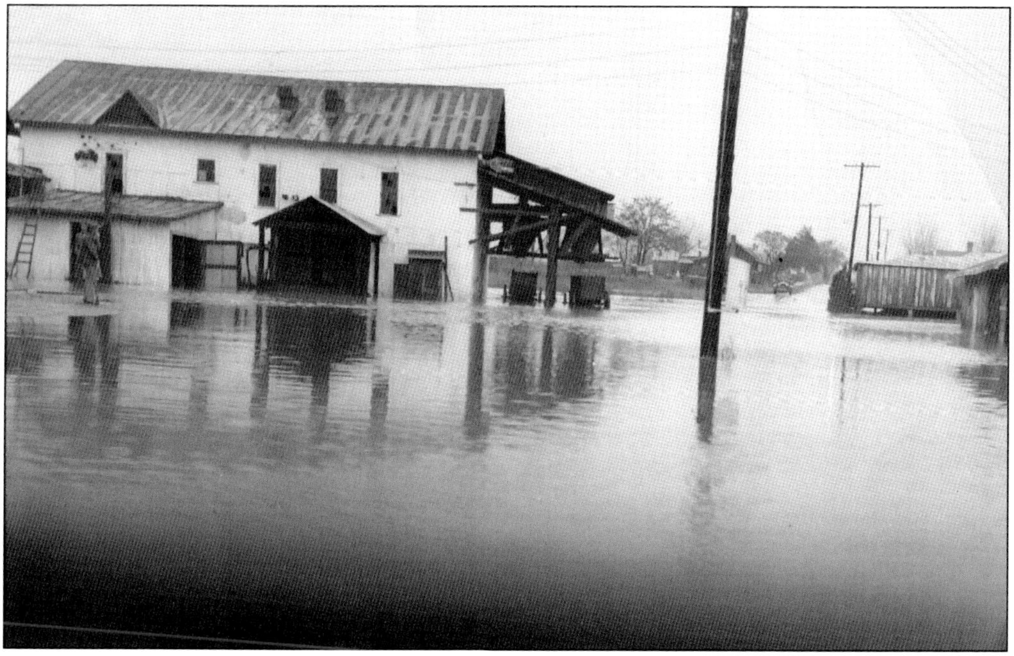

Established in 1901, the Cochran Oil Mill and Ginnery on Ash Street sustained a major flood in the 1930s, when the "Big Ditch" system of Cochran flooded. The "Big Ditches" were built in the early 1900s to drain the town and prevent malaria outbreaks from mosquitoes.

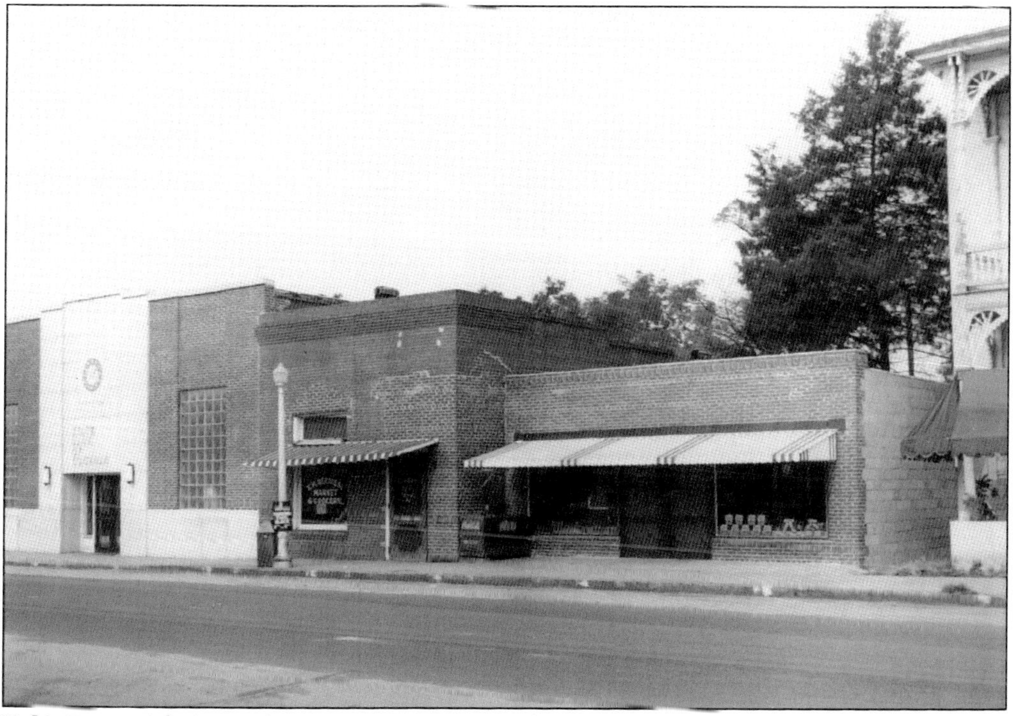

T. H. Reeves Market and Grocery was on Second Street in Cochran between the State Bank of Cochran (1921–1973) and the Cochran Hotel (right), which later became Calvin's Cleaners. (Photograph by George A. Noah. Courtesy of Bertha Noah and Leanna Noah.)

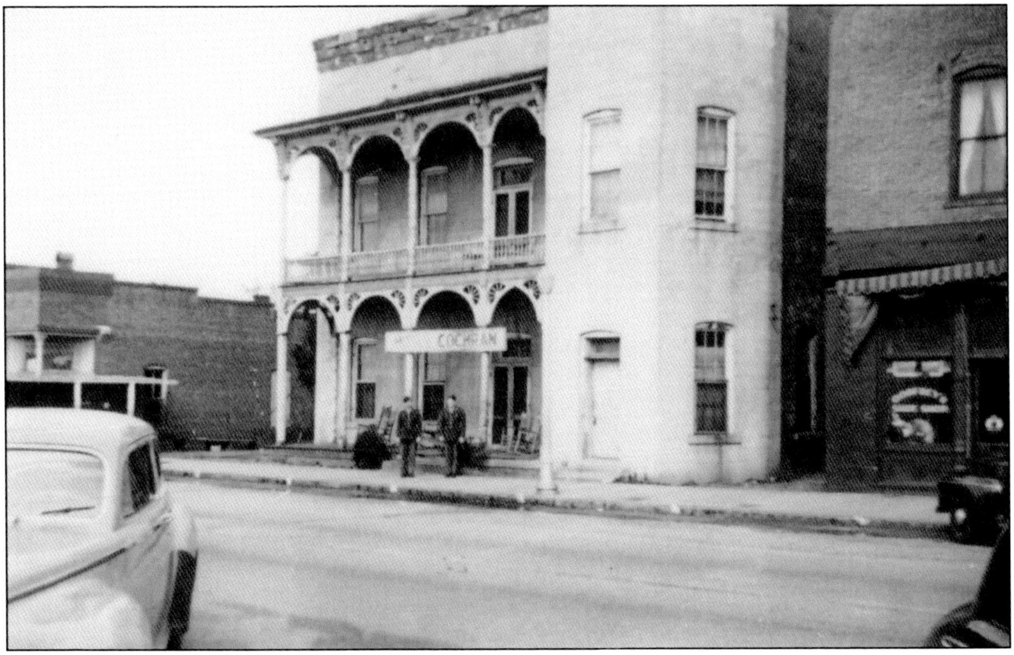

The hotel in Cochran was built in 1898 and remained open until the 1960s. After the death of Thomas Howard Reeves, his wife, Emmie Hendricks Reeves, sold the hotel property to Mr. and Mrs. A. T. "Red" Dykes (Bert), who operated R&B Appliances and R&B Jewelry until 2006. Note the window of Godfrey's Shoe Shop next door. (Courtesy of Cochran-Bleckley Chamber of Commerce, Kathryn Davis Fisher, director.)

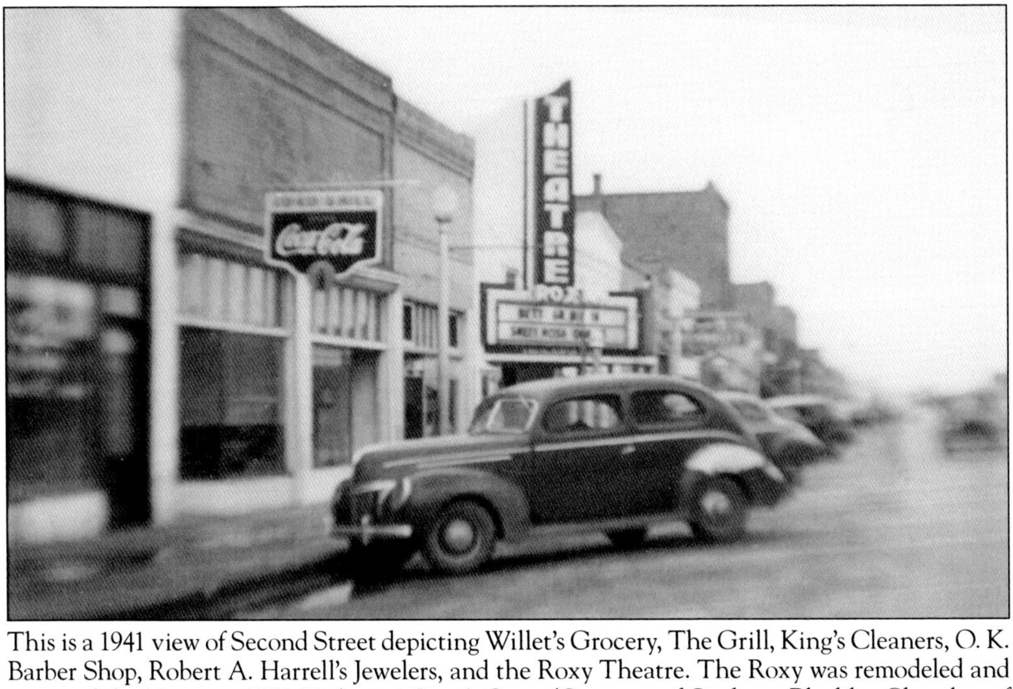

This is a 1941 view of Second Street depicting Willet's Grocery, The Grill, King's Cleaners, O. K. Barber Shop, Robert A. Harrell's Jewelers, and the Roxy Theatre. The Roxy was remodeled and renamed the Vogue in 1953. Today it is Jerry's Gym. (Courtesy of Cochran-Bleckley Chamber of Commerce, Kathryn Davis Fisher, director.)

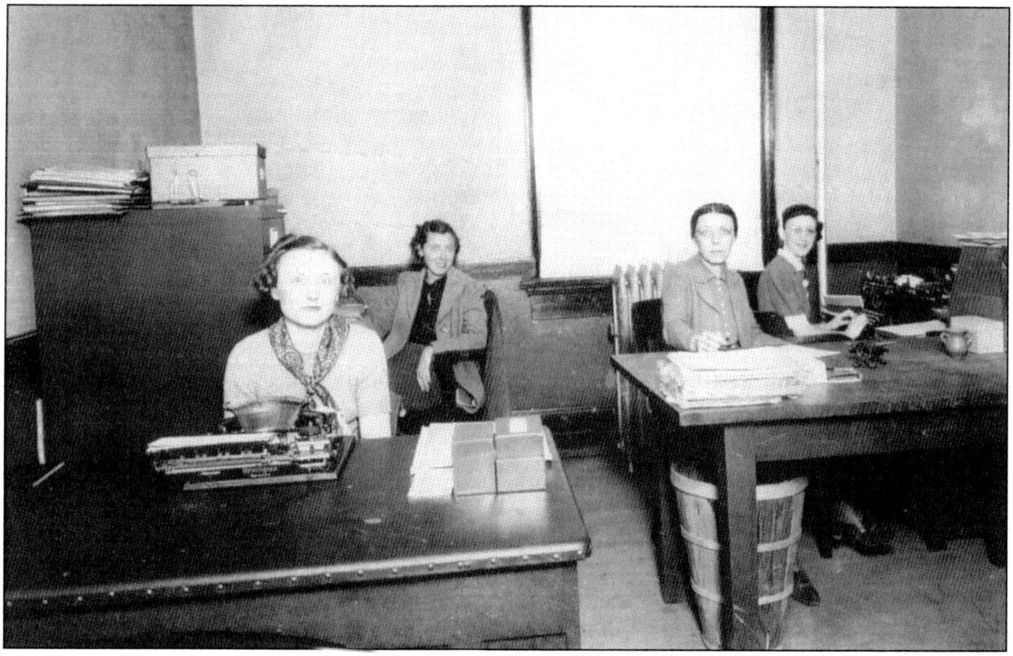

A small room contained the original welfare department of Bleckley County, Georgia, in 1936. The courthouse office was directed by Margaret Cook Hendricks, assisted by Sarah Anne Peacock Roth with typist Ollene Graham Shelton and file clerk Kathryn Norris Roland. Today this is the office of J. David Brown, tax commissioner of Bleckley County, Georgia. (Courtesy of Barney Wilson Hendricks Jr.)

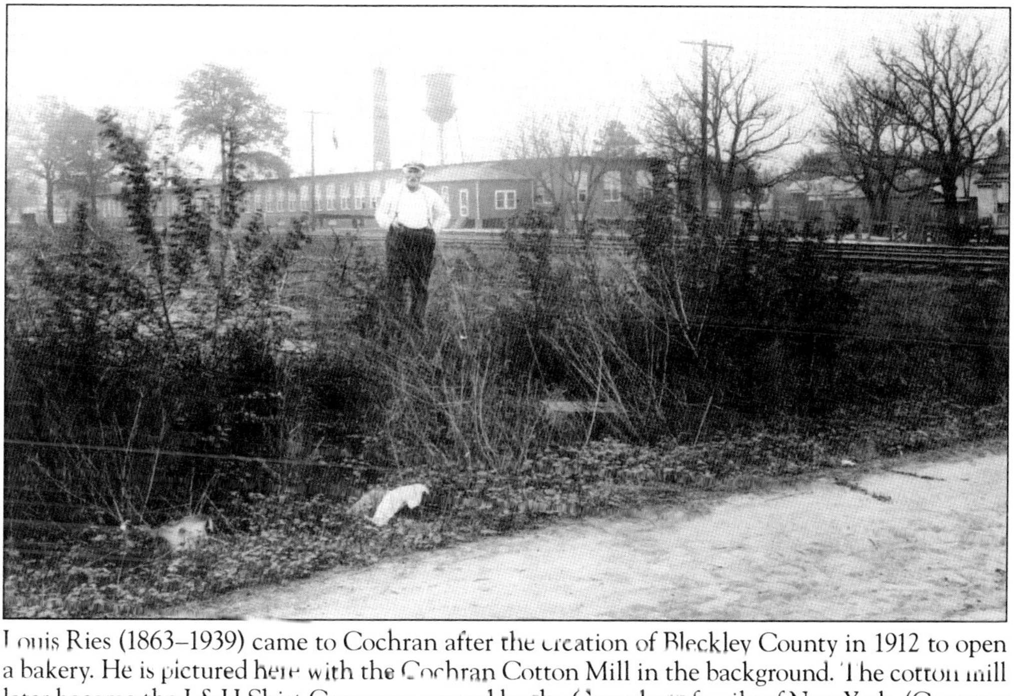

Louis Ries (1863–1939) came to Cochran after the creation of Bleckley County in 1912 to open a bakery. He is pictured here with the Cochran Cotton Mill in the background. The cotton mill later became the L&H Shirt Company, owned by the Greenberg family of New York. (Courtesy of Virginia Stephens Smith.)

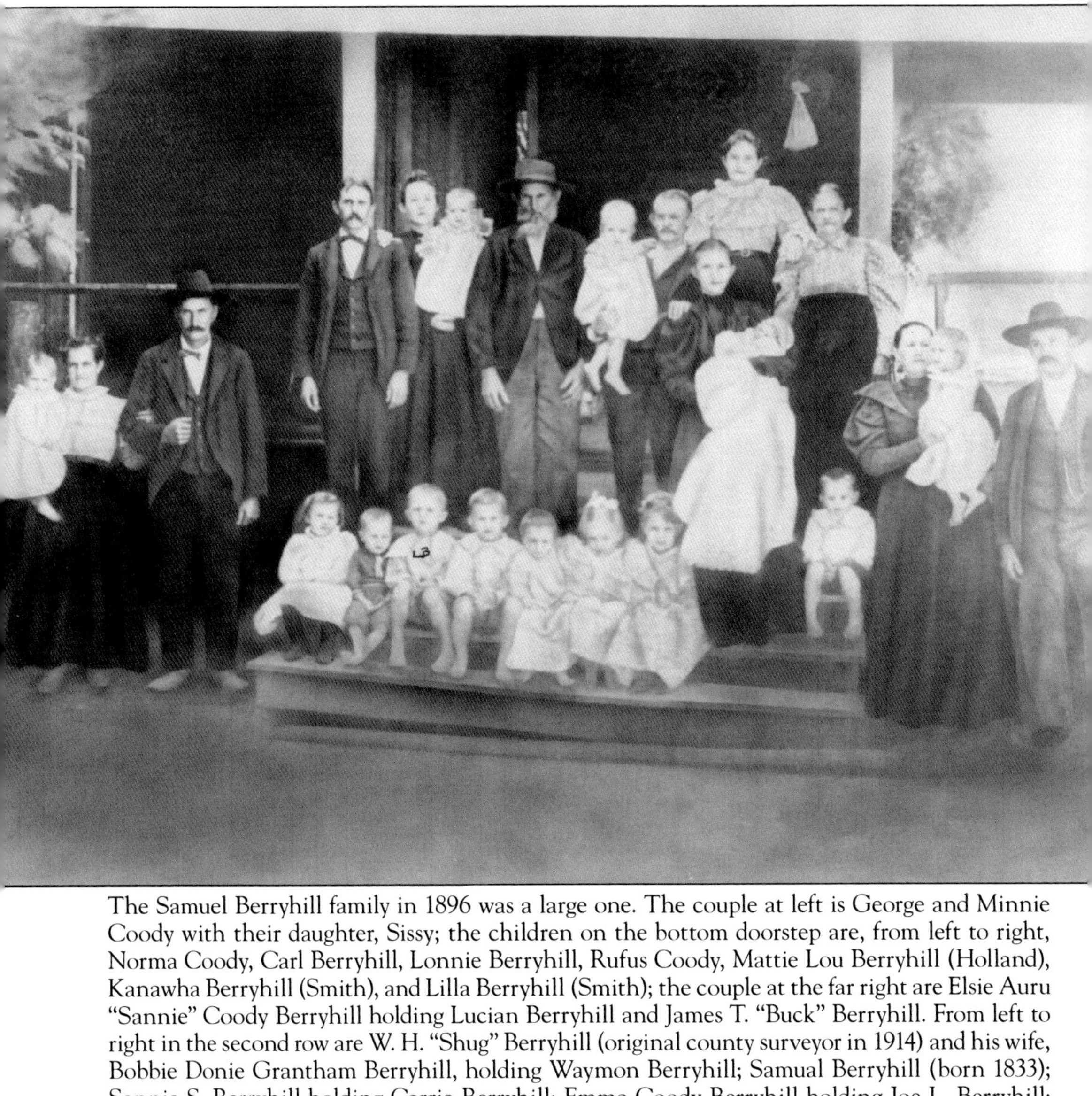

The Samuel Berryhill family in 1896 was a large one. The couple at left is George and Minnie Coody with their daughter, Sissy; the children on the bottom doorstep are, from left to right, Norma Coody, Carl Berryhill, Lonnie Berryhill, Rufus Coody, Mattie Lou Berryhill (Holland), Kanawha Berryhill (Smith), and Lilla Berryhill (Smith); the couple at the far right are Elsie Auru "Sannie" Coody Berryhill holding Lucian Berryhill and James T. "Buck" Berryhill. From left to right in the second row are W. H. "Shug" Berryhill (original county surveyor in 1914) and his wife, Bobbie Donie Grantham Berryhill, holding Waymon Berryhill; Samual Berryhill (born 1833); Sannie S. Berryhill holding Carrie Berryhill; Emma Coody Berryhill holding Joe L. Berryhill; Laura Antionette Sauls Berryhill (wife of Samuel); and Jim Sam Berryhill (seated). Dora Berryhill stands in the third row. (Courtesy of Nettie Smith Godfrey.)

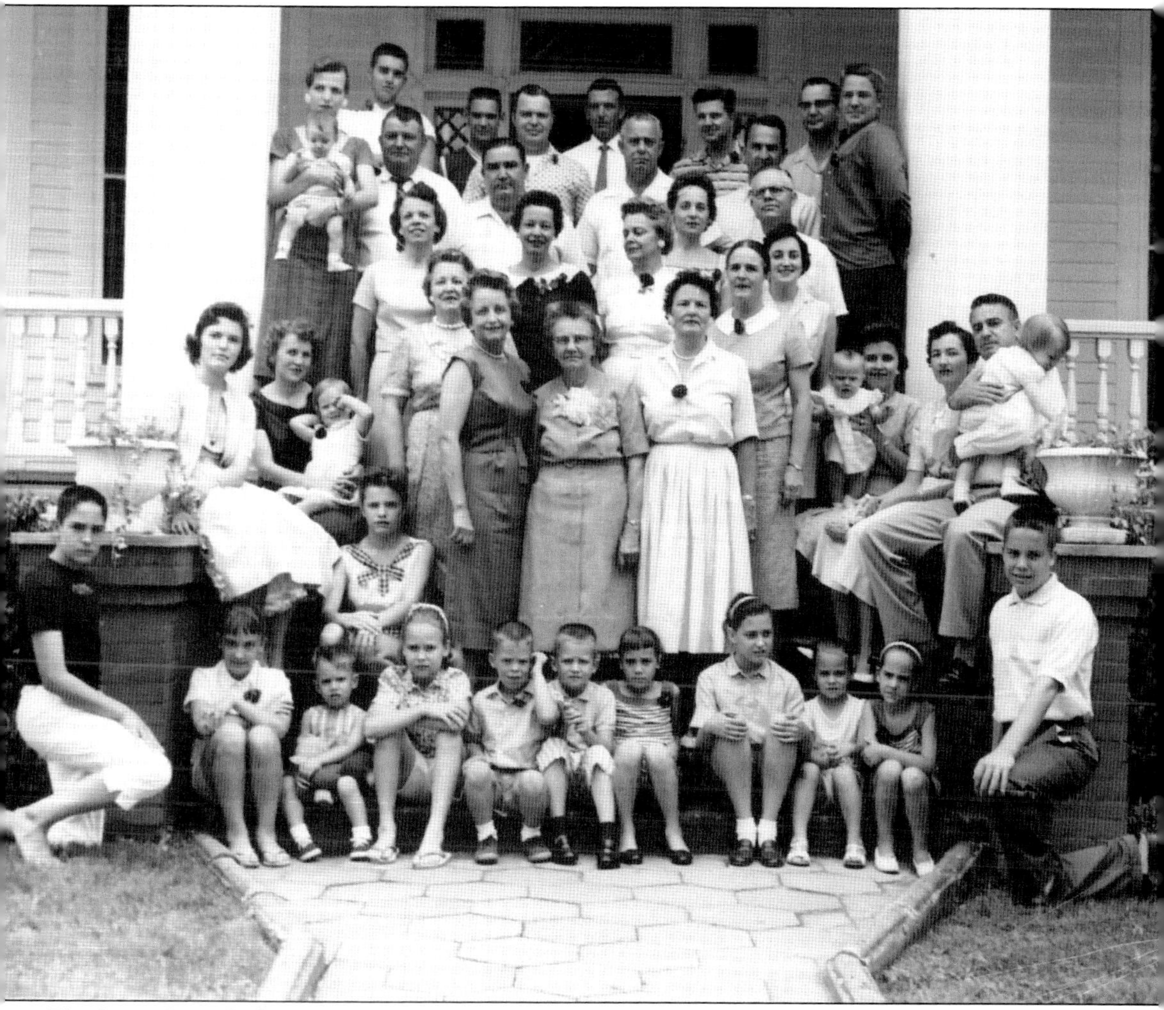

The James Perry Dykes and Susie Petty Dykes family met in March 1959 for Susie's birthday of Susie. From left to right are (first row) William E. "Bill" Dykes, Janet Dykes, John Turner, Donna Turner, Perry Dykes, Brad Turner, Carol Dykes, Beckey Robinson, Marie Turner, Kathy Dykes, Johnny Coffee; (on the left buttress) Susan Dykes Holmes, Vickey Finney, and baby Nancy; (on the right buttress) Sue Marie holding baby Sally Turner, Quinion Dykes, and David W. Dykes Sr. holding baby Julie Dykes; (seated on the second doorstep) Dianne Dykes; (second row) Marie Dykes Thompson, Susie Petty Dykes (with corsage), and Pearl Dykes Hemphill; (third row) Nellie Dykes Roberts, Evelyn Finney, and Linda Dykes Padgett; (fourth row) Corrine Dykes, Marjorie Dykes Coffee, and Hurly Dykes; (fifth row) Martha Eleanor Bryan holding baby Tina Bryan, Sam Dykes, James M. Dykes, Roy Dykes, Kathryn Crooms Dykes, and Grady Coffee; (sixth row) Jimmy Finney, Jim Dykes, Jerry Dykes, Sidney Bryan, Ralph Finney Jr., Wyndell Dykes, and John M. Dykes. (Photograph by George A. Noah; courtesy of Bertha H. Noah and Leanna Noah.)

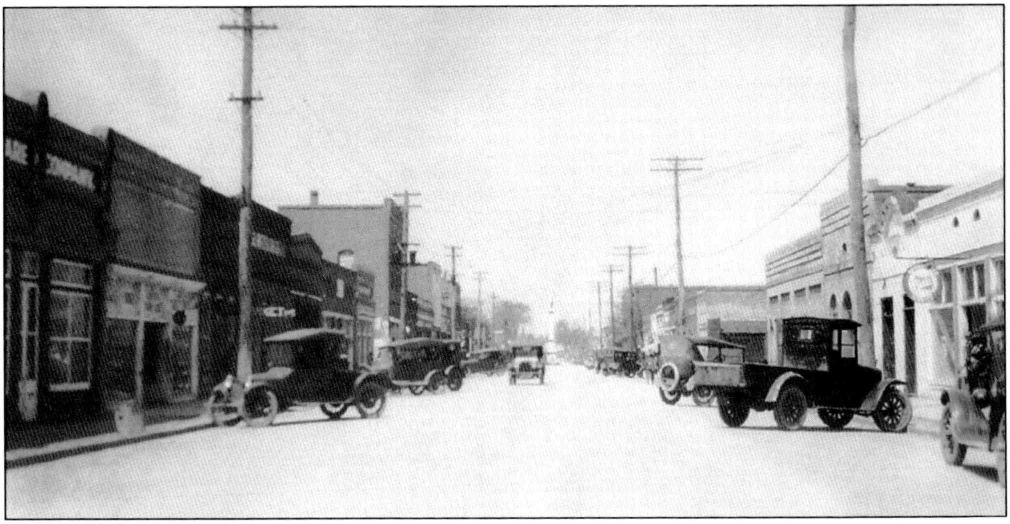

A 1923 scene of Second Street, Cochran, Georgia, shows the dirt street of the day. (Photograph by Virginia Speer Harris.)

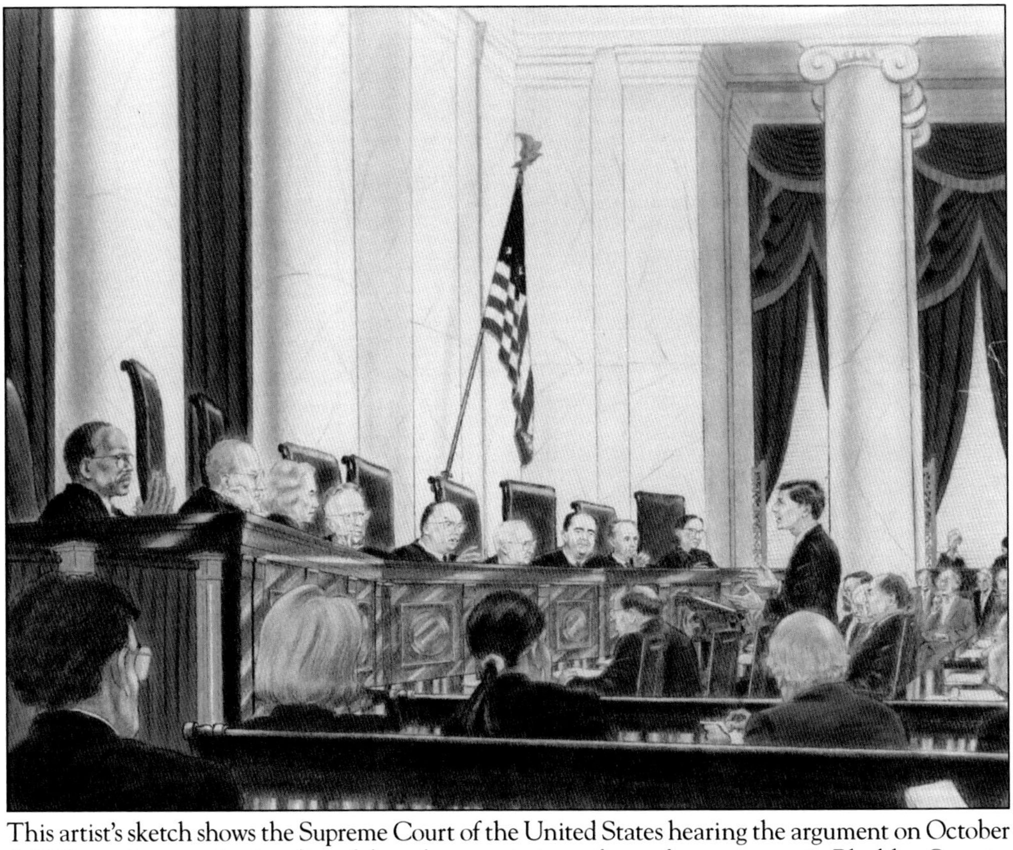

This artist's sketch shows the Supreme Court of the United States hearing the argument on October 5, 1993, on the constitutionality of the sole commissioner form of government in Bleckley County, Georgia. The court ruled five to four in favor of Bleckley County. Seated at the appellant's table is Lonnie Barlow; standing to argue the case is R. Napier Murphy; and seated at the appellee's table are Chris Coats and Laughlin McDonald.

Two

SCHOOLS

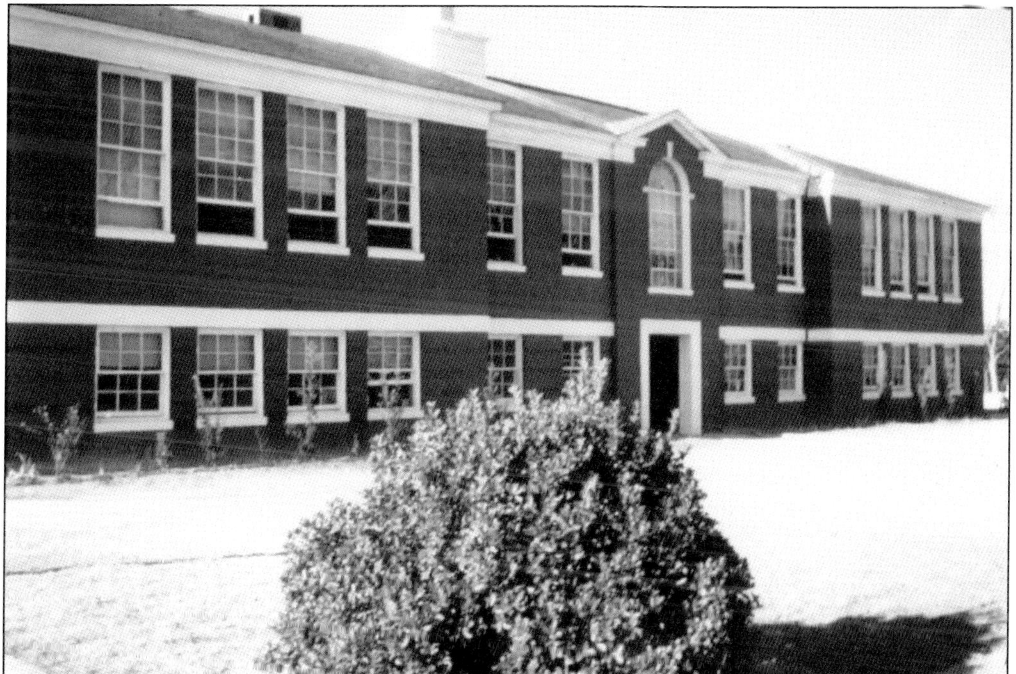

Cochran High School's class building and library were built on Third Street and served the community until the 1960s.

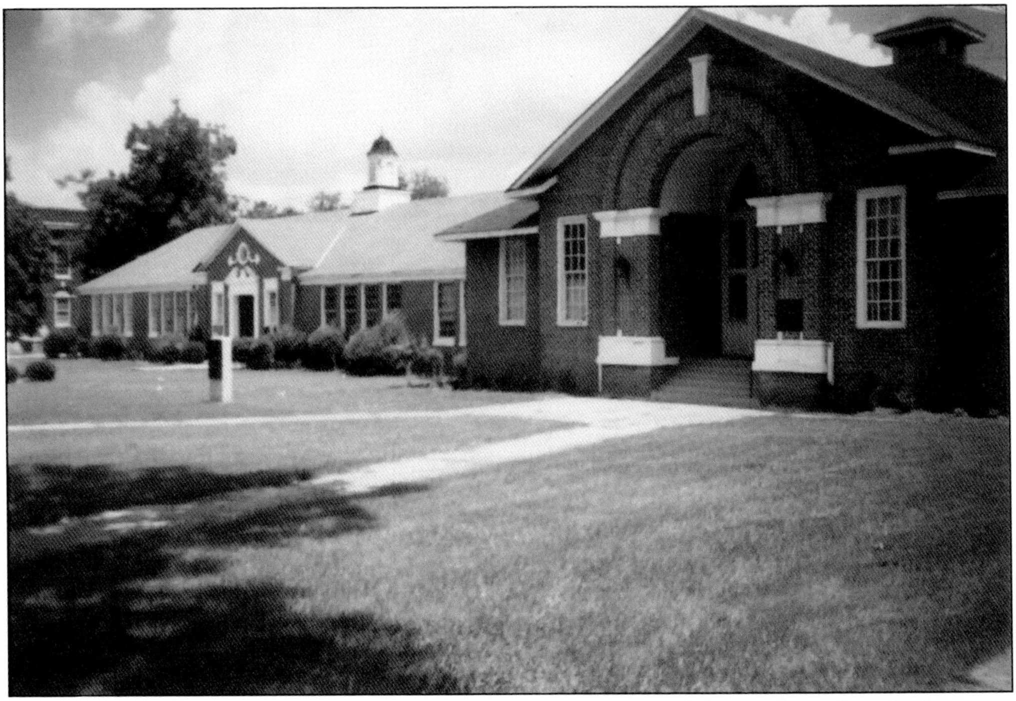

Cochran Elementary School, built in 1940 under the WPA, joined the Cochran City Auditorium, where graduations were held until the early 1960s.

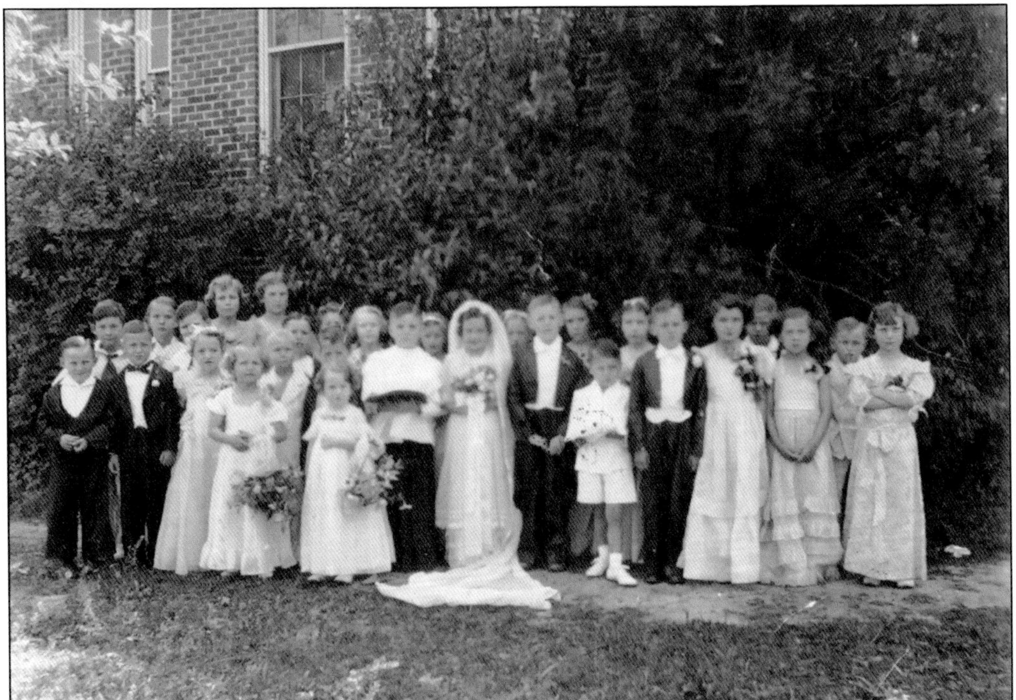

In the 1937 Tom Thumb wedding held in the Cochran City Auditorium, the two little girls holding flower baskets are Sara Ann Harrell (right) and Nola Jean Barlow.

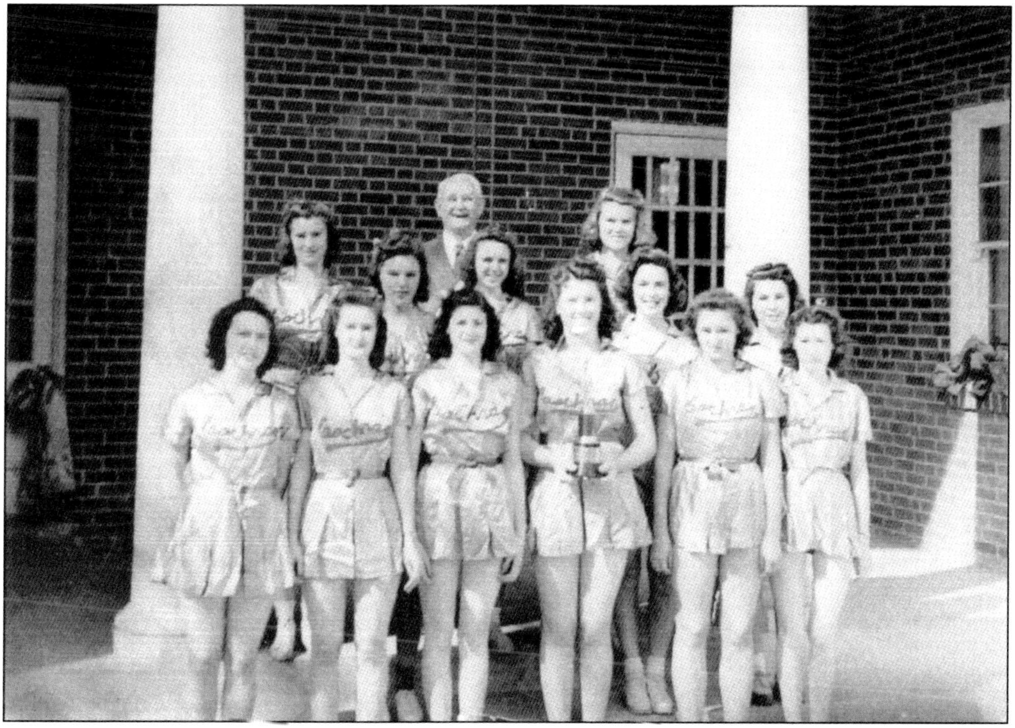

In 1942, Cochran High School girls won the basketball trophy. From left to right are (first row) Jackie Stokes Harper, Rubye NeSmith Erwin, Lilla Lee Lyles Purser, Frances Collier Perkins, Ellen Dykes Cote, and Polly Jones; (second row) Dollie Lucas Grinstead, Wynelle Skipper, Elizabeth Willingham, Carolyn Collins Smith, and Jewel Lawson NeSmith; (third row) Thomas Malcom Purcell Sr., coach and superintendent of schools, and Inez Collier Ware.

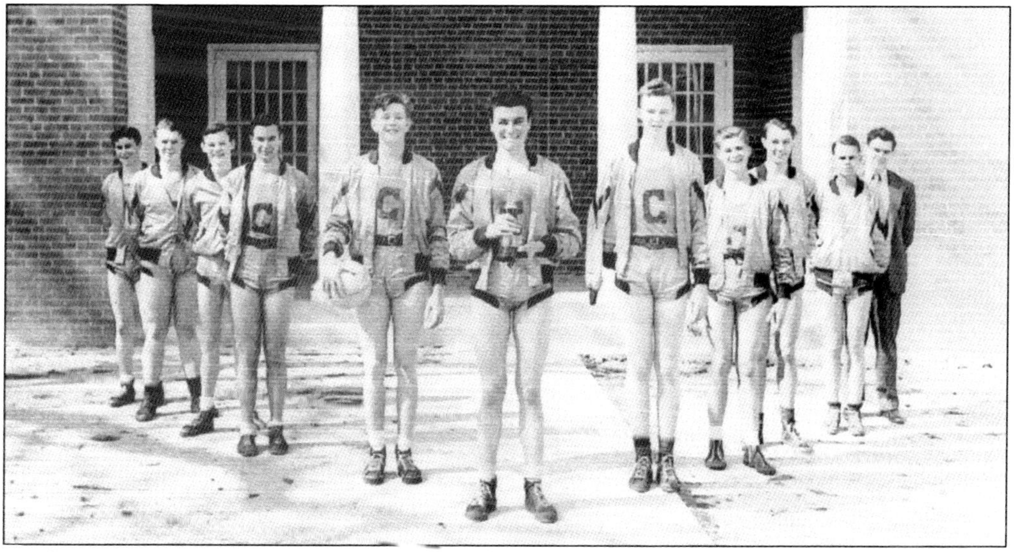

In 1942, Cochran High School boys won the basketball trophy. Pictured, from left to right, are Leonard Coley, Colonel Lucas, Dan Dillashaw, Allie Pace, George "Red" Love, Roy Willard Coley, Kindred H. Thompson, Carlton "Cottie" Wade, Barney Hendricks, Hayward "Hap" Jones, and coach Norman Faircloth.

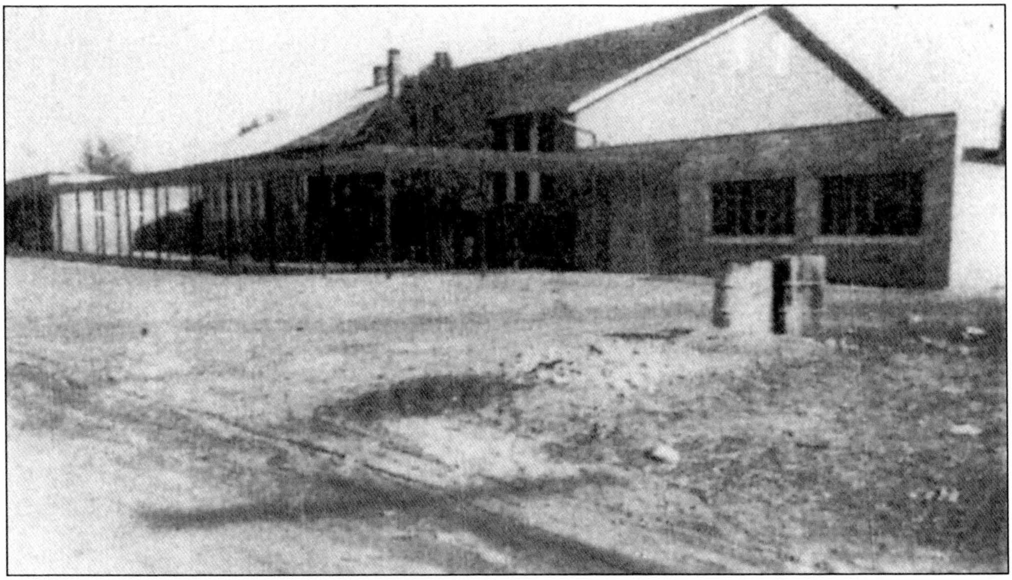

Thompson Street School was part of the Cochran School System until consolidation. (Courtesy of Dr. Peyton Williams, assistant state school superintendent for Georgia.)

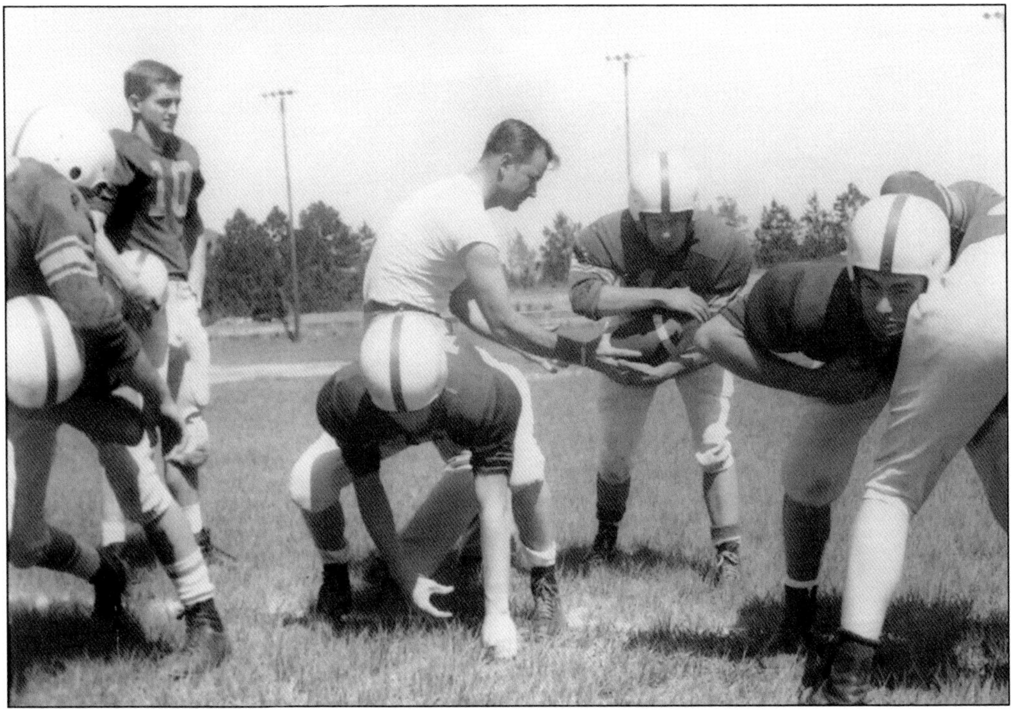

This photograph shows a 1955 football practice at Cochran High School, with coach Shelley Hayes passing the ball to Billy Ray Godfrey, who is guarded by Jerry Rambo as Roy Mullis (left) looks on. Others are Benny Braddy (center), Neal Hill, and Ben Dykes. Billy Ray Godfrey became the only man ever elected as mayor of Cochran and as sole commissioner of Bleckley County. Roy Mullis was clerk of the City of Cochran. (Photograph by George A. Noah; courtesy of Bertha Noah and Leanna Noah.)

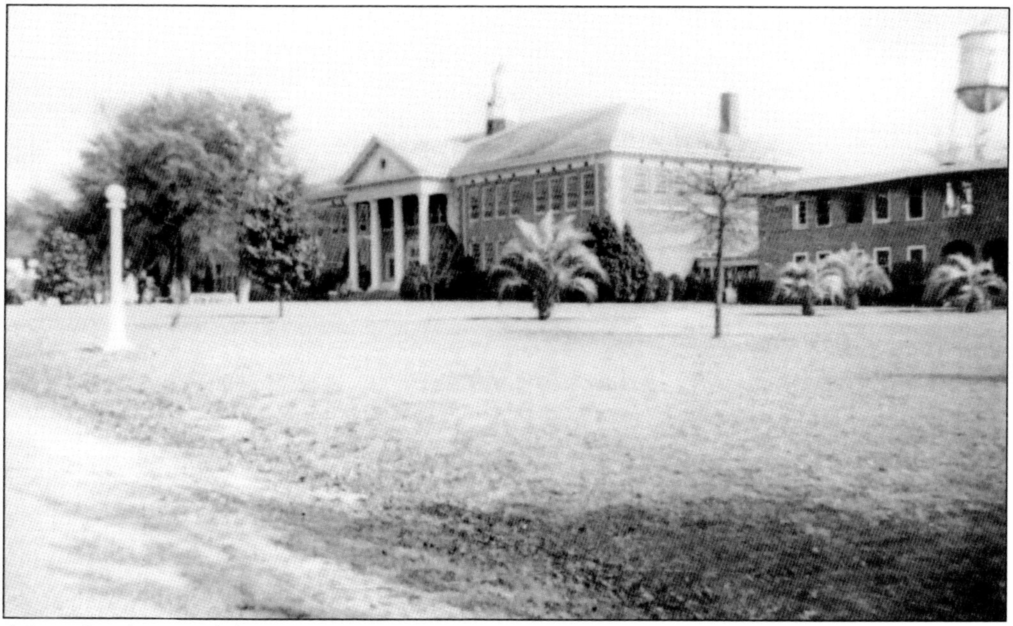

After a fire destroyed the 1884 octagonal building of Middle Georgia College, Walker Auditorium was constructed in 1926 at the college. It was named for Dr. Thomas Duhart Walker Sr., a local physician, farmer, and civic leader who promoted the college as a unit of the University System of Georgia when it became Middle Georgia College in 1931. To the right is Peacock Hall, a boys' dormitory named for Dr. John B. Peacock. (Courtesy of Paul Robards, MLS, Middle Georgia College.)

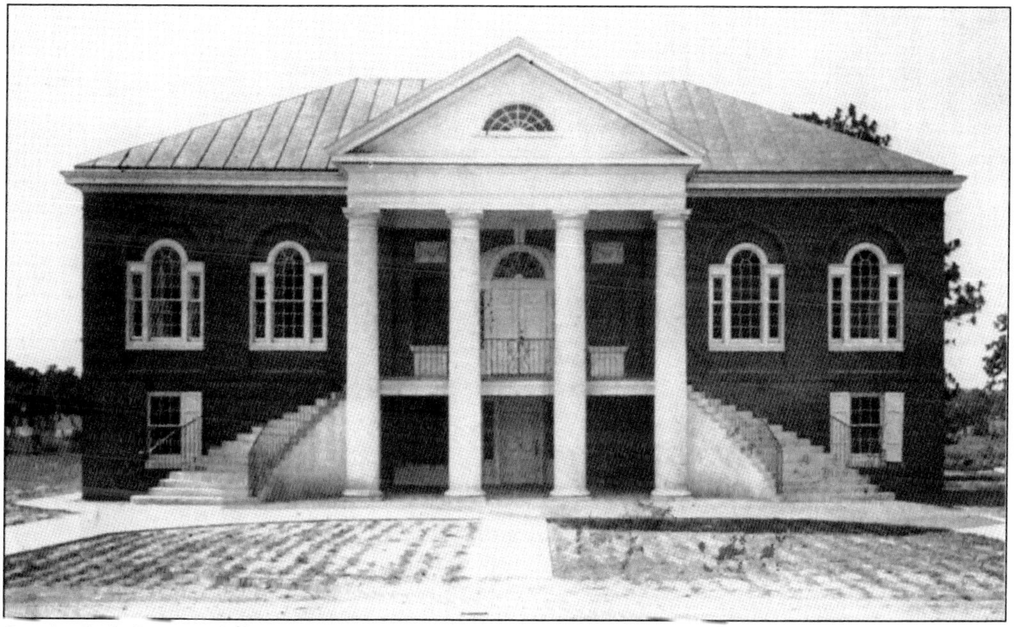

Sanford Hall at Middle Georgia College was built as part of the WPA grants in the 1930s. Originally it housed the library and administrative offices. Today the library is in a separate building. (Courtesy of Paul Robards, MLS, Middle Georgia College.)

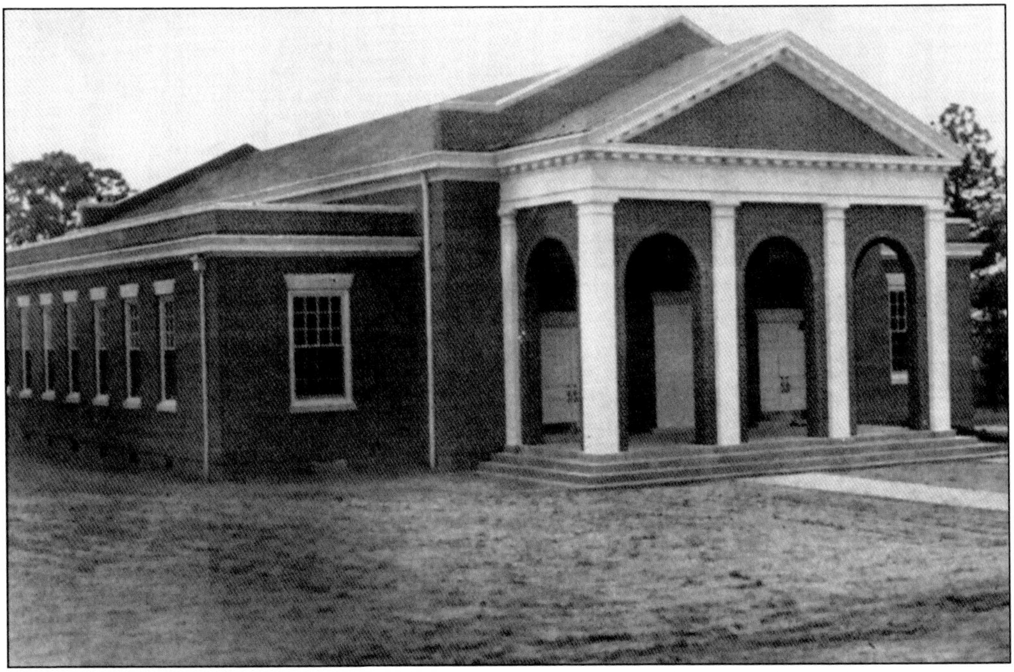

Originally constructed as the dining hall of Middle Georgia College, this building was later known as Memorial Hall. Today it houses classrooms and administrative offices. (Courtesy of Paul Robards, MLS, Middle Georgia College.)

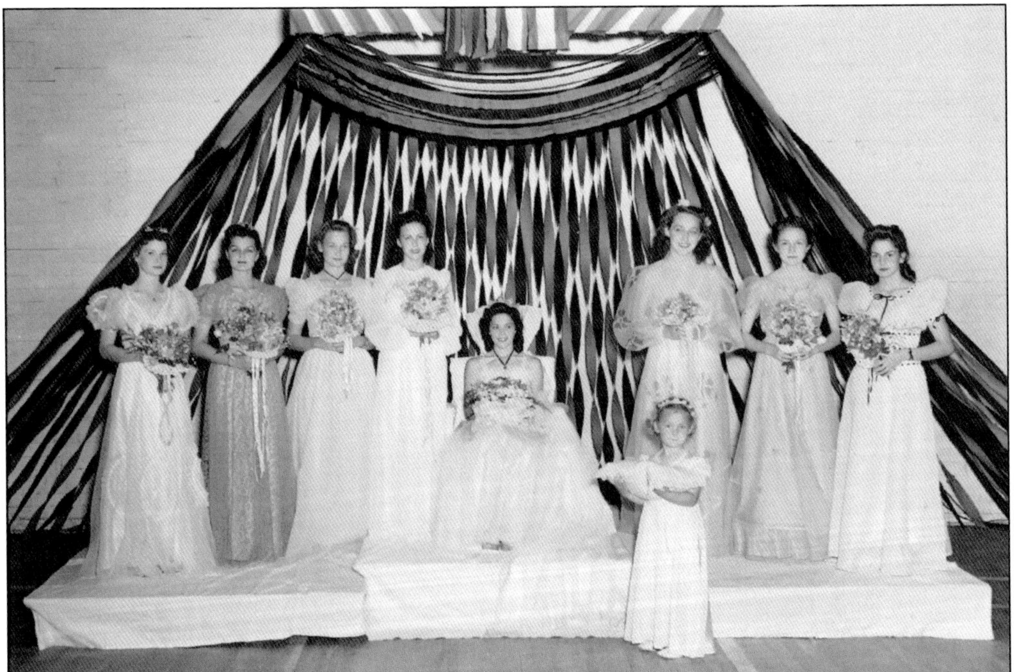

Louise Lyles (seated) was the 1938 Queen of May at Middle Georgia College. The other ladies and the crown bearer are unidentified. Miss Lyles married Richard L. Smith Sr., who was a prominent physician in Cochran for 50 years until his death in 1998.

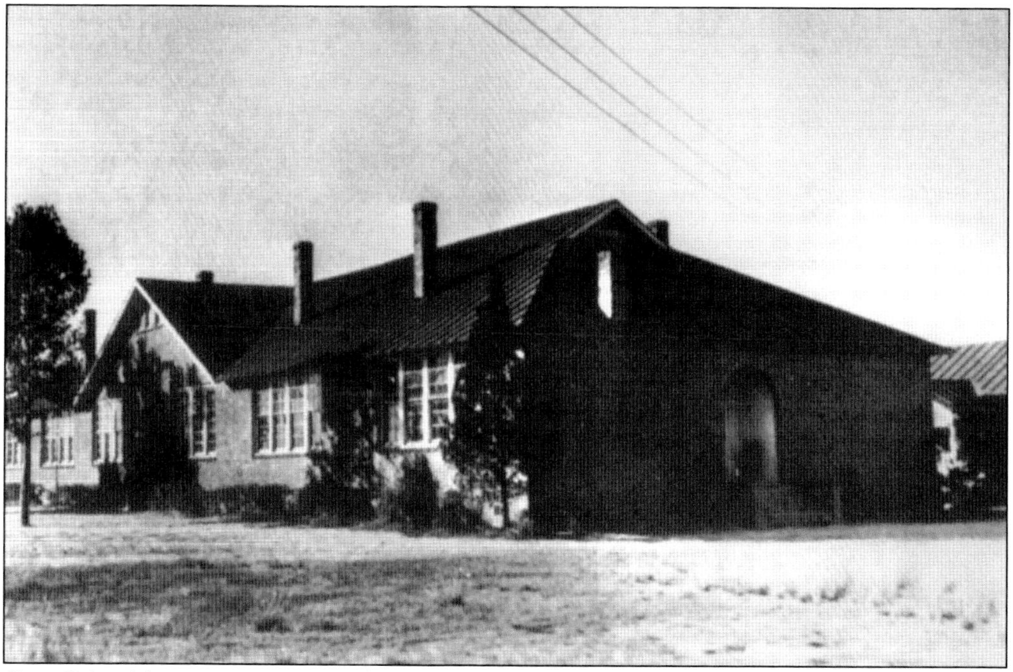

Cary School began operation in the 1800s in a frame building that was replaced with a brick structure in 1929. It closed in 1963, when all Bleckley County elementary schools were consolidated. (Courtesy of Jack Lucas.)

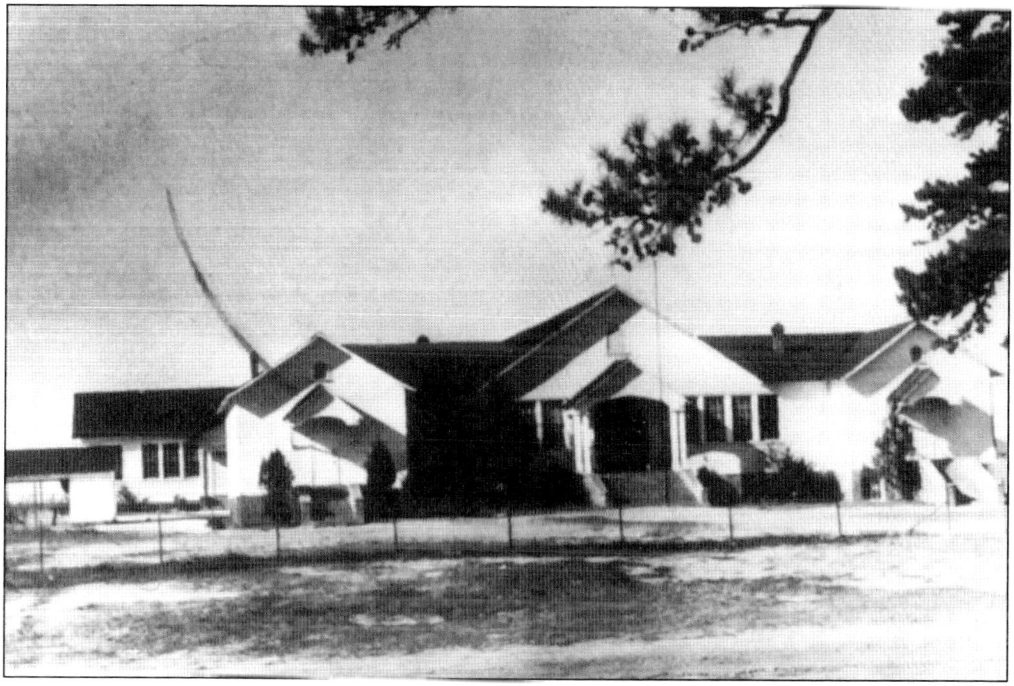

Salem School, located on Georgia Highway 26 across from Salem Baptist Church, began in the late 1850s, and by 1940, it was the largest of the county schools. It closed with the consolidation in 1963. (Courtesy of Jack Lucas.)

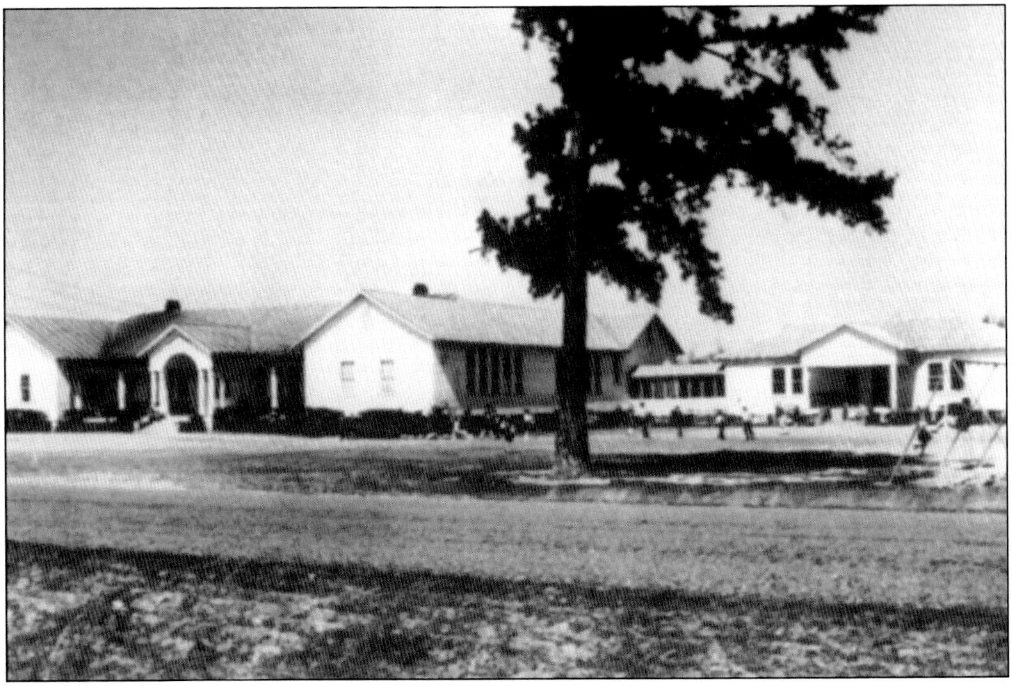

Limestone School opened in September 1932 and was a consolidation of the Davis School (on Chicken Road) and the Smith School (on Limestone Road). Later Sunnyside School (on Georgia Highway 26) became part of Limestone. Limestone closed with the consolidation in 1963. (Courtesy of Jack Lucas.)

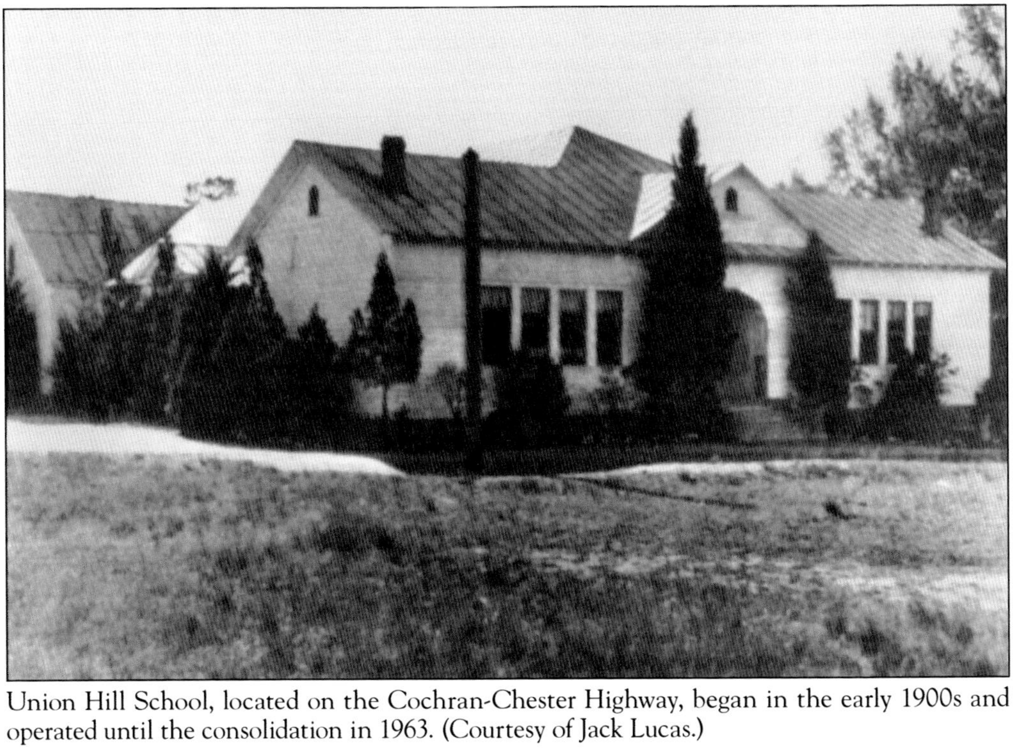

Union Hill School, located on the Cochran-Chester Highway, began in the early 1900s and operated until the consolidation in 1963. (Courtesy of Jack Lucas.)

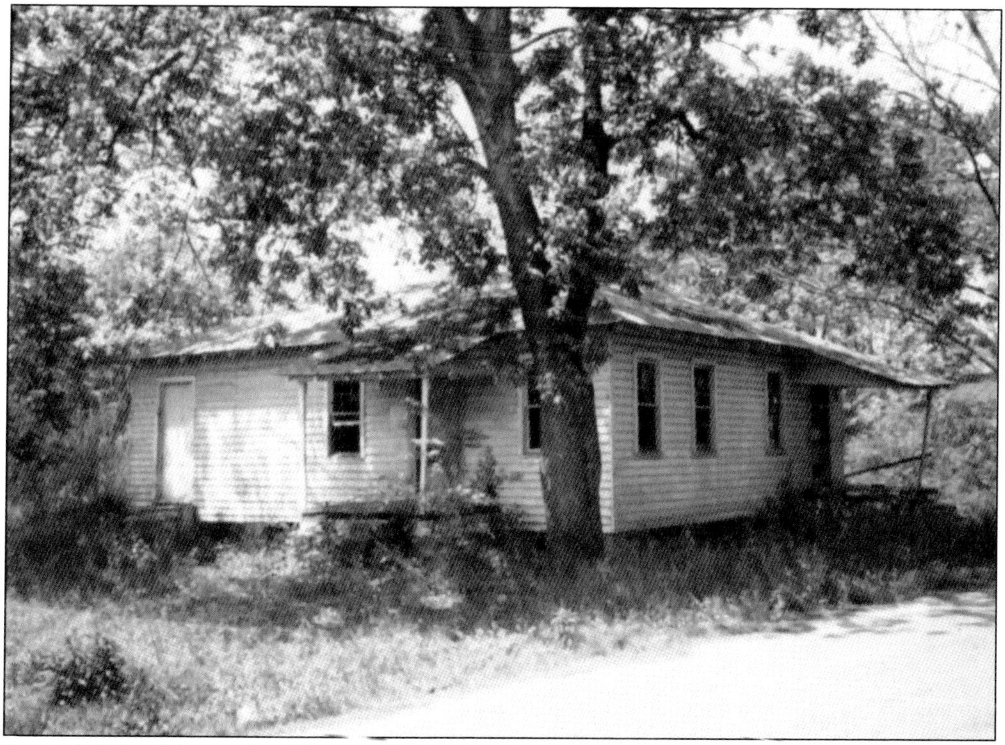

Antioch School, located on Thigpen-Barlow Road across from Antioch Church, was in operation in 1912, when Bleckley County was created. The land for the school was a gift from Tobe and Ella Pusser Young. (Courtesy of Jack Lucas.)

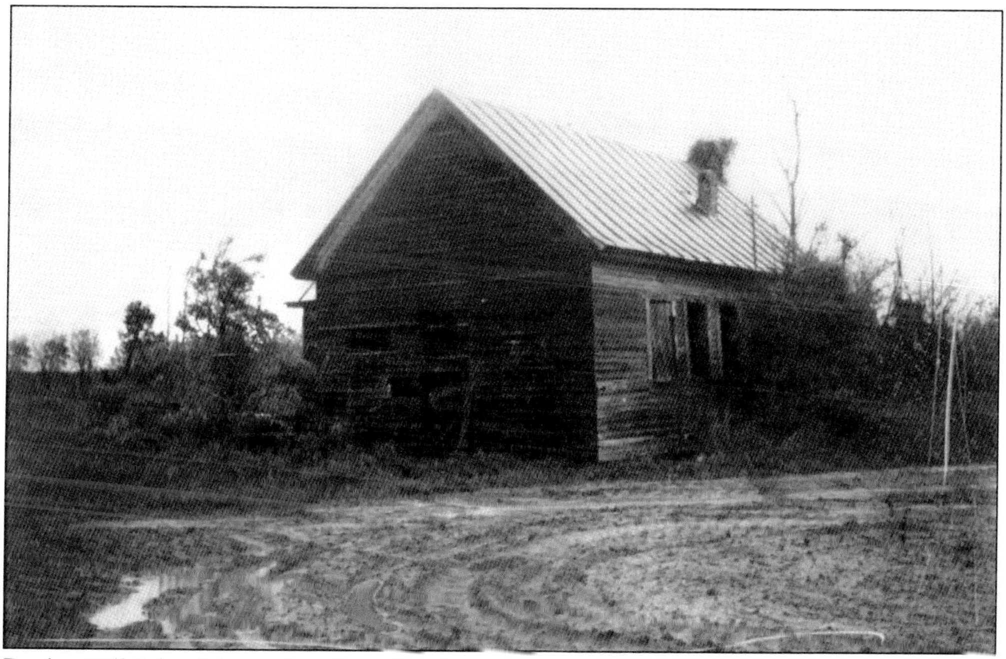

Bunker Hill School, located on Butts Road, was in operation in the early 1900s. When it closed, students transferred to Salem School. (Courtesy of Jack Lucas.)

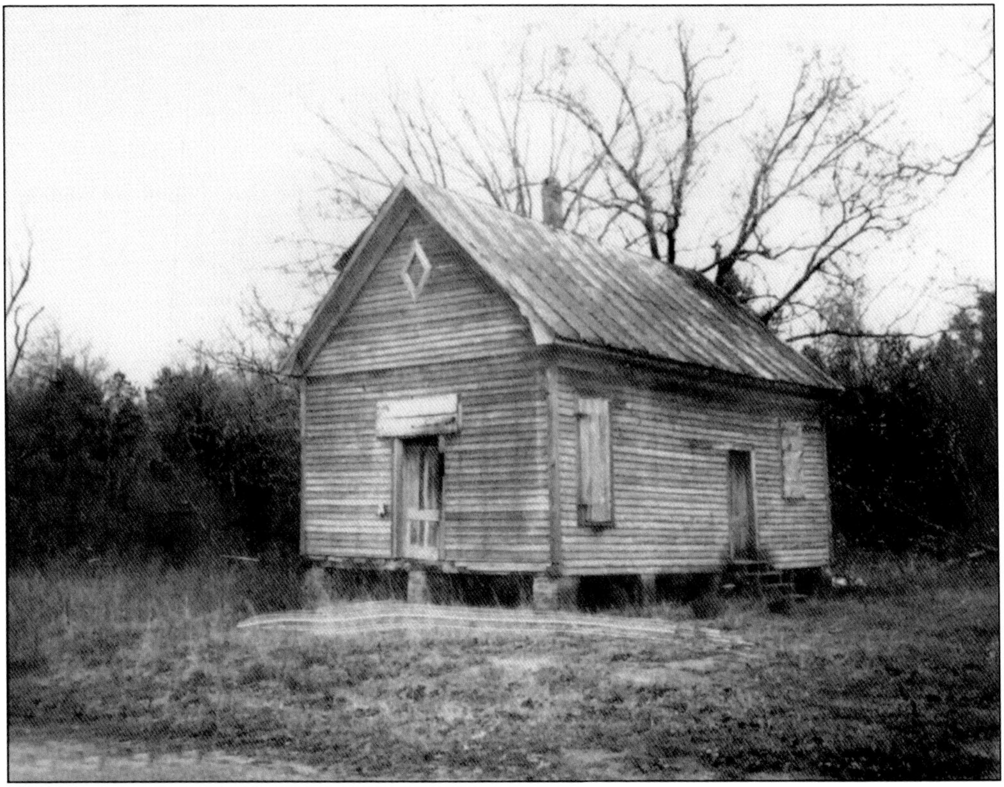

Collins School operated from 1910 to 1919. (Courtesy of Jack Lucas.)

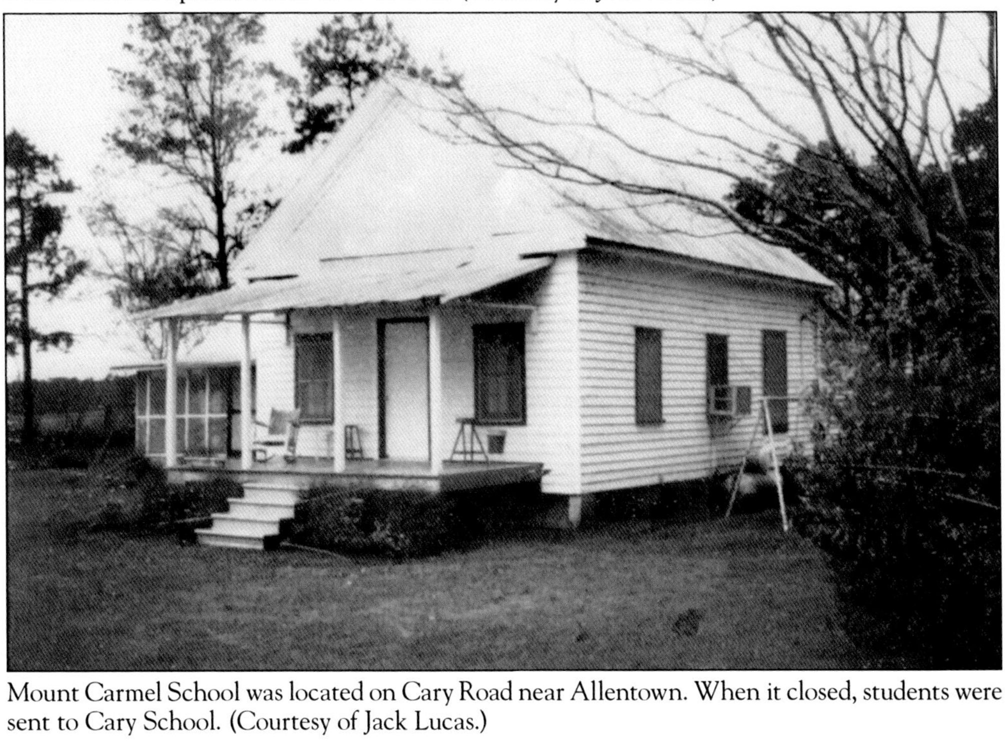

Mount Carmel School was located on Cary Road near Allentown. When it closed, students were sent to Cary School. (Courtesy of Jack Lucas.)

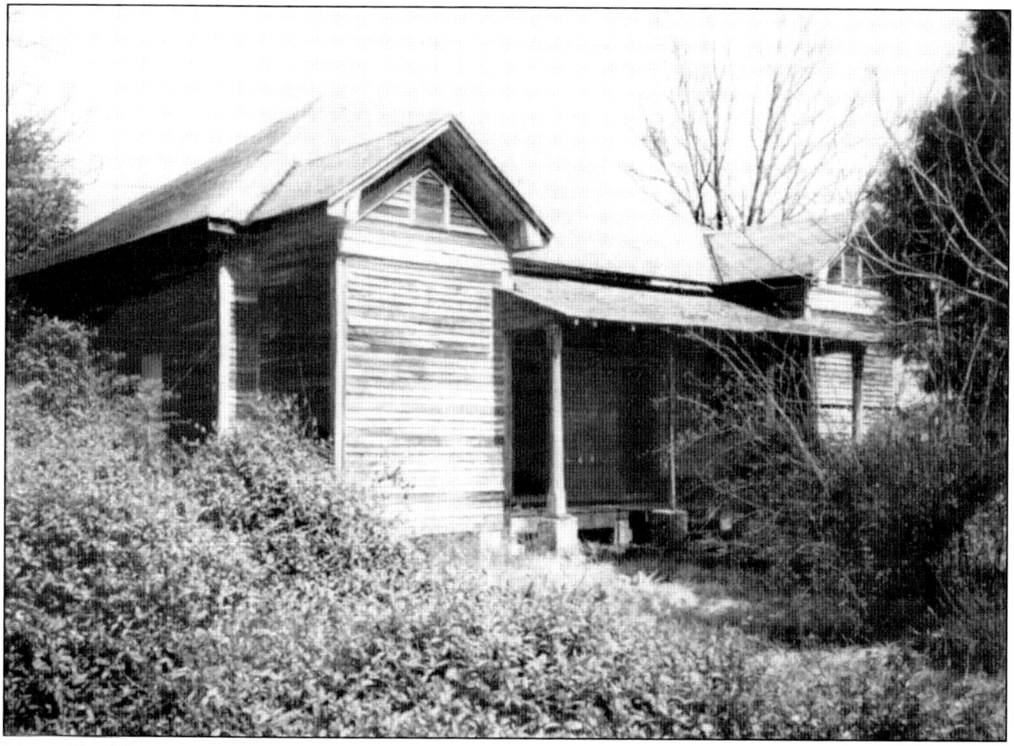

New Bleckley School was located on Cary Road. It was later the home of the Sapp family. (Courtesy of Jack Lucas.)

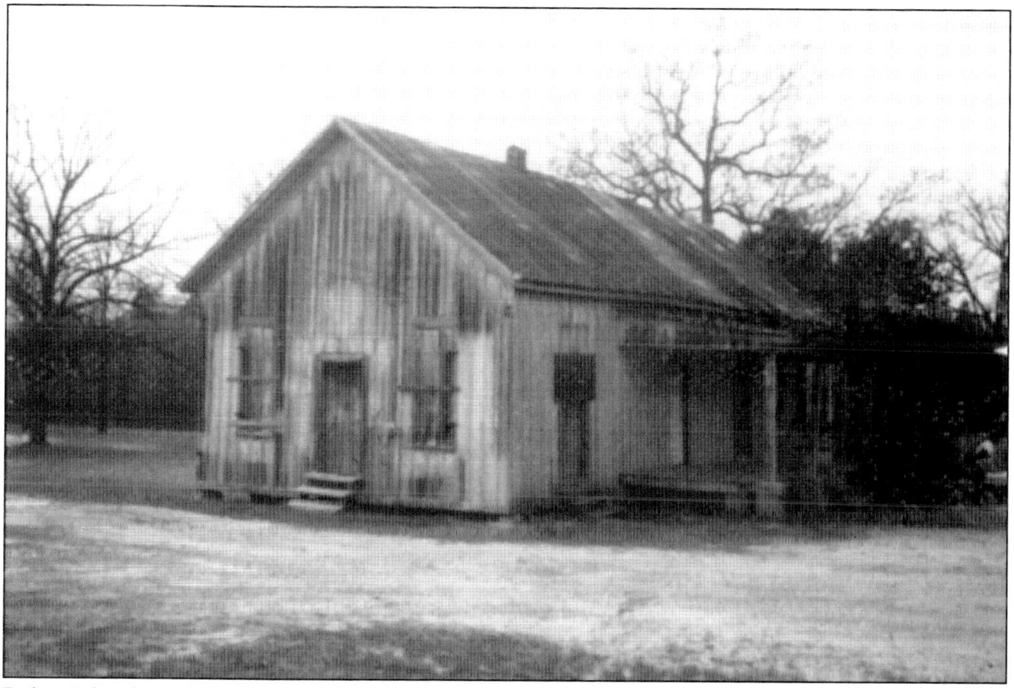

Rebie School was located near Little Bethel Church. It operated from 1912 until it was consolidated with Salem in 1937. (Courtesy of Jack Lucas.)

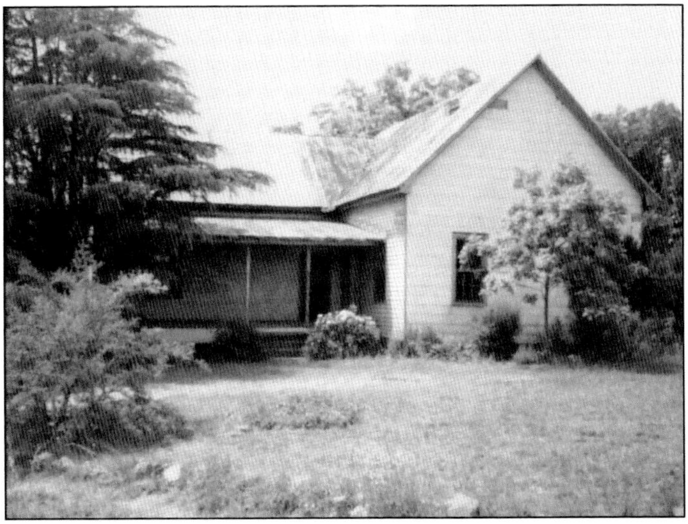

Walker School was located on Frank Cook Road. It operated from 1906 to 1920. (Courtesy of Jack Lucas.)

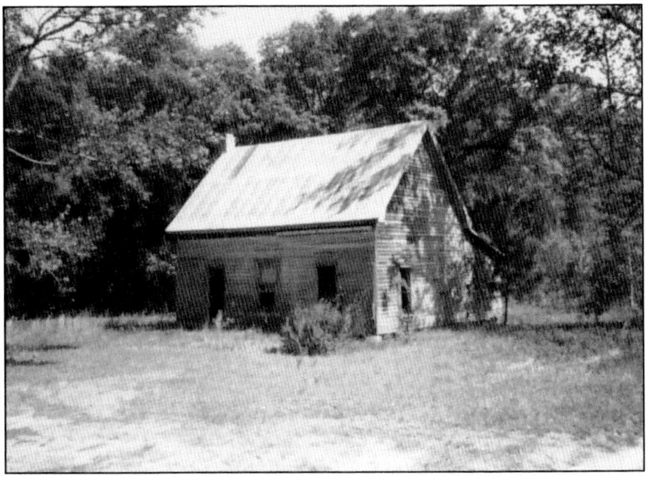

White's Chapel School was located on the W. B. English farm on Dublin Highway. It was consolidated with Salem in 1922. (Courtesy of Jack Lucas.)

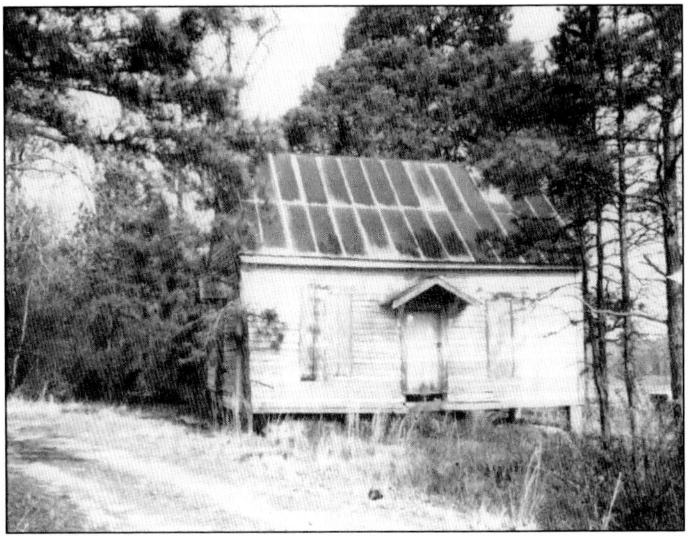

Arde School was located on the Cochran-Montrose Road. (Courtesy of Jack Lucas.)

Brown Hill School, on the Cary-Allentown Road, was in operation from 1879 to 1965. (Courtesy of Jack Lucas.)

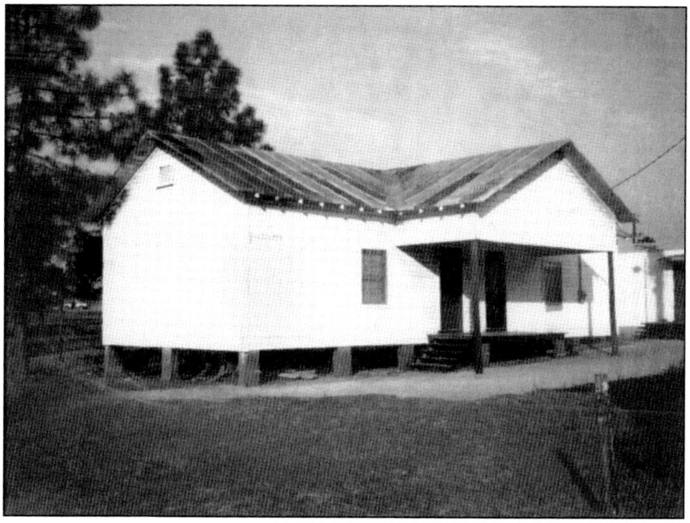

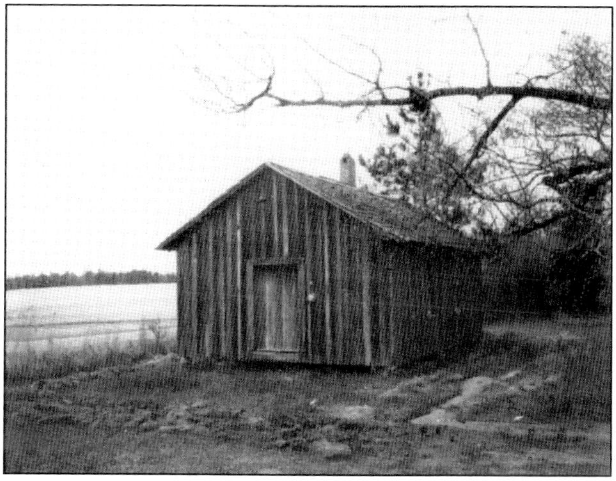

Dennis Gift was a school near the Dodge-Pulaski-Bleckley County lines near New Zion Church. (Courtesy of Jack Lucas.)

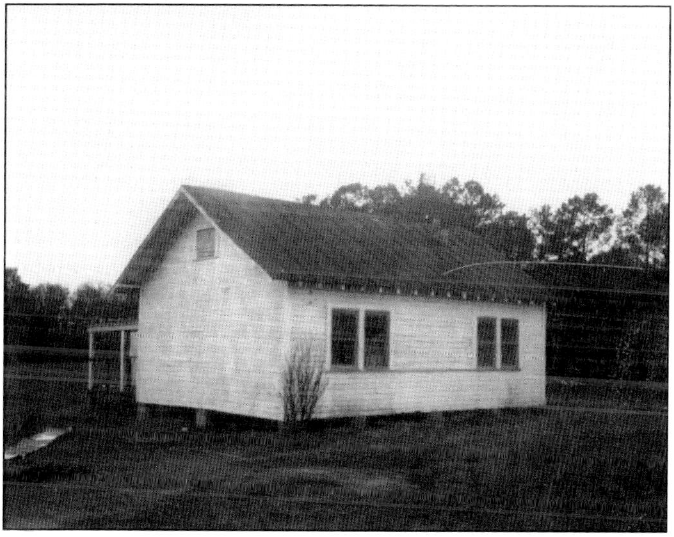

Green Grove School was located on the Macon State Highway across from the Collier home. It closed with consolidation. (Courtesy of Jack Lucas.)

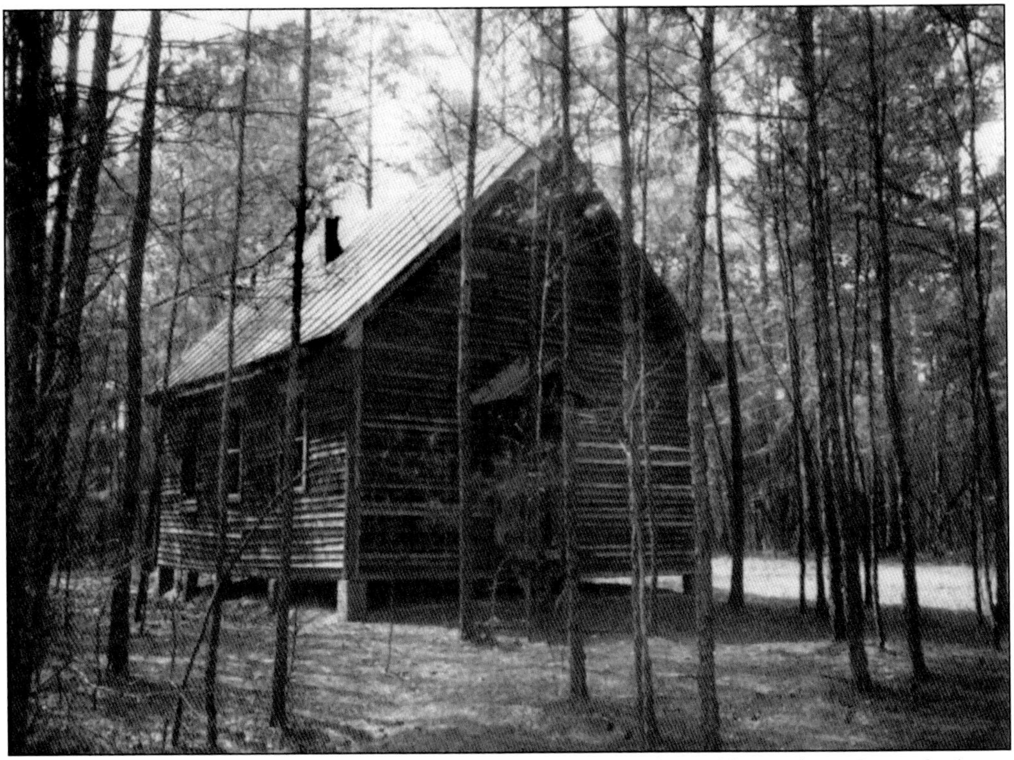

Mae Chapel was a school located on the farm of William Perry on the Dublin Highway. It is today being restored by the Bleckley County Association of Retired Educators. (Courtesy of Jack Lucas.)

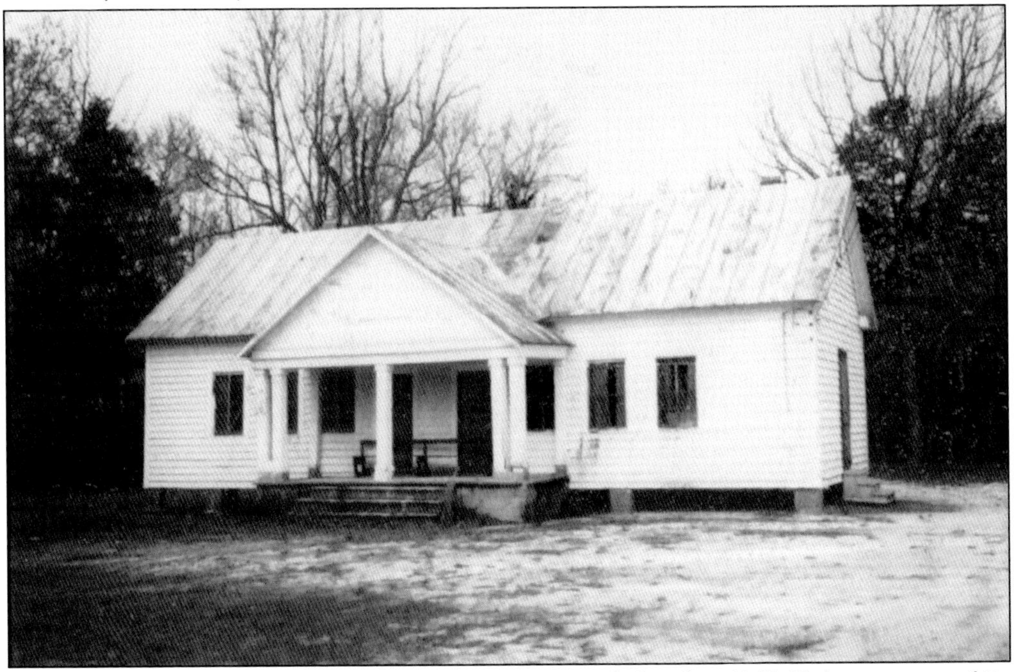

St. Paul School, located on Cary Road, began in 1880 and closed in 1965. Today it is part of St. Paul Church. (Courtesy of Jack Lucas.)

Three

Churches up to 1976

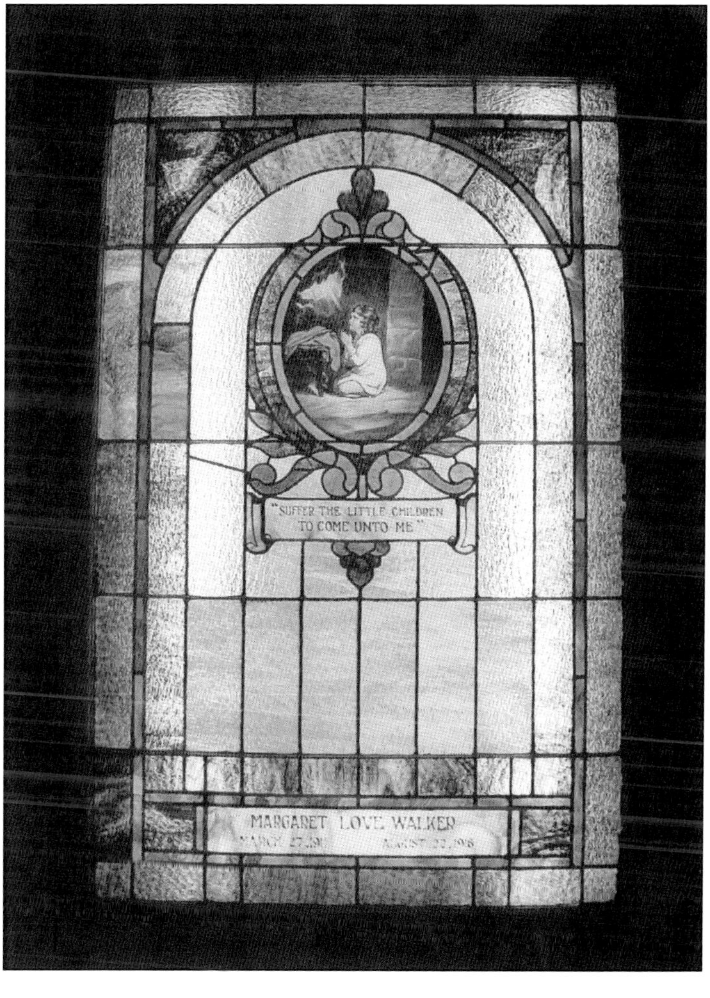

This Little Samuel stained-glass window in the First Baptist Church of Cochran is in memory of six-year-old Margaret Love Walker, daughter of Dr. and Mrs. T. D. Walker Jr. and granddaughter of Dr. and Mrs. Thomas Duhart Walker Sr. In an epidemic in 1916, she died and was buried in Cedar Hill Cemetery in Cochran, Georgia.

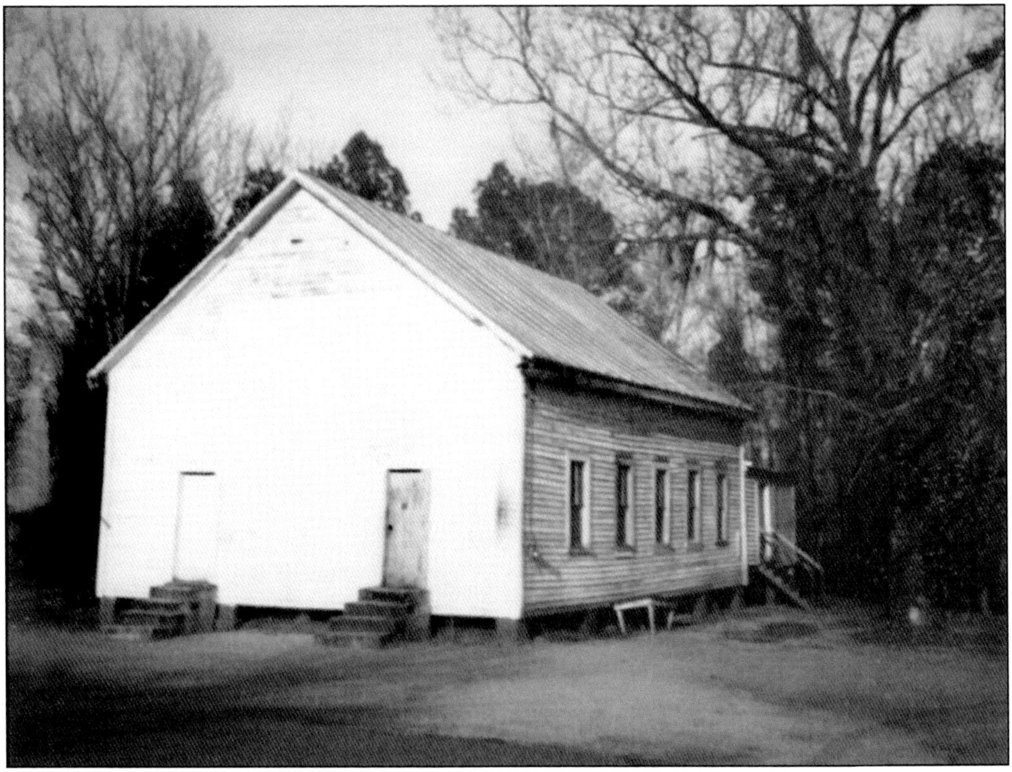

Antioch Baptist Church has been a place of worship for African Americans for almost a century. (Courtesy of Jack Lucas.)

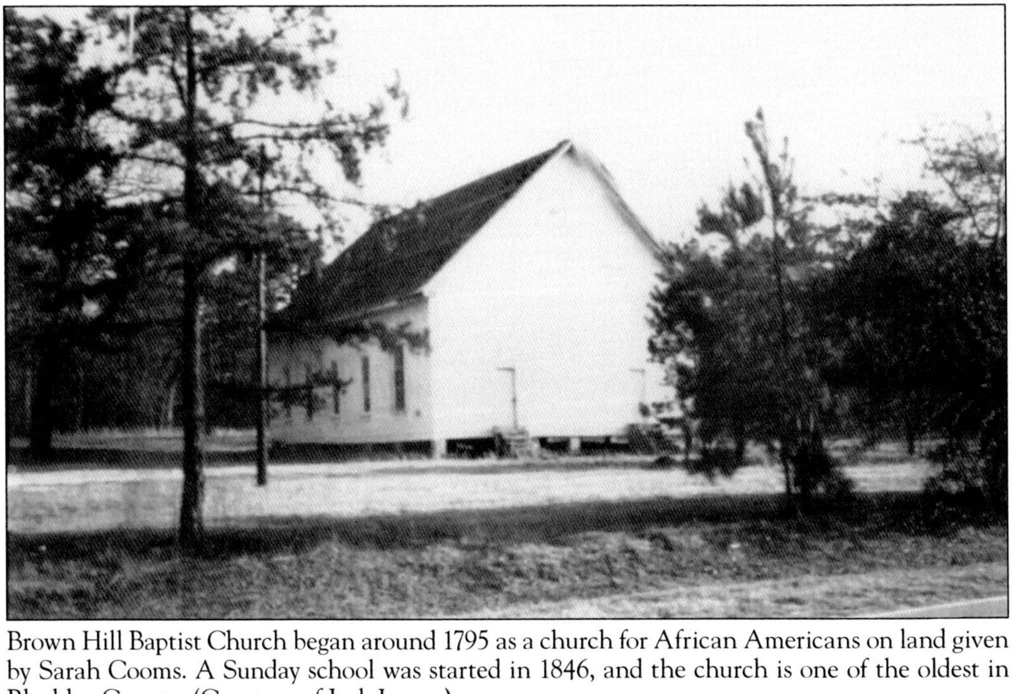

Brown Hill Baptist Church began around 1795 as a church for African Americans on land given by Sarah Cooms. A Sunday school was started in 1846, and the church is one of the oldest in Bleckley County. (Courtesy of Jack Lucas.)

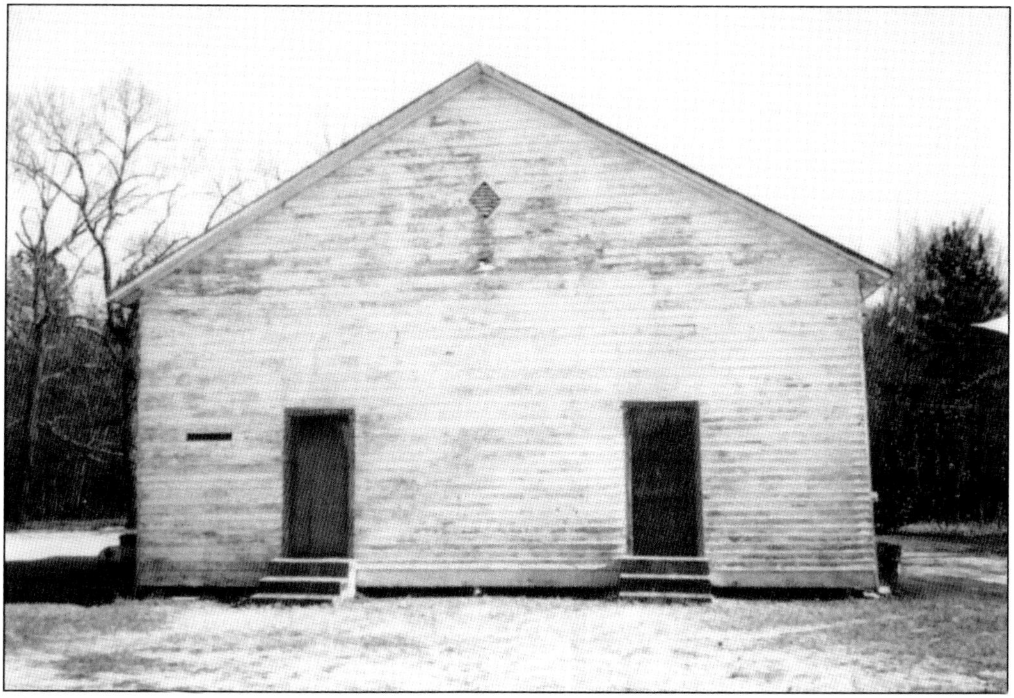

Christian Hope Baptist Church began in 1882 as a mission church of Salem Baptist Church for African Americans and continues to the present time. (Courtesy of Jack Lucas.)

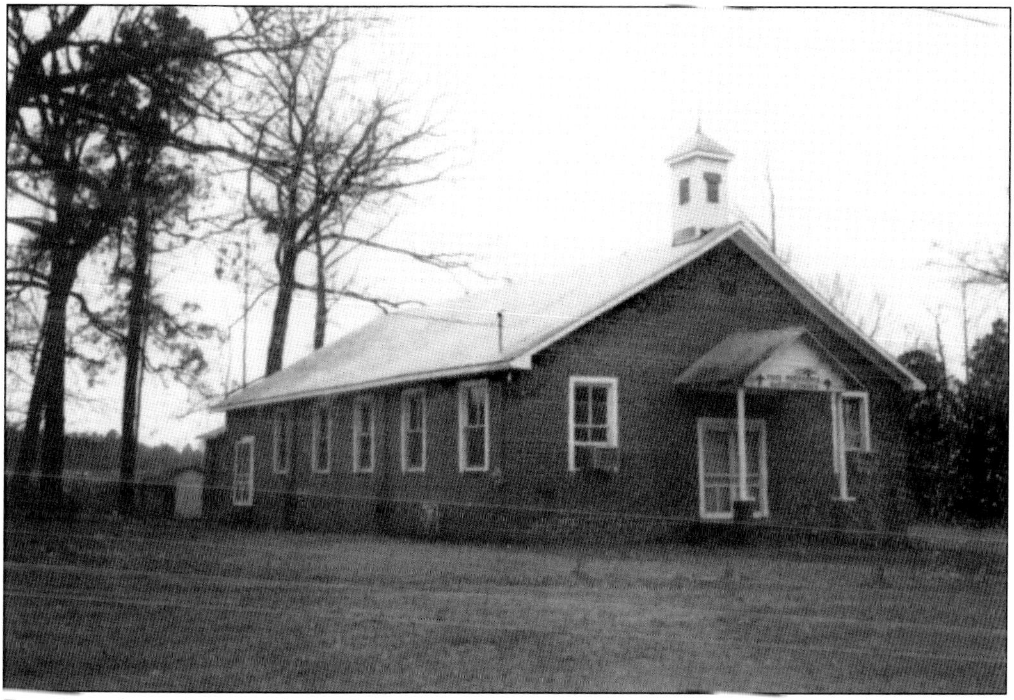

Free Providence Baptist Church began in 1873 for African Americans. The first meetinghouse was a log cabin, which was later enlarged. It was torn down to build the present brick church. (Courtesy of Jack Lucas.)

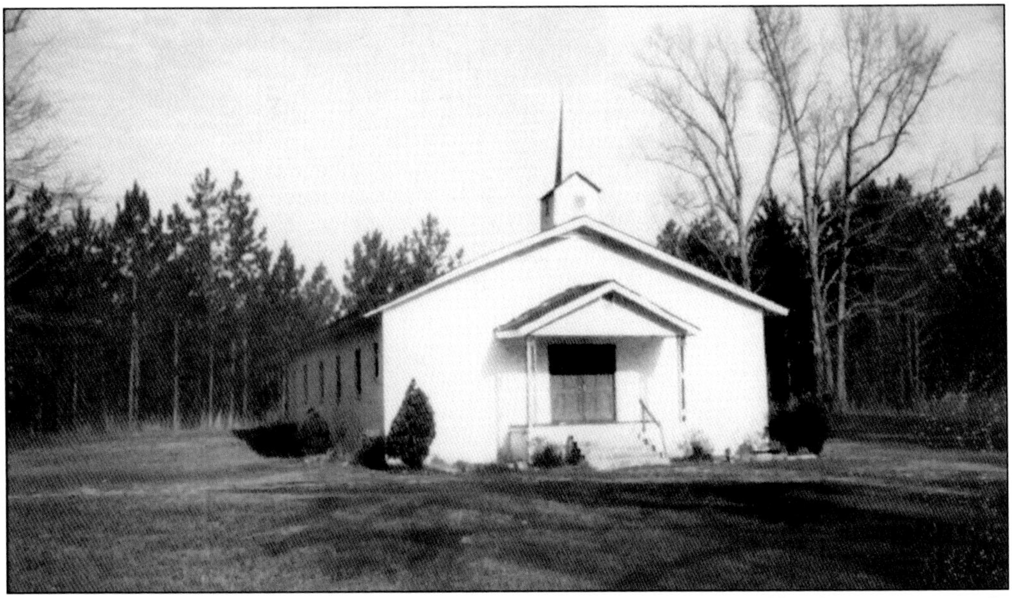

Longstreet Baptist Church was founded in 1883 for African Americans and has been continuously in operation for more than a century. (Courtesy of Jack Lucas.)

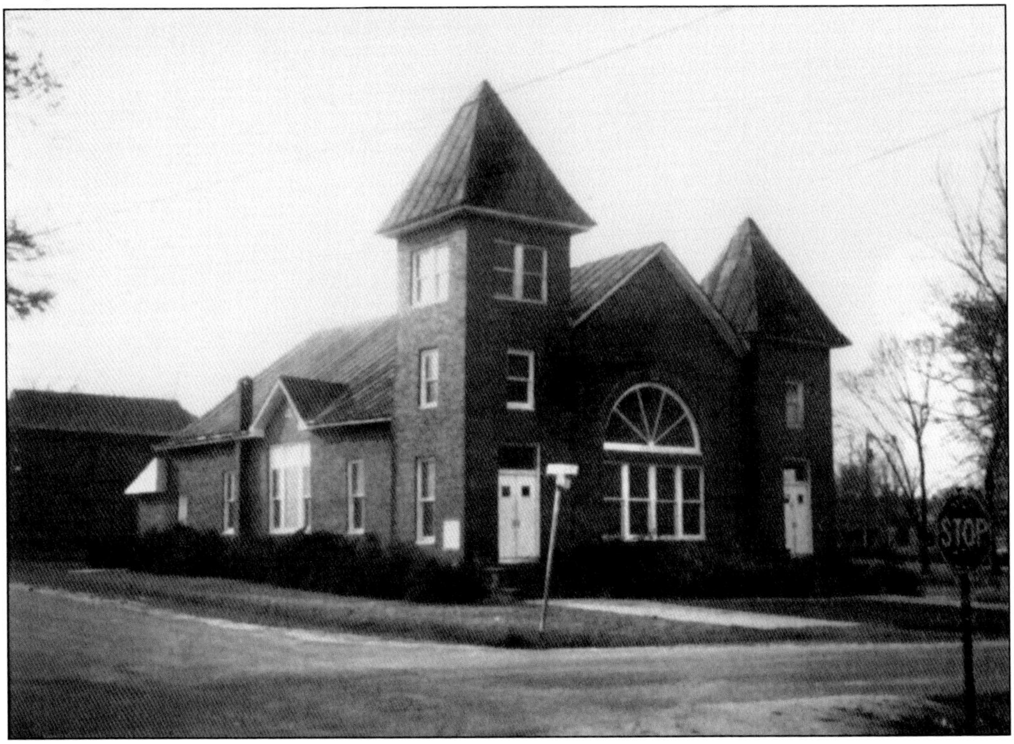

Marthann Baptist Church on Dinah Street in Cochran was formed for African Americans on September 29, 1881, and continues to the present time. Named for Sr. Martha Henderson, the church has stood as a monument pointing all in a heavenly way. In the midst of strife and war and when world ideals were crumbling, this church held high the banner of Christ. (Courtesy of Jack Lucas.)

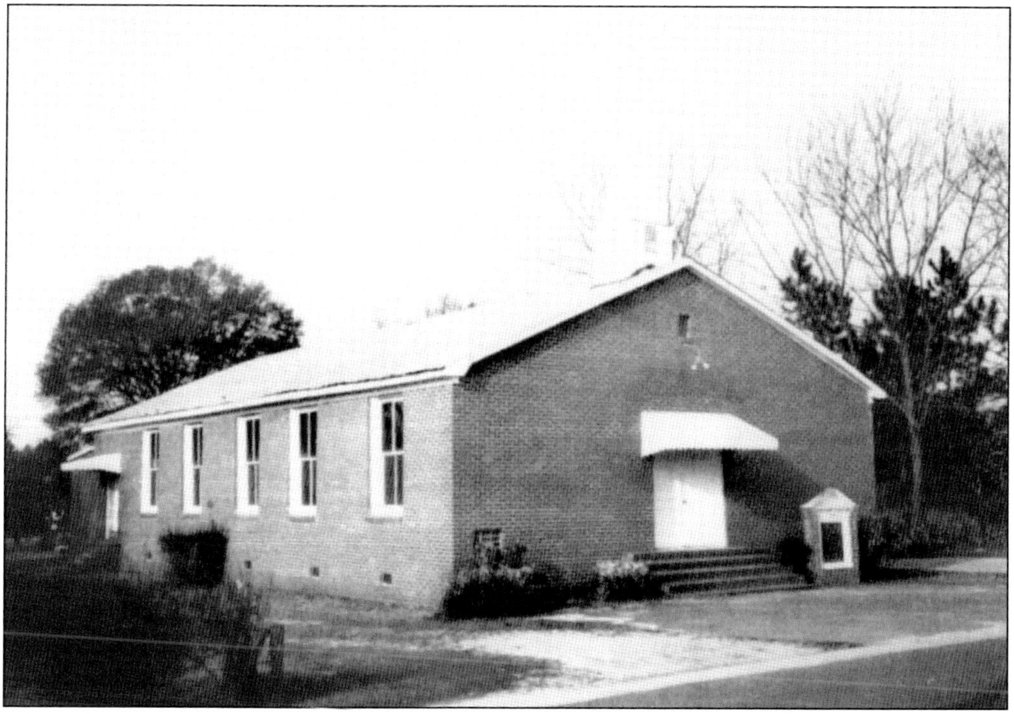

Mount Zion Baptist Church was founded in 1872 on Fifth Street in the Whipple town section of Cochran. It continues as a thriving congregation for African Americans. (Courtesy of Jack Lucas.)

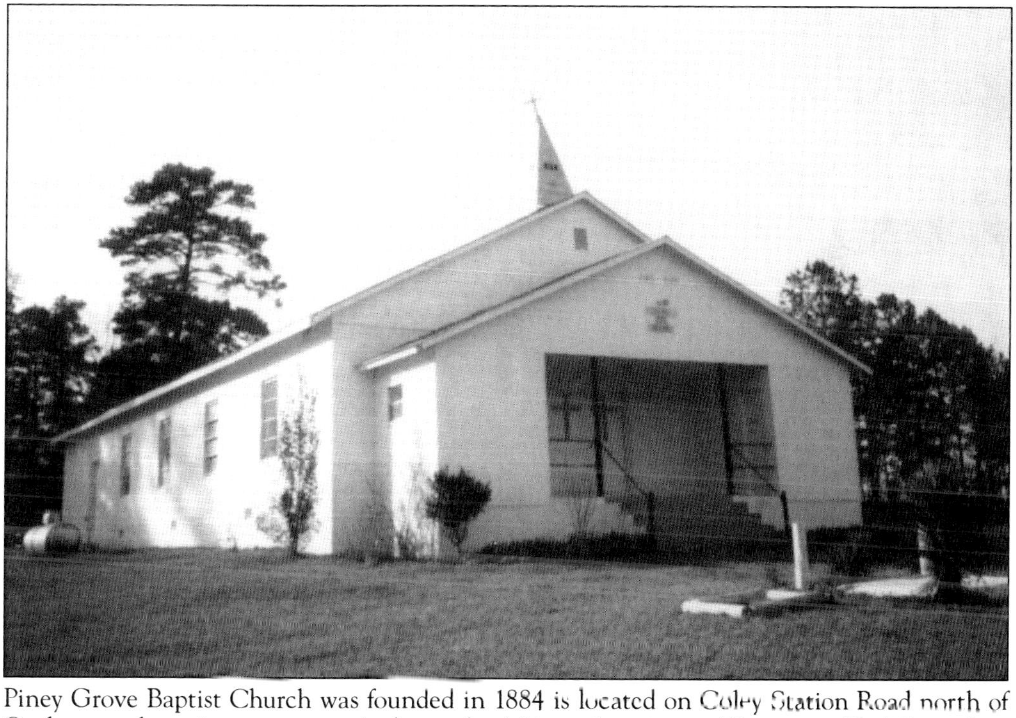

Piney Grove Baptist Church was founded in 1884 is located on Coley Station Road north of Cochran and continues as a meetinghouse for African Americans. (Courtesy of Jack Lucas.)

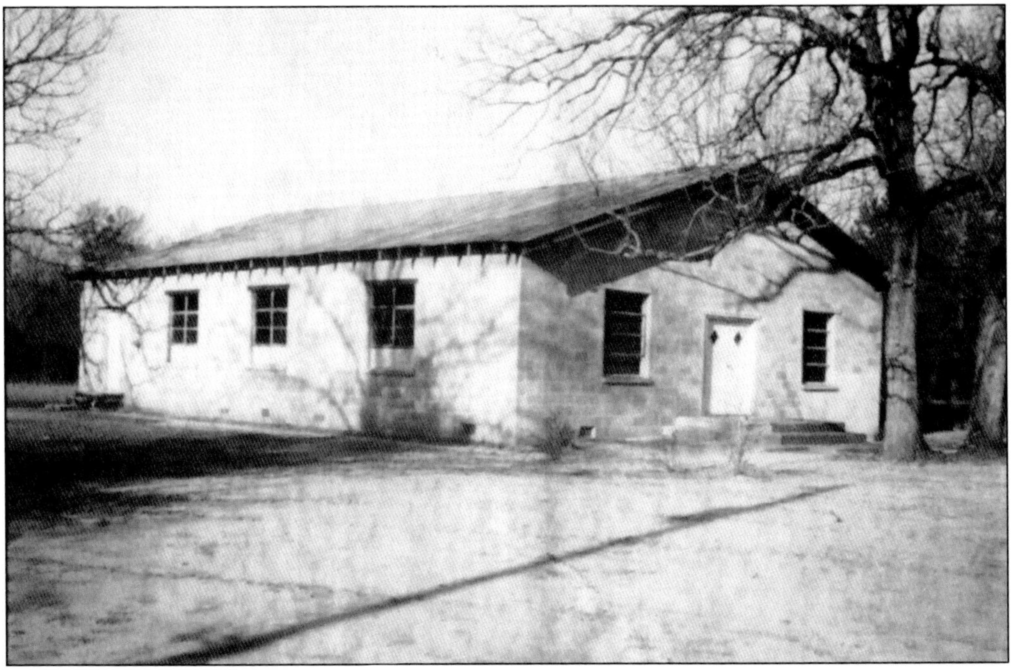

St. James A.M.E. Church began in 1875. The abbreviation indicates that the church was African Methodist Episcopal in belief. The African American congregation removed the original wooden structure in 1955 and built the present brick meetinghouse in 1962. (Courtesy of Jack Lucas.)

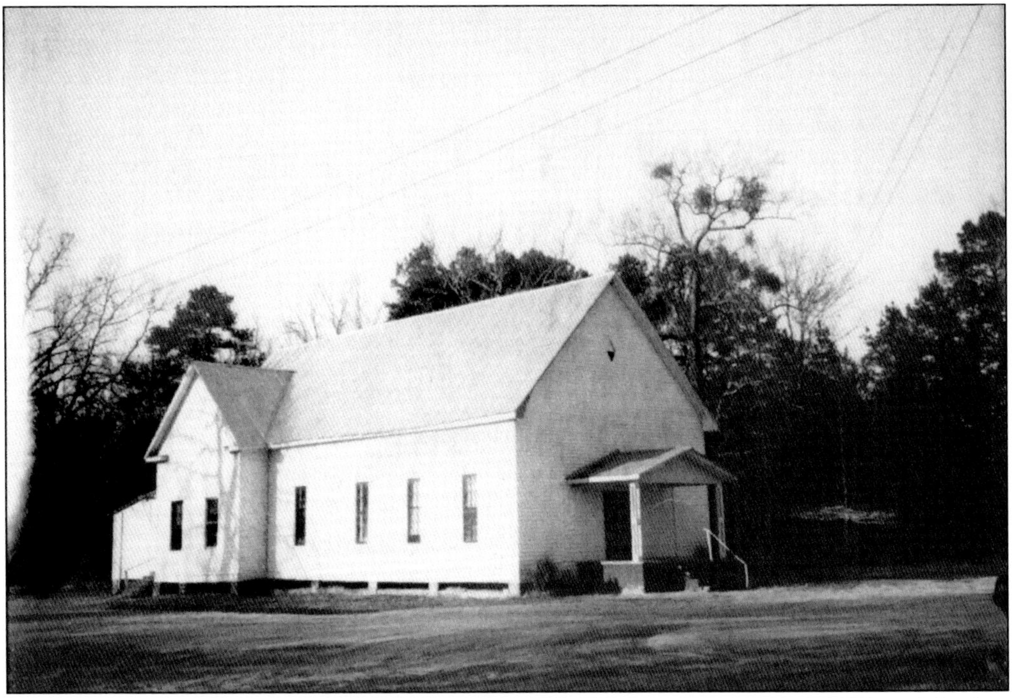

St. Paul Baptist Church on Cary Road was organized by African Americans in 1874, and the first sanctuary was built in 1886. A nearby school of the same name was added to the church after the consolidation of schools. (Courtesy of Jack Lucas.)

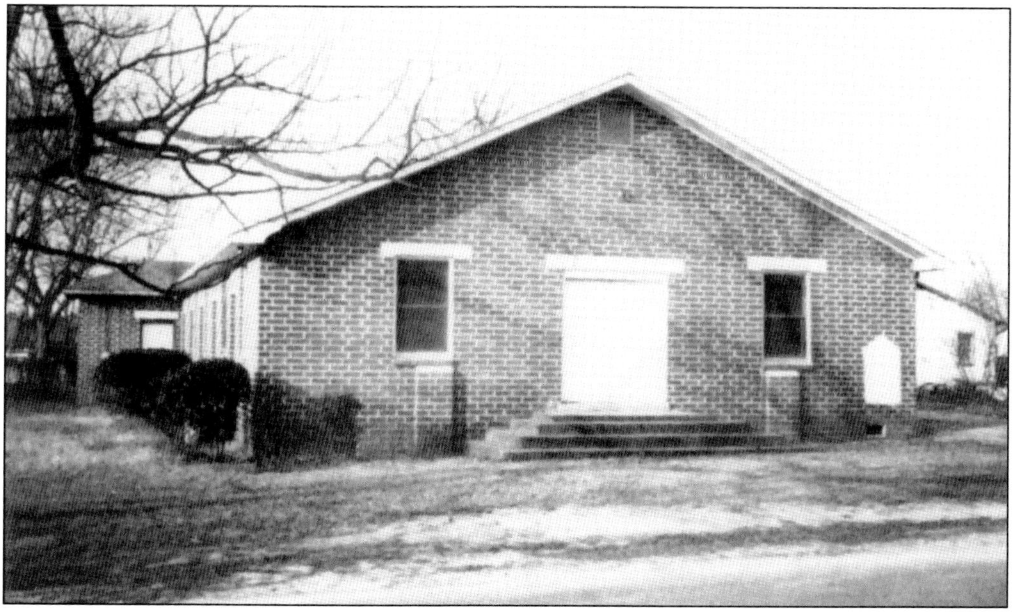

Turner Chapel A.M.E. Church in Cochran began as part of the African Methodist Episcopal movement in 1867 on land given by the Mullis family near the railroad tracks. In 1890, the church was rebuilt, and it was remodeled in 1918. It is one of the strongest churches in Bleckley County. (Courtesy of Jack Lucas.)

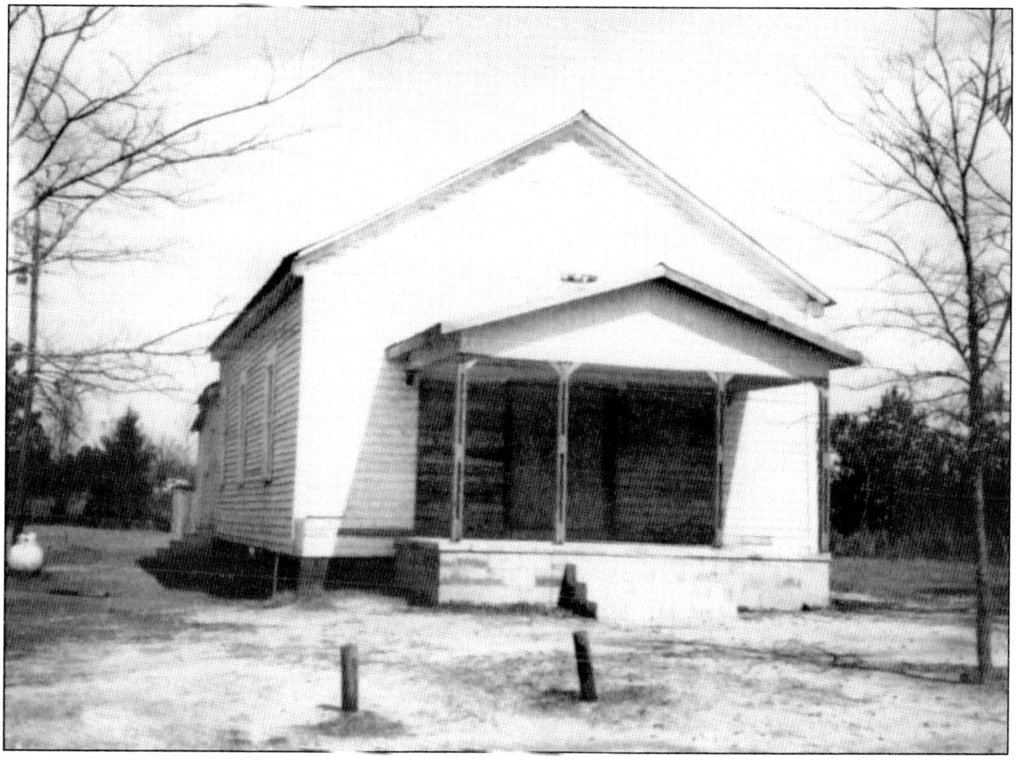

Ward Hill Baptist Church, in the southern part of the county, was organized by African Americans in 1911. (Courtesy of Jack Lucas.)

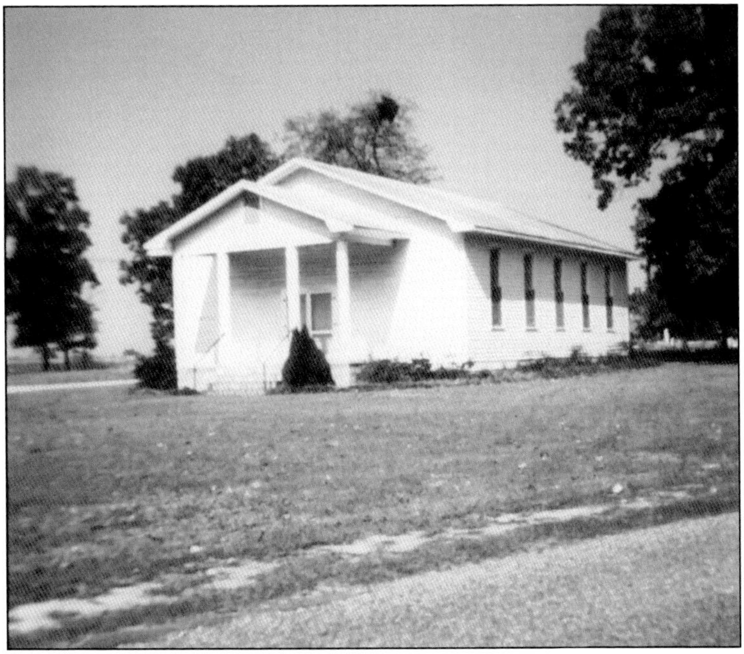

Antioch Methodist Church was established on lands given by the family of John Pusser and Edith Helms Pusser. The sanctuary was built in 1896. It burned in the 1970s. (Courtesy of Jack Lucas.)

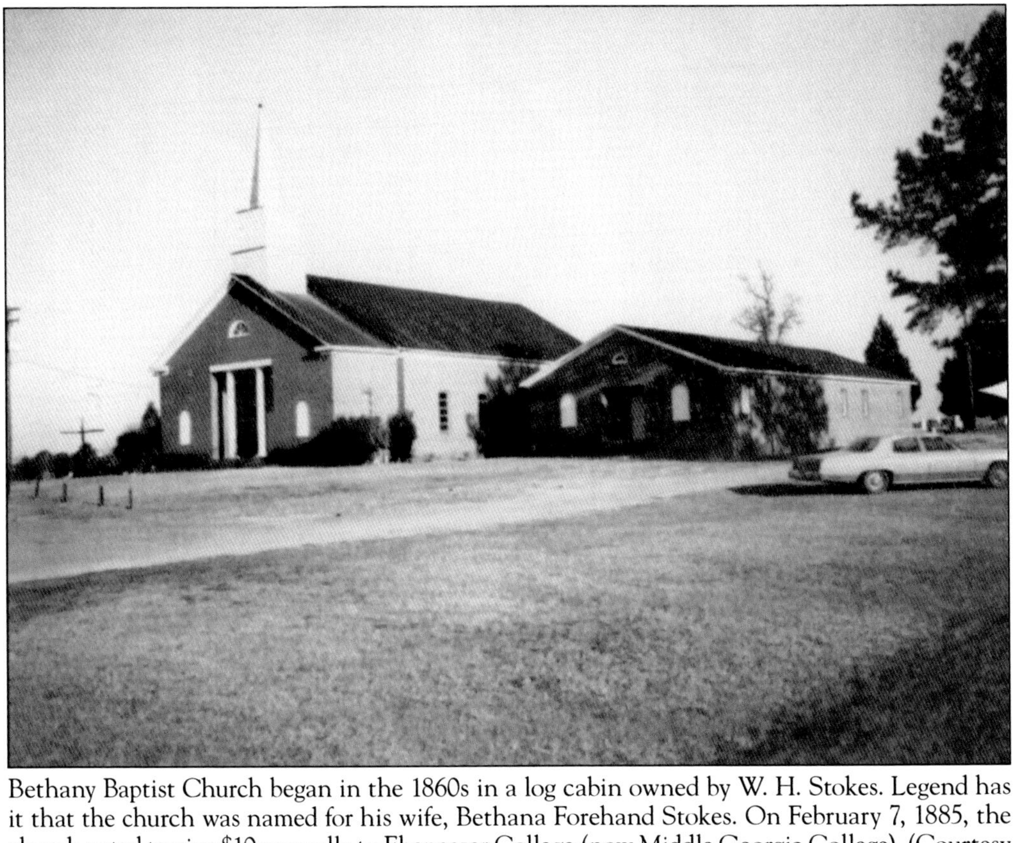

Bethany Baptist Church began in the 1860s in a log cabin owned by W. H. Stokes. Legend has it that the church was named for his wife, Bethana Forehand Stokes. On February 7, 1885, the church voted to give $10 annually to Ebeneezer College (now Middle Georgia College). (Courtesy of Jack Lucas.)

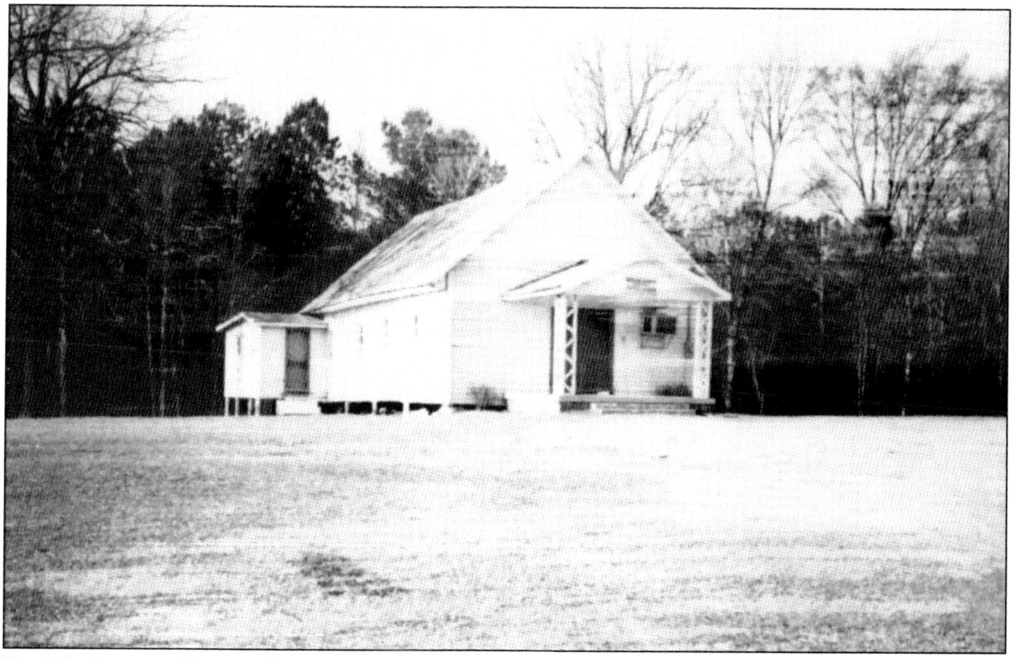

Beulah Springs Free Will Baptist Church was founded in 1924 on lands given by Barkwell Thompson. (Courtesy of Jack Lucas.)

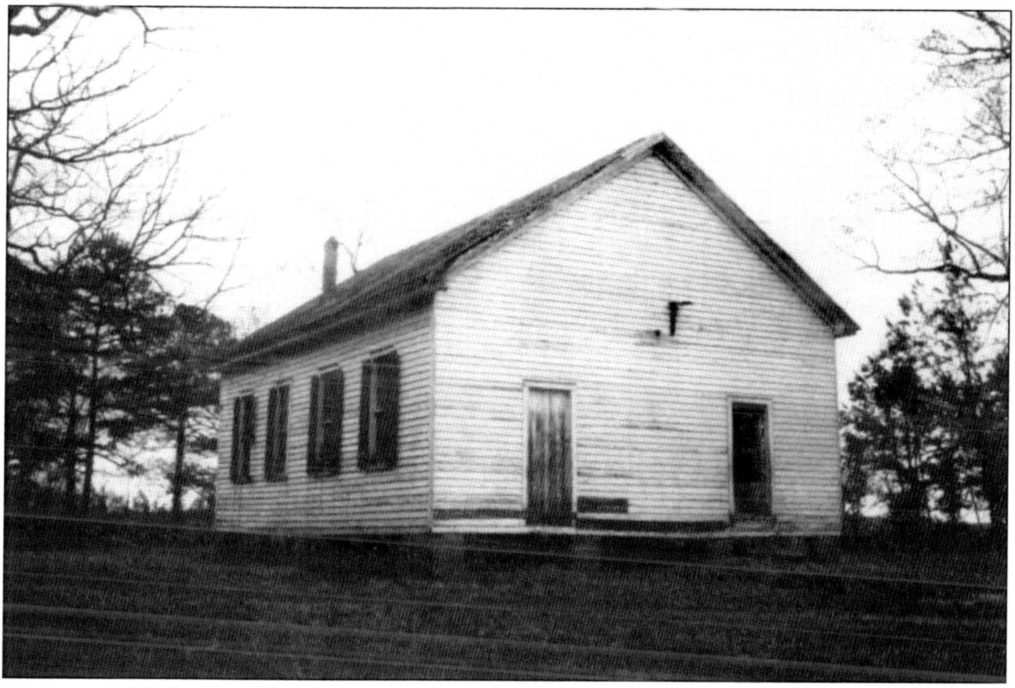

Centenary Methodist Church was organized in 1884. Prominent families were the Helms, Meadows, Porter, and Trunnell families. On March 21, 1939, the entire membership of Centenary Methodist Church was transferred to the Cochran Methodist Episcopal Church. The church meetinghouse was sold to the Bleckley County Board of Education. It later became the home of the Diller family. (Courtesy of Jack Lucas.)

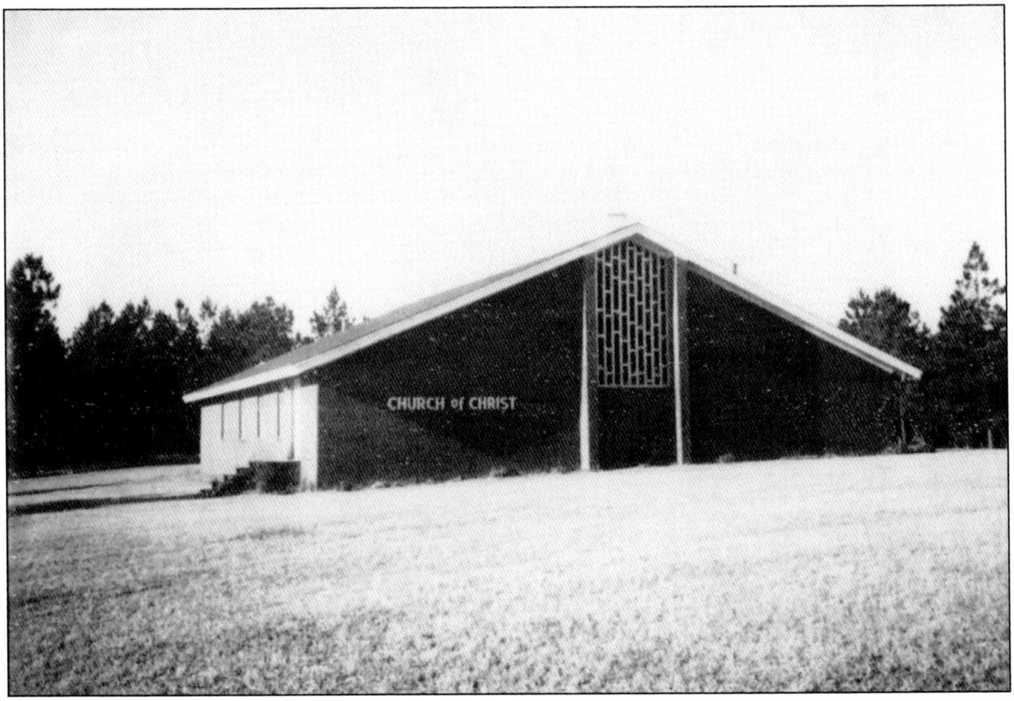

The Church of Christ in Cochran was established in February 1970, and a brick sanctuary was built in 1972. Located on the Eastman Highway south of Cochran, the church has provided for many missions through the years. (Courtesy of Jack Lucas.)

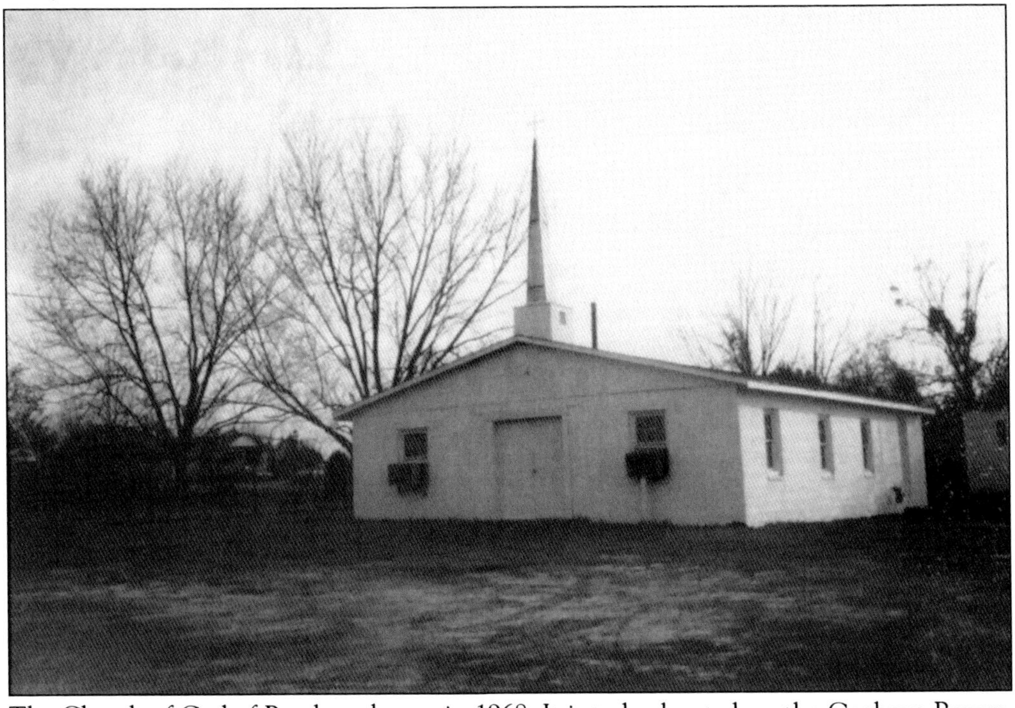

The Church of God of Prophecy began in 1968. It is today located on the Cochran Bypass. (Courtesy of Jack Lucas.)

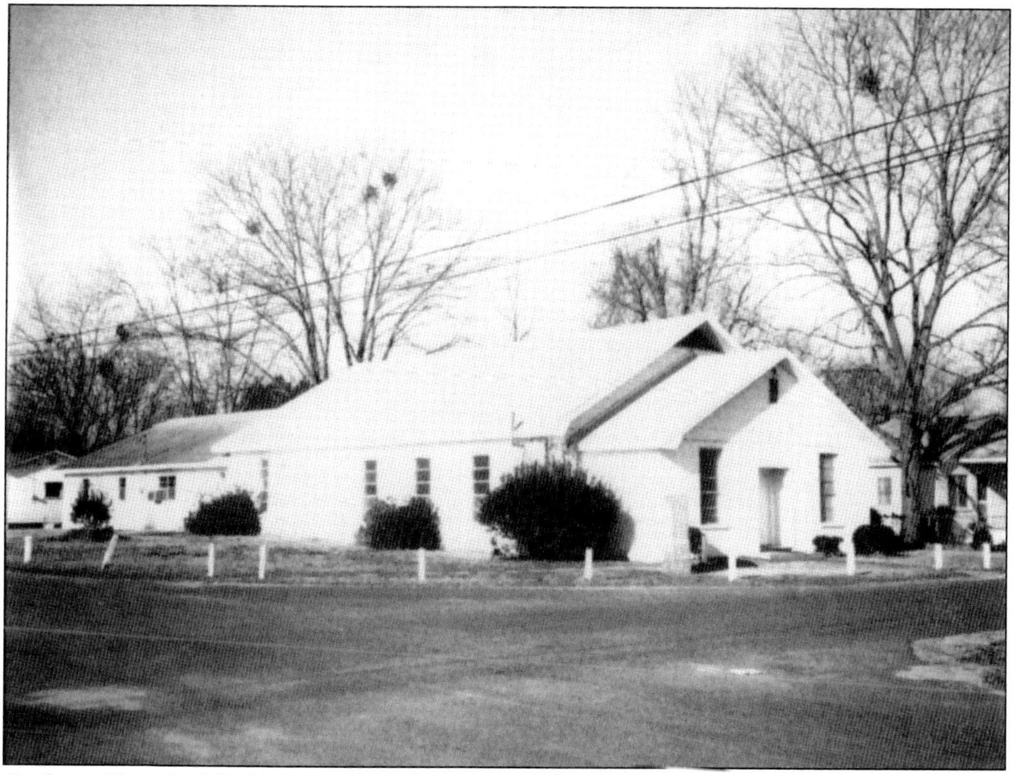

Cochran Church of God began in March 1946 on Oak Street. Due to limitations of space for class rooms, it was moved to a new facility on the Hawkinsville Highway. The original 1946 structure became My Father's House, which also later moved to a larger facility. (Courtesy of Jack Lucas.)

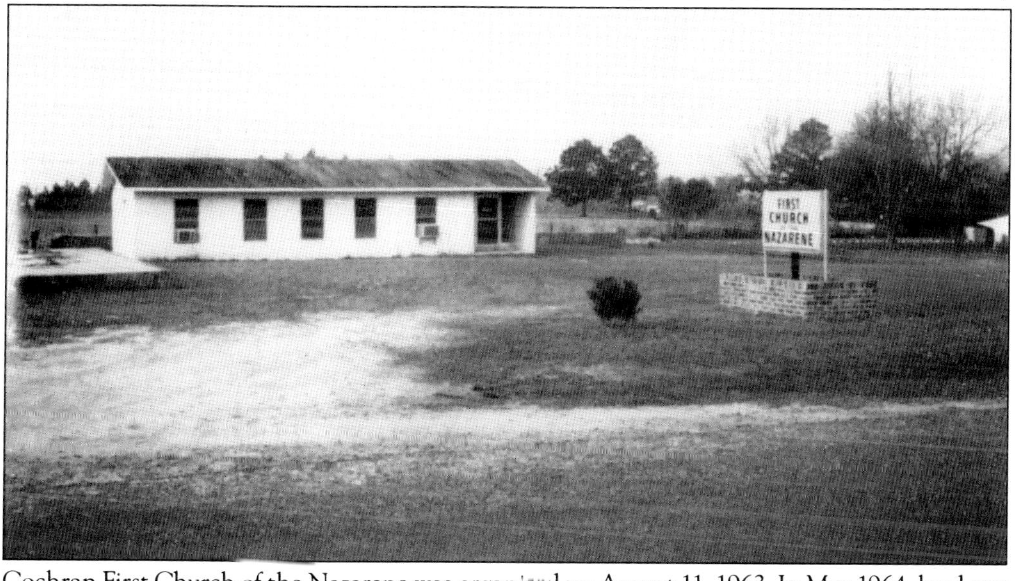

Cochran First Church of the Nazarene was organized on August 11, 1963. In May 1964, land was acquired for a church building, and Rev. John W. Dye Sr. became pastor in 1965. The church has had sustained growth and today enjoys a new sanctuary facility in the Suburban Acres subdivision north of Cochran. (Courtesy of Jack Lucas.)

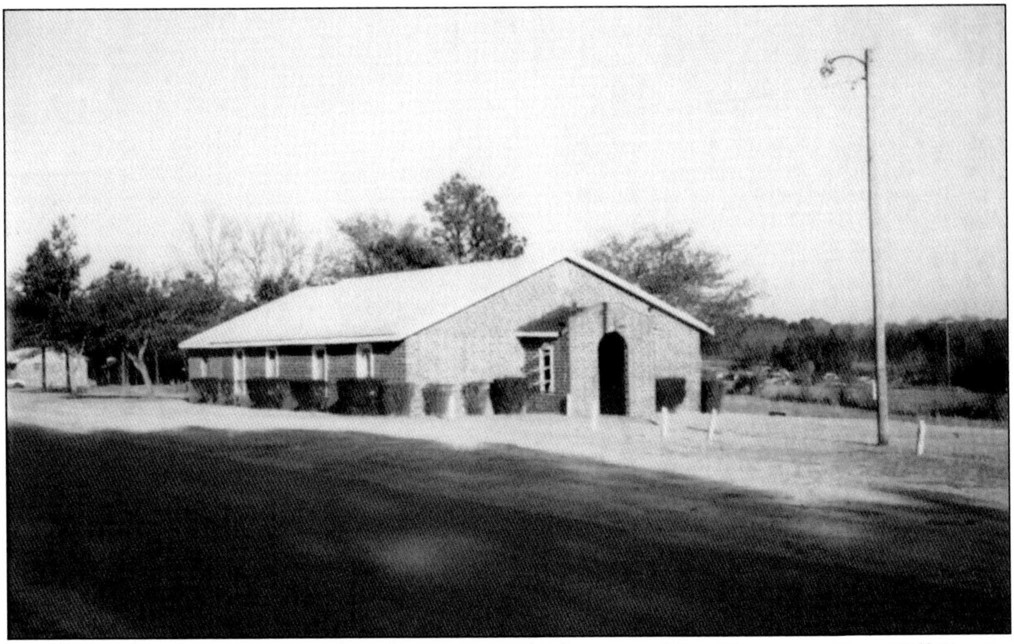

Cross Roads Free Will Baptist Church was originally known as New Ebeneezer Free Will Baptist Church when it was established in 1910. The church has continued to grow to the present time. (Courtesy of Jack Lucas.)

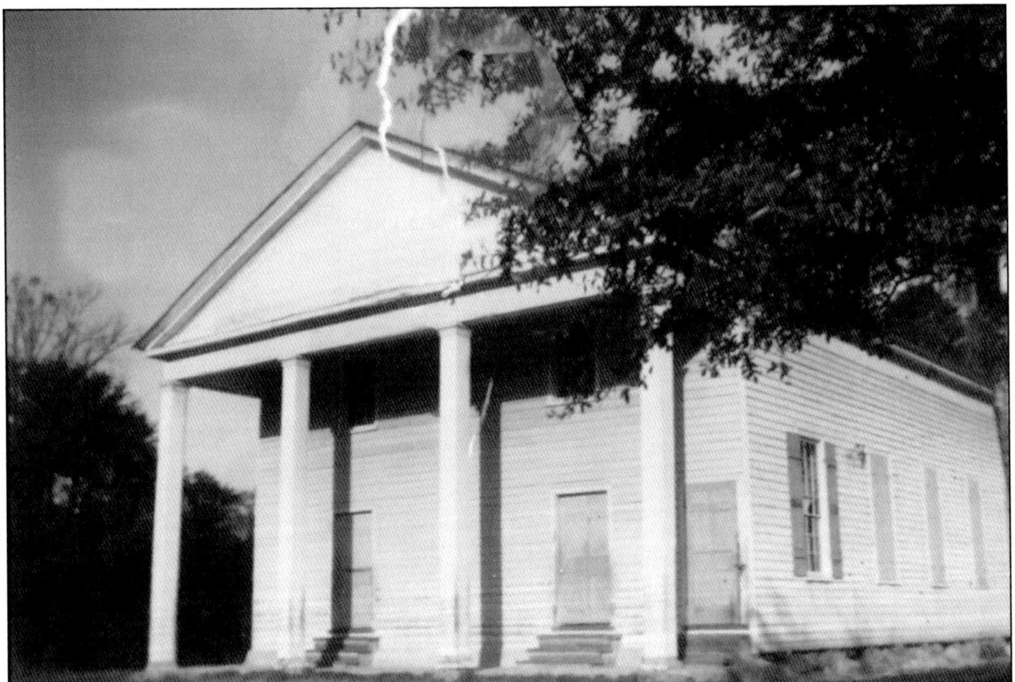

Evergreen Baptist Church was constituted in 1809. Originally known as Mount Horeb, the name was changed to Evergreen in 1844. It is the only church in Bleckley County that held a balcony for slaves. Note the three doors: the left for men, center for women, and right for slaves. The slave door and separate doors were removed in the 1980s. (Courtesy of John B. Peacock.)

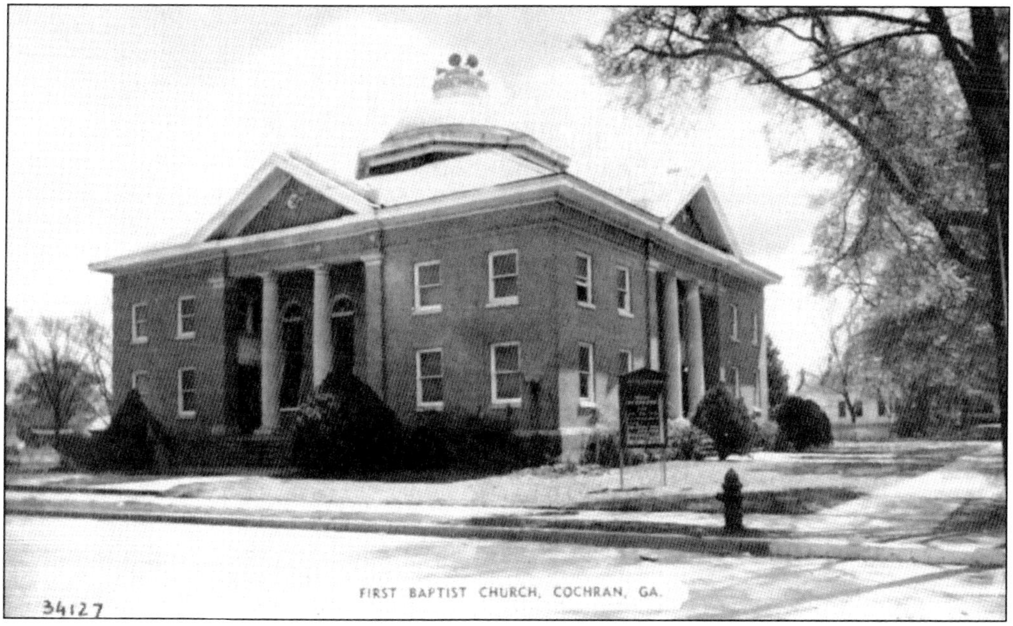

First Baptist Church of Cochran began in 1868. The first sanctuary was built in 1881 on lands given by Burrell B. Dykes. The present sanctuary was built in 1917, with several additions of land and facilities being added through the years.

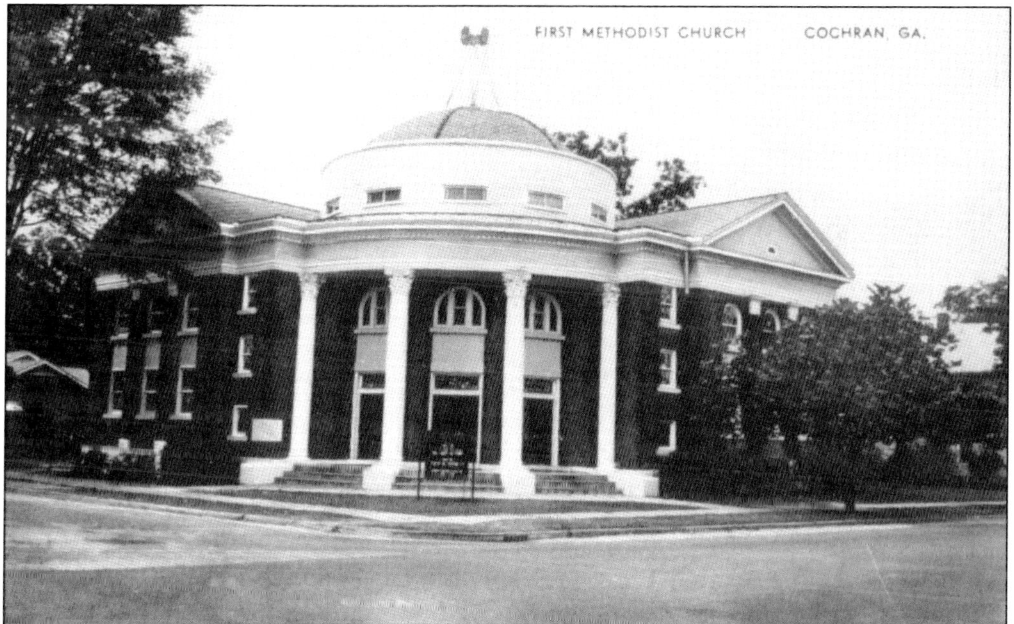

First United Methodist Church of Cochran began in 1868, and the original wooden meetinghouse was shared with Baptist and Episcopal congregations. The present brick structure was built in 1916.

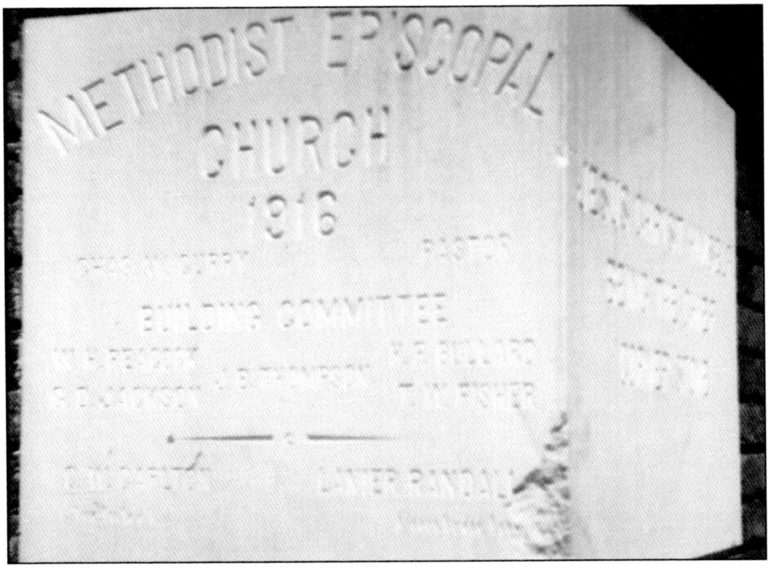

This corner stone of Cochran Methodist Episcopal Church in 1916 lists Charles W. Curry as pastor, with the building committee composed of Walter Hunt Peacock, R. D. Jackson, J. Barkwell Thompson, H. F. Bullard, and T. W. Fisher Sr.

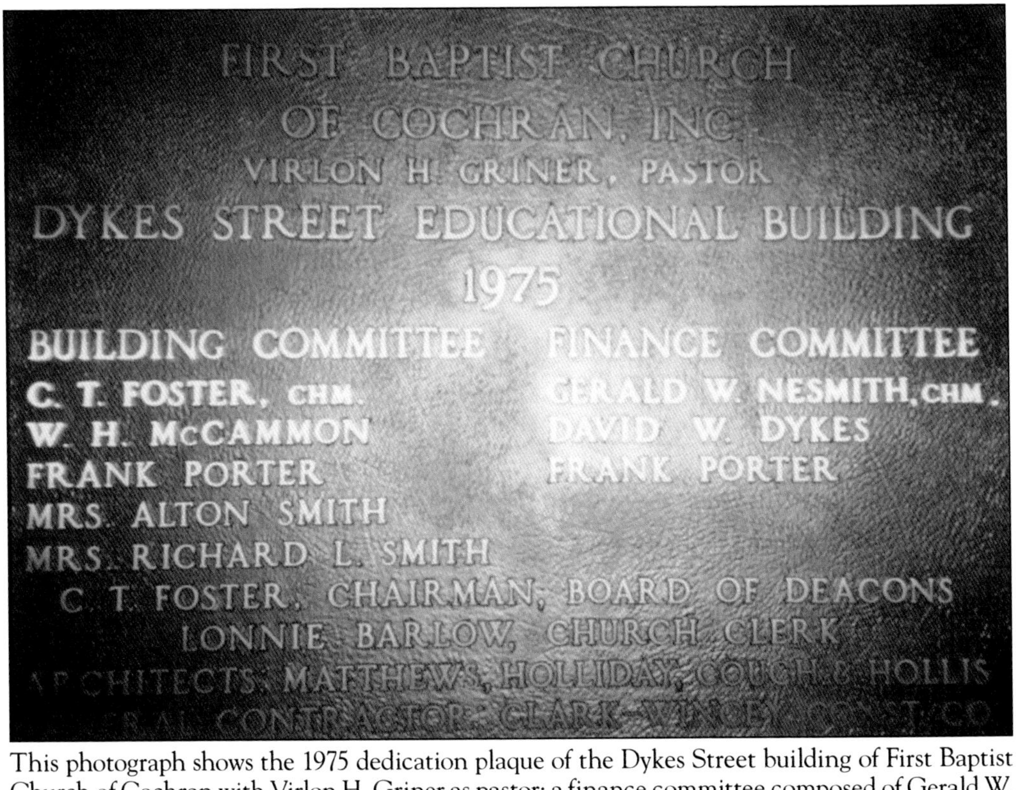

This photograph shows the 1975 dedication plaque of the Dykes Street building of First Baptist Church of Cochran with Virlon H. Griner as pastor; a finance committee composed of Gerald W. NeSmith (chairman), David W. Dykes Sr., and Frank Porter; and a building committee composed of C. T. Foster (chairman), W. H. McCammon, Frank Porter, Mrs. Alton Smith, Mrs. Richard L. Smith, and Lonnie Barlow (church clerk).

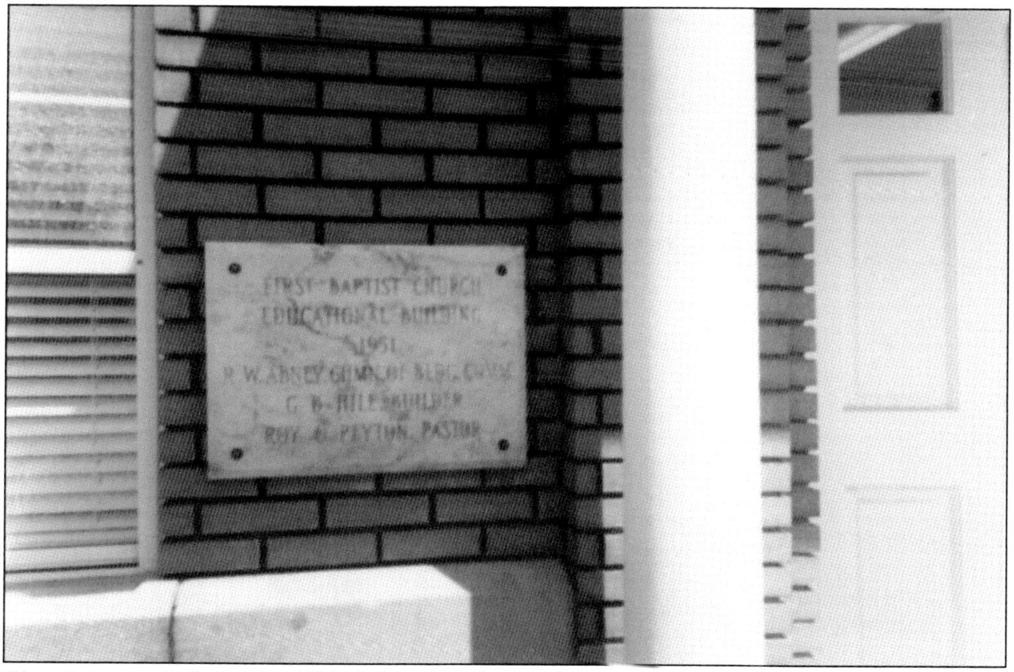

This photograph shows the 1951 dedication plaque of the Second Street building of First Baptist Church of Cochran with Roy O. Peyton as pastor, Ralph W. Abney Sr. as building chairman, and G. B. Hill as builder.

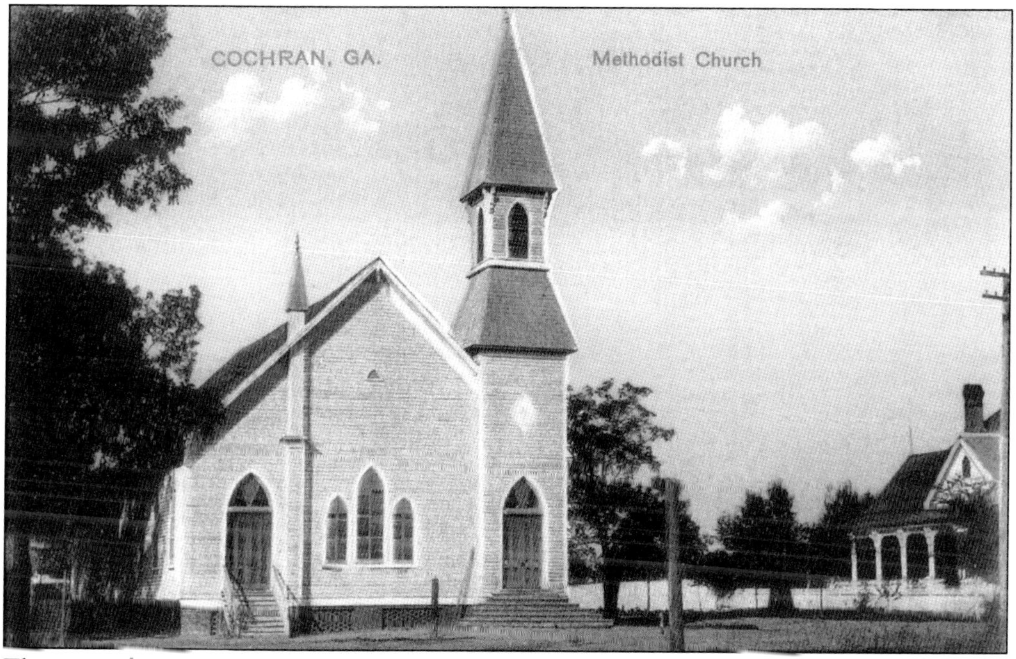

The original common meetinghouse of Methodists, Episcopals, and Baptists on Third Street in Cochran was removed in 1916 to build the present First United Methodist Church. Across the street is the Arthur Wiggs home (later the Robert A. Harrell home).

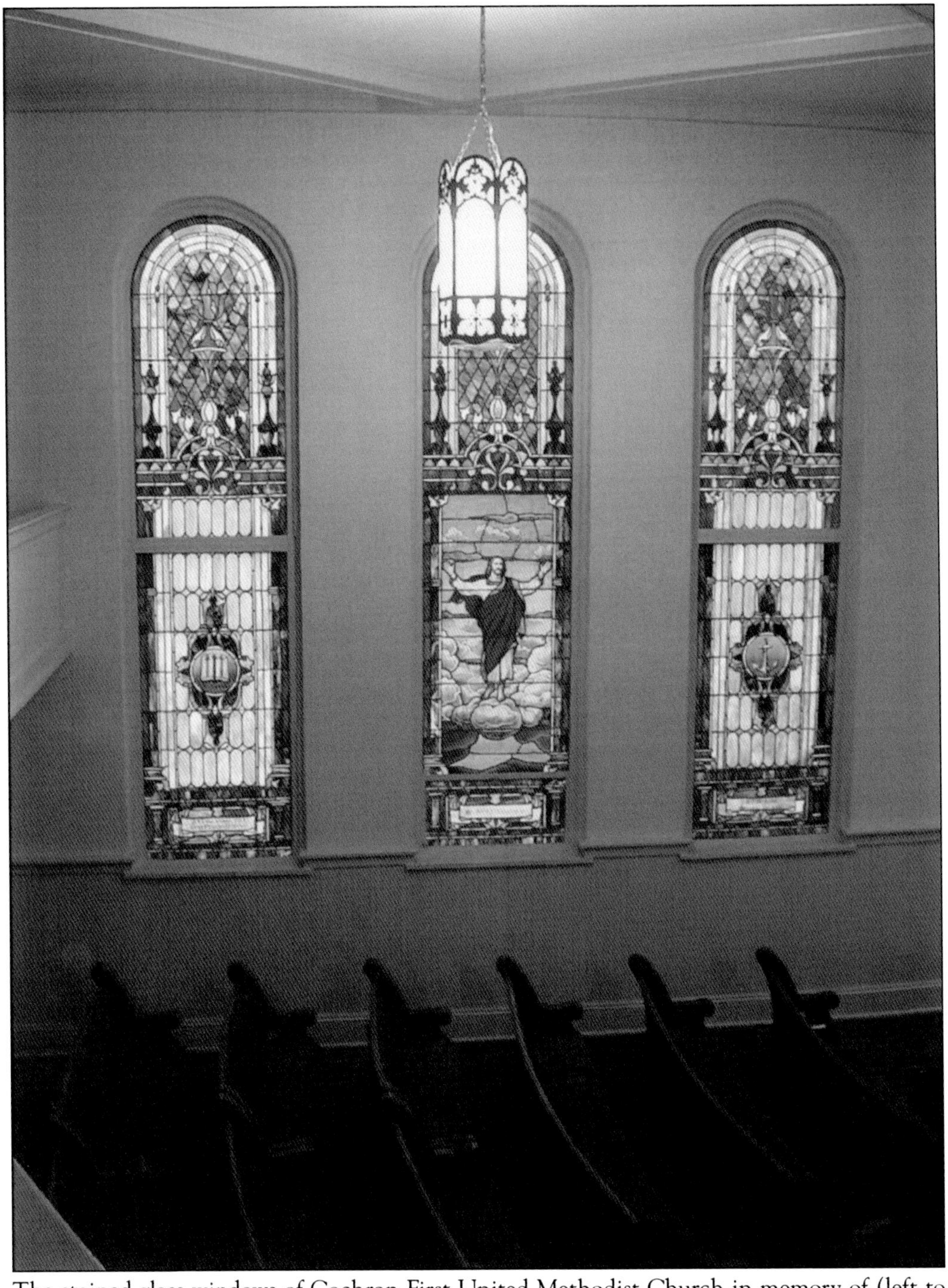

The stained-glass windows of Cochran First United Methodist Church in memory of (left to right) Anna Phoebe Grimsley, A. J. Thompson, and Robert Toombs Jackson were installed in 1916. (Courtesy of Deborah L. Ellis.)

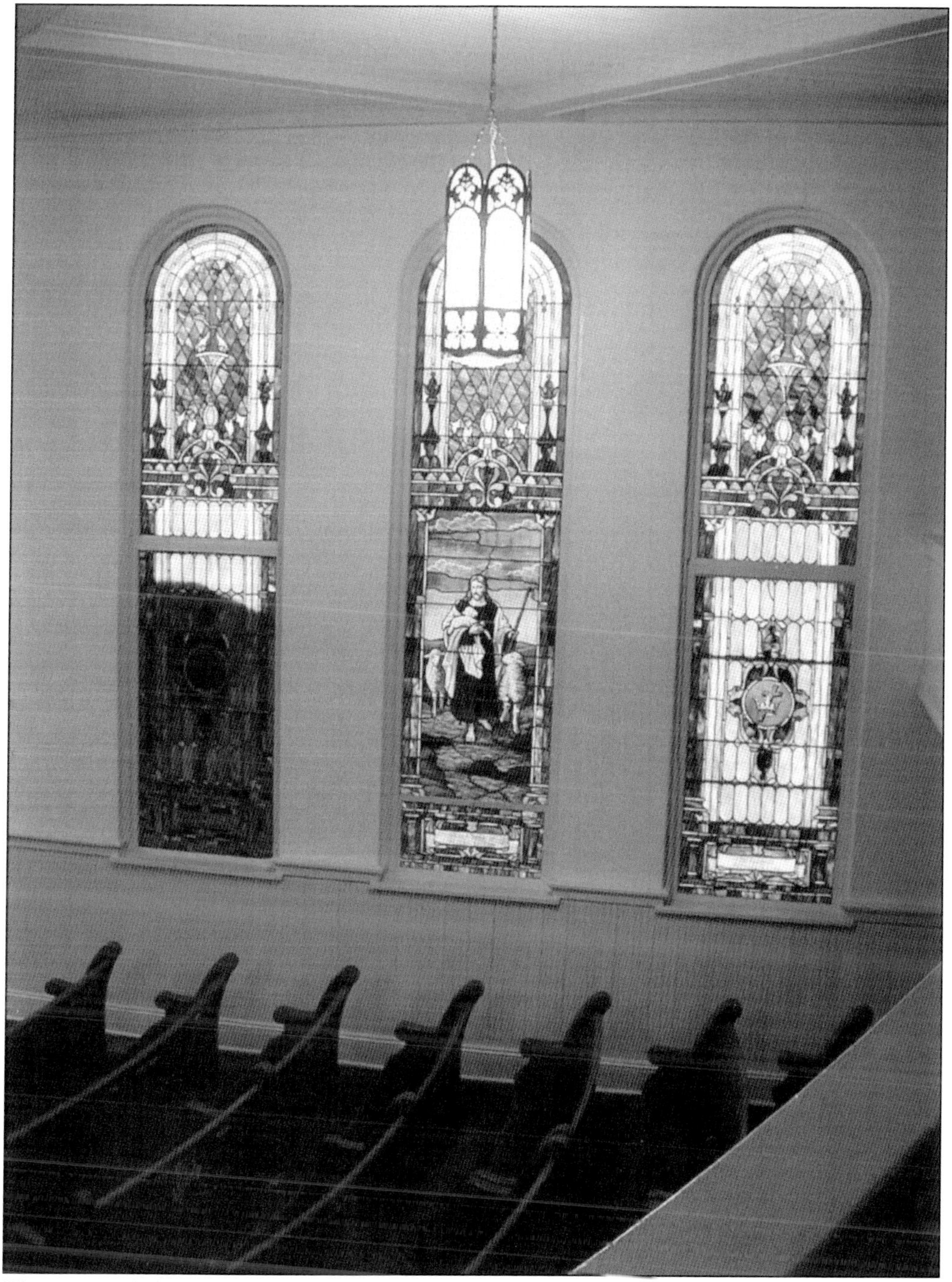

These stained-glass windows of Cochran First United Methodist Church are in memory of (left to right) Jesse W. Wynne, J. J. Taylor, and John C. Dunham. These three men were all born around 1850 and all died about the same time in 1914–1915. They were childhood friends at Longstreet Road. Each constructed store buildings in downtown Cochran and were successful merchants. (Courtesy of Deborah L. Ellis.)

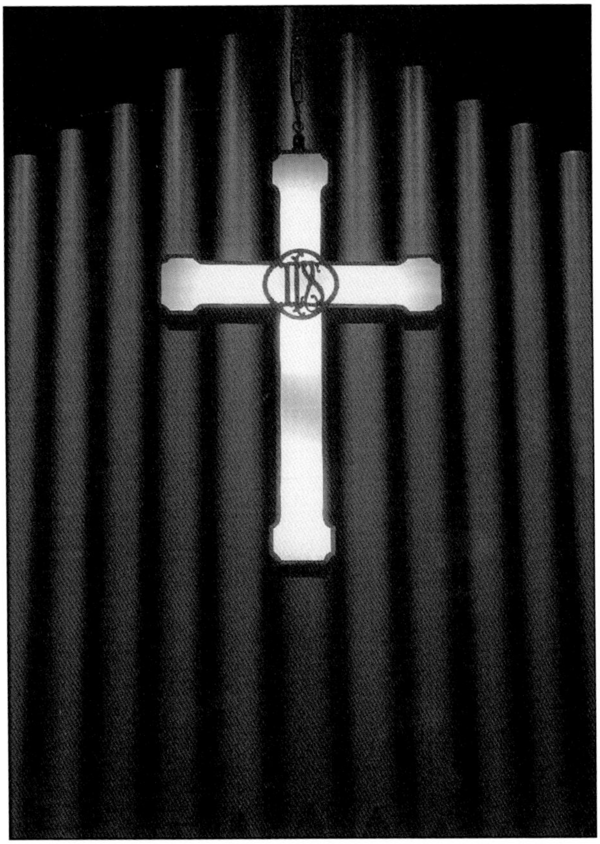

The cross above the altar in Cochran First United Methodist Church was installed in 1953 by the Andrew Lewis Thompson family. (Courtesy of Deborah L. Ellis.)

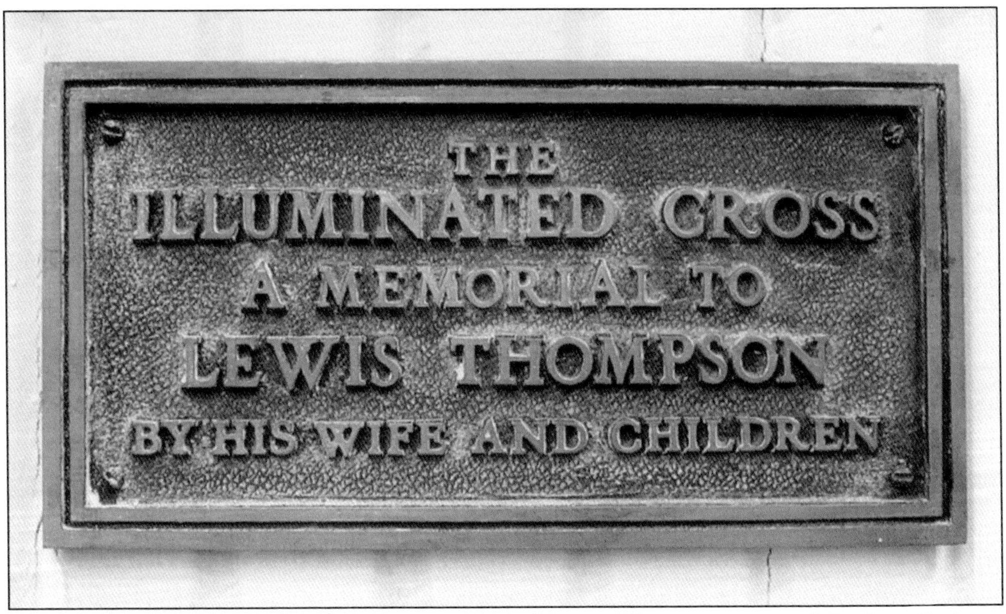

This photograph shows the plaque in memory of Lewis Thompson, son of Andrew Jackson Thompson and Kemper Peacock Thompson, located in the Cochran First United Methodist Church. (Courtesy of Deborah L. Ellis.)

This stained-glass window in Cochran First United Methodist Church is in memory of Sallie Birch McVay. (Courtesy of Deborah L. Ellis.)

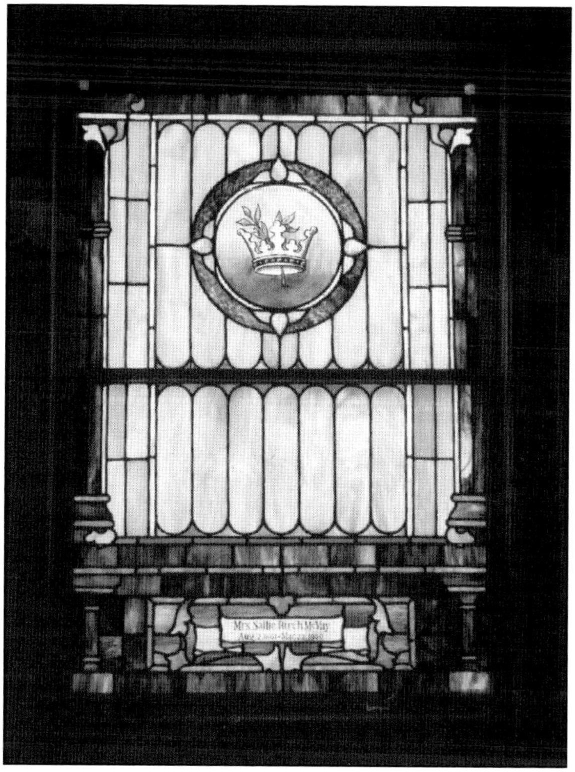

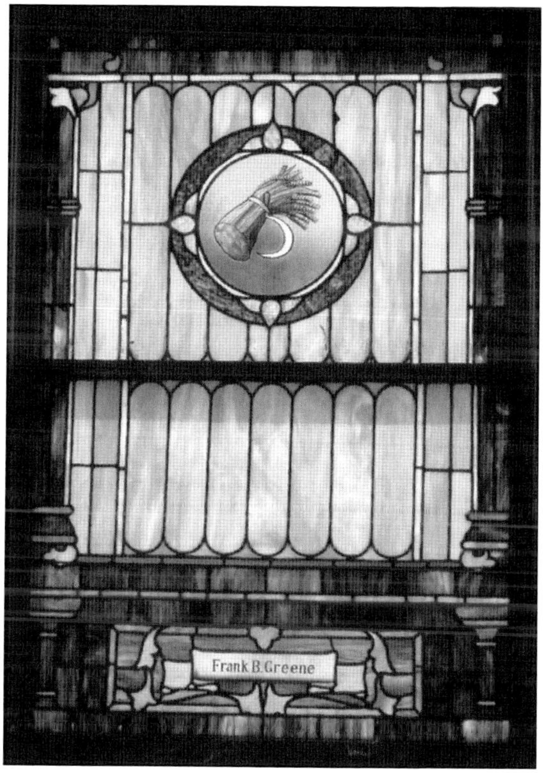

This stained-glass window in Cochran First United Methodist Church is in memory of Frank B. Greene. (Courtesy of Deborah L. Ellis.)

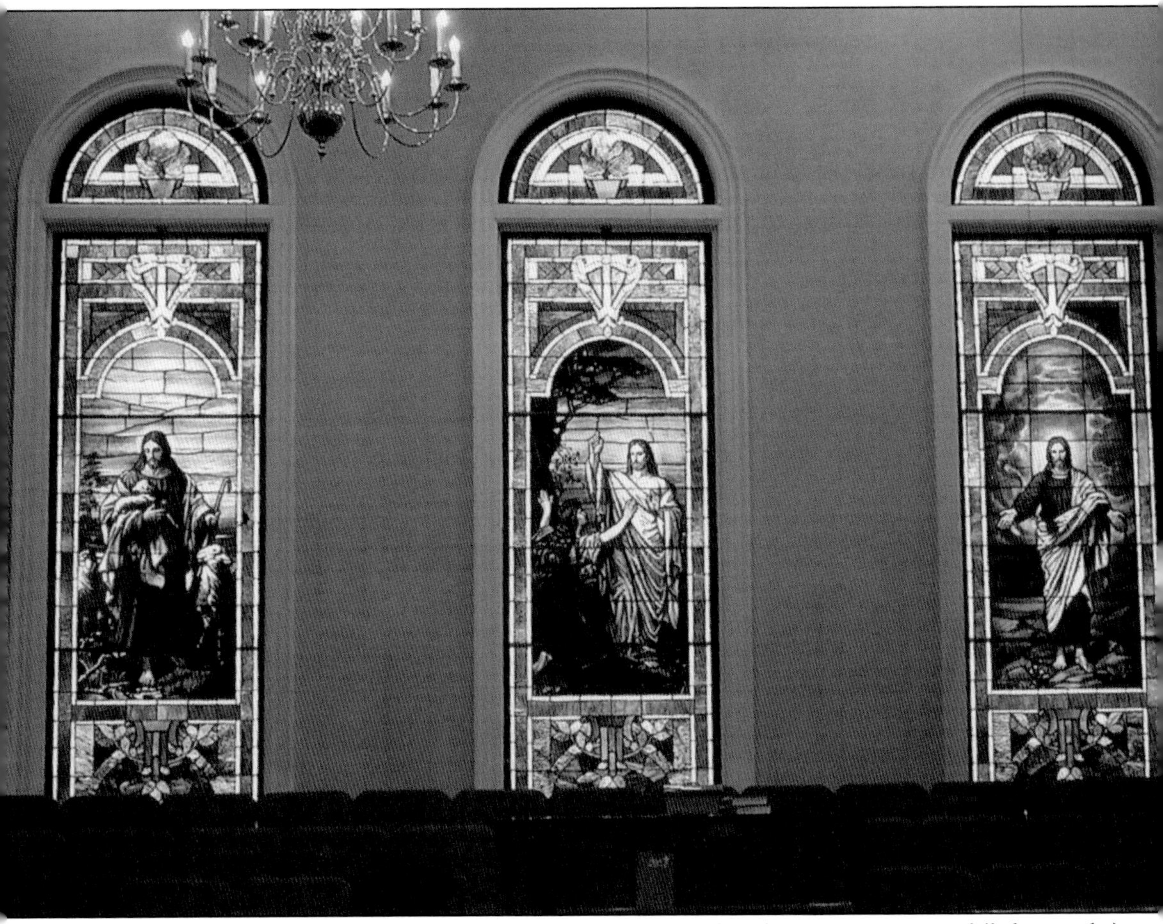

These stained-glass windows of Cochran First Baptist Church are in memory of (left to right) Wilson Hendricks and Elizabeth Hendricks, Martha Dykes Bullard, and Elijah Cook Sr. The Hendricks's daughter, Leila, married the Cooks' son, Elijah Cook Jr. Martha Dykes Bullard was the daughter of Burrell B. Dykes, who gave the land on which the church was first built in 1881. (Courtesy of Deborah L. Ellis.)

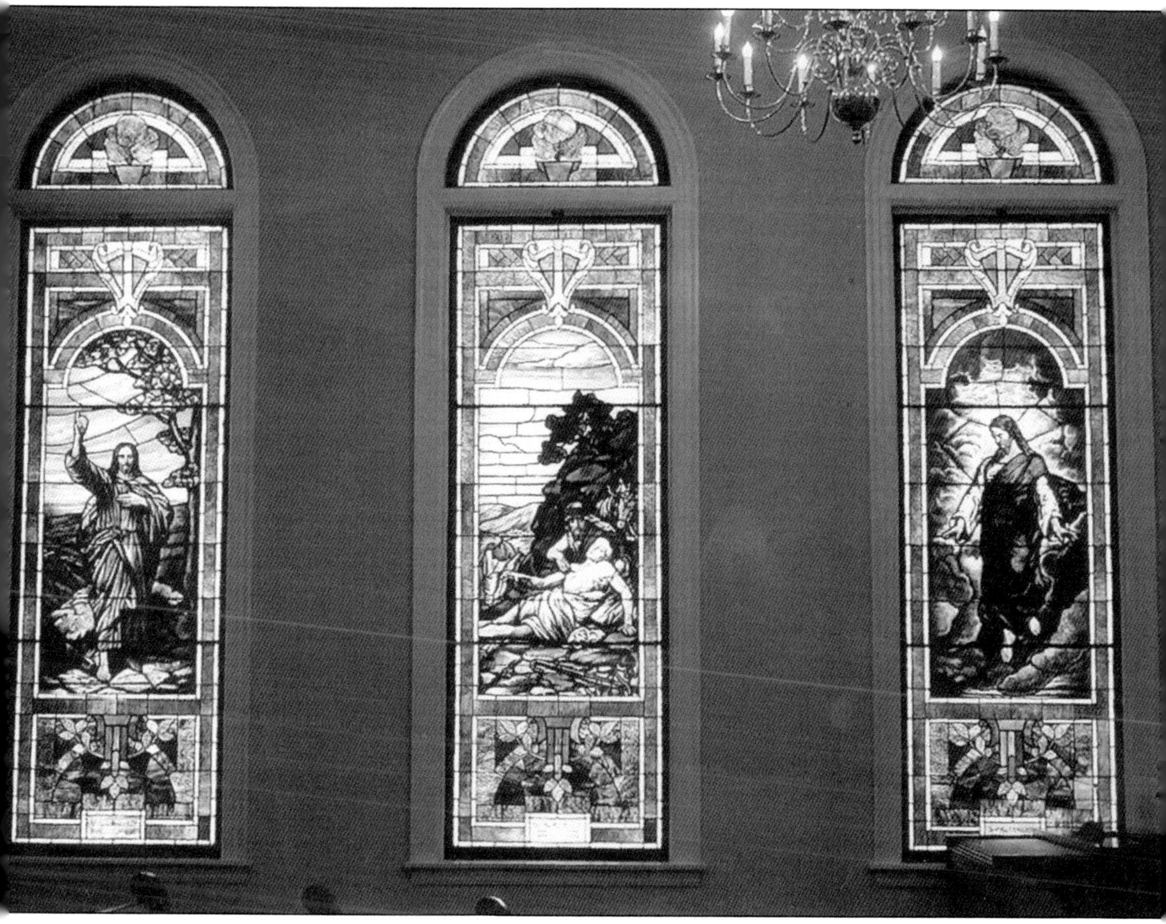

The stained-glass windows of Cochran First Baptist Church in memory of (left to right) Burrell B. Dykes, W. J. Mullis, and Thomas Duhart Walker Sr. were installed in 1917. (Courtesy of Deborah L. Ellis.)

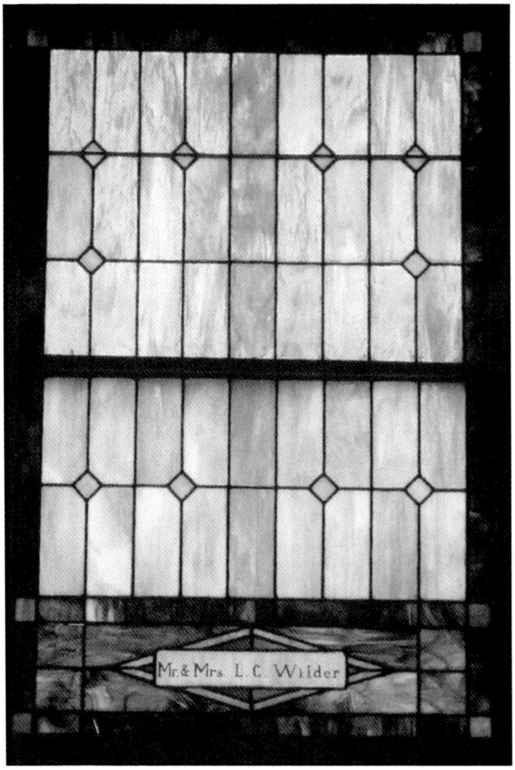

This stained-glass window of Cochran First United Methodist Church is in memory of Mr. and Mrs. Leighton C. Wilder (Mabel). (Courtesy of Deborah L. Ellis.)

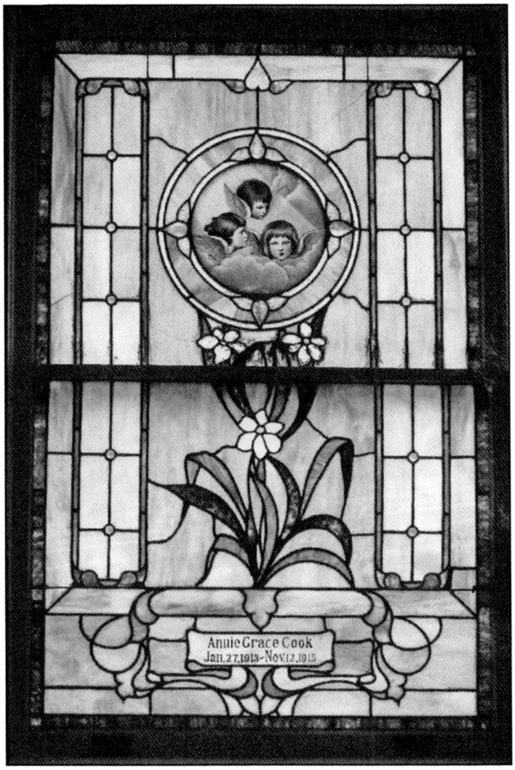

The stained-glass window in the choir room of Cochran First United Methodist Church is in memory of Annie Grace Cook, the two-year-old daughter of James E. Cook and Lottie Taylor Cook. (Courtesy of Deborah L. Ellis.)

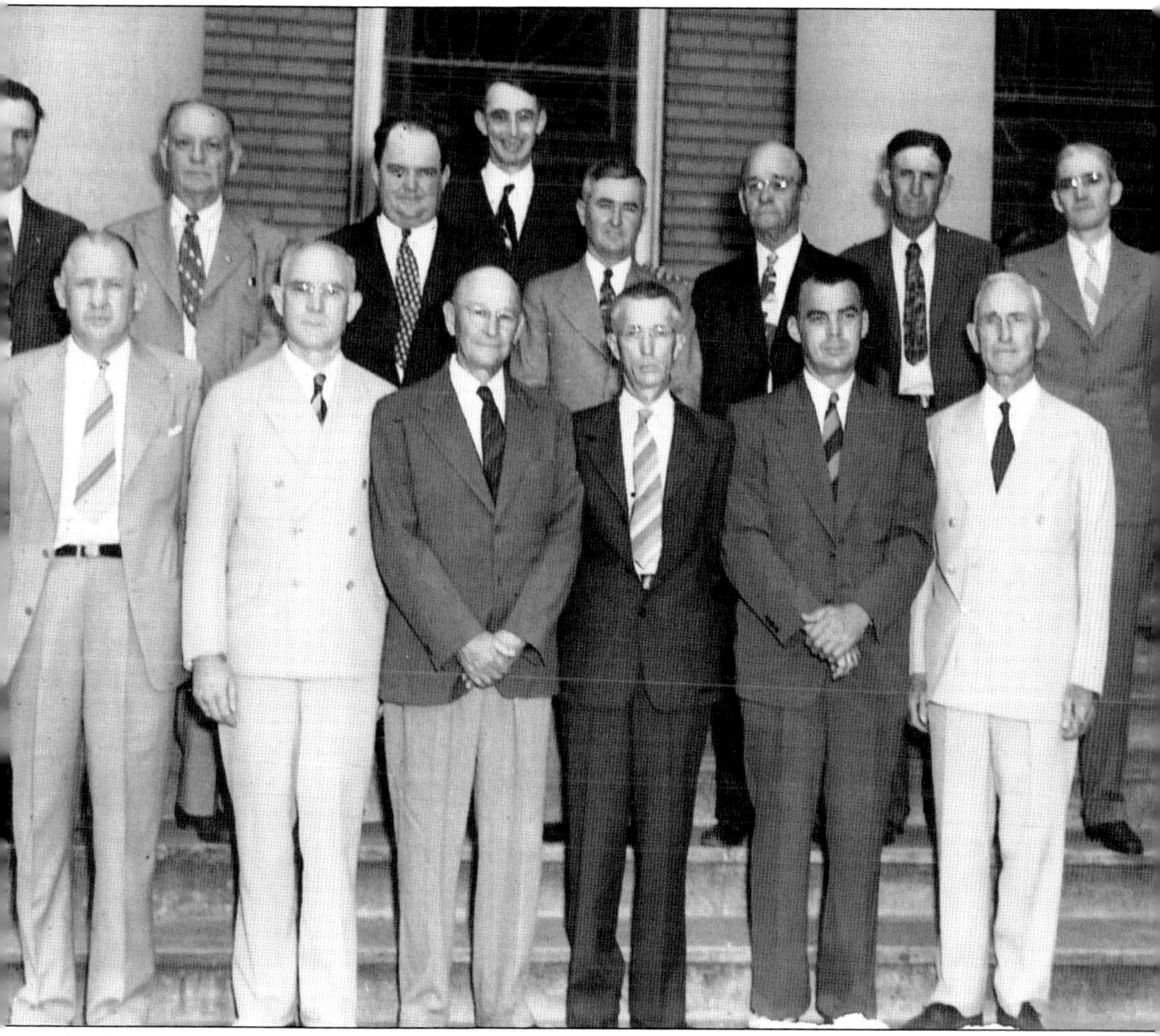

The deacons of Cochran First Baptist Church in 1946 were, from left to right, (first row) John T. "Jake" Morris (coach and dean of Middle Georgia College), A. A. Holcombe (Cochran grocer), Lucian A. Whipple (Cochran attorney of more than 70 years), Valda L. "Stratty" Adams, Whit Reeves, and Dr. Leo H. Browning (president of Middle Georgia College); (second row) Bennie Meadows, Dr. J. M. Smith, Leo L. Phillips Sr., pastor Lee Knowles, John D. NeSmith (clerk, Bleckley Superior Court), Dr. Robert L. Whipple (Cochran physician of many years), Dr. Thomas White (veterinarian), and Joe Lyles (Cochran merchant). (Courtesy of Lilla Lee Purser, daughter of Joe Lyles Sr. and daughter-in-law of Oliver Purser.)

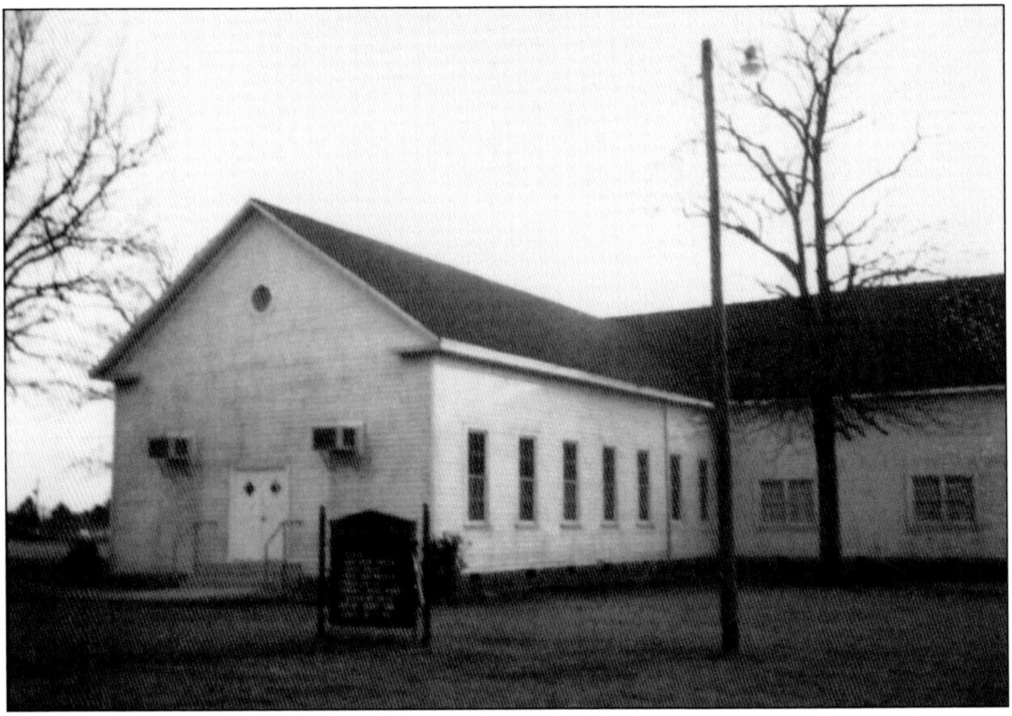

Lakeview Baptist Church was founded in 1960 and has had continued growth since that time. (Courtesy of Jack Lucas.)

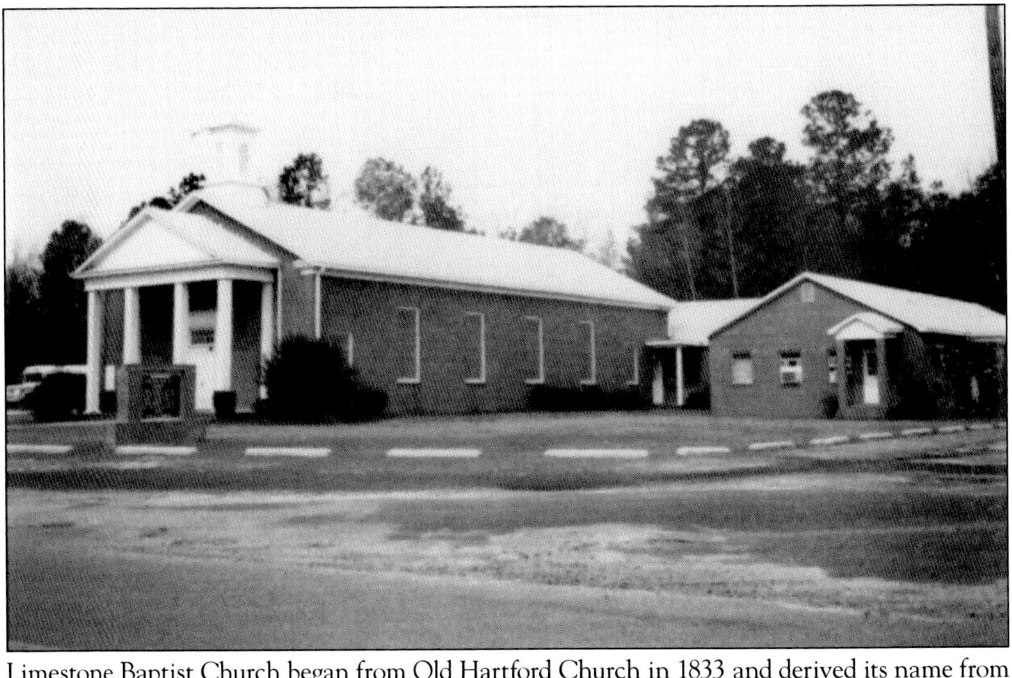

Limestone Baptist Church began from Old Hartford Church in 1833 and derived its name from its location on the banks of Limestone Creek. From an initial log building, two previous frame structures, and two devastating fires, the present brick structure has been in use for 25 years. (Courtesy of Jack Lucas.)

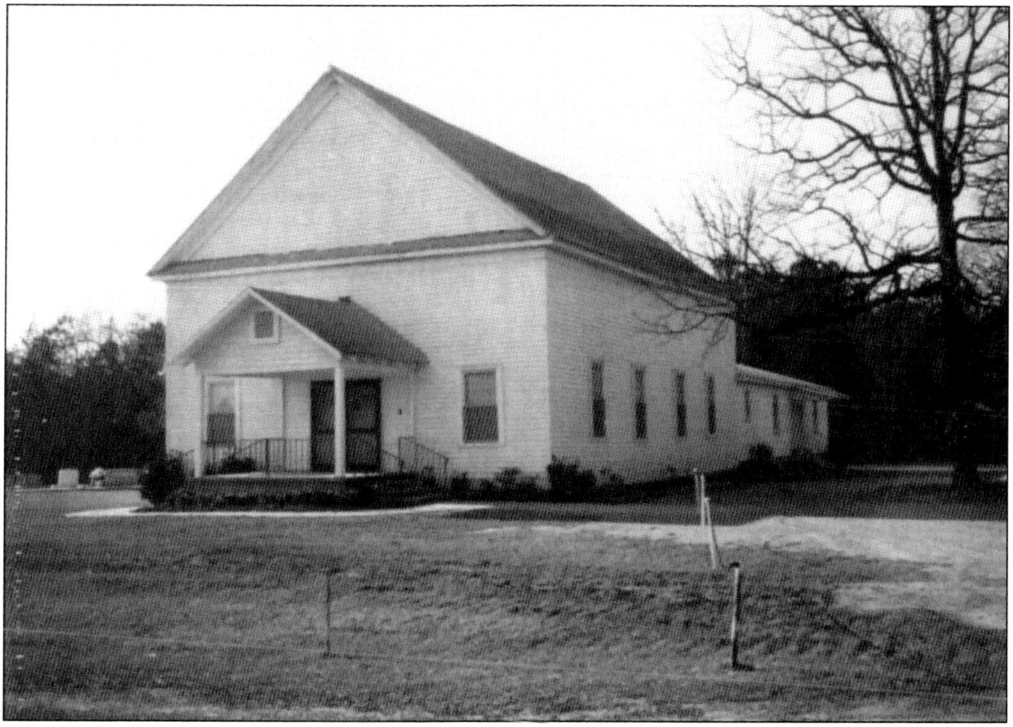

Little Bethel Free Will Baptist Church began in 1913 and acquired land the next year from Sarah A. Davis. A frame structure was erected in 1915, and a first revival was held. Although improvements have been made from time to time, church services have been held in the original structure in the same location for over 95 years. (Courtesy of Jack Lucas.)

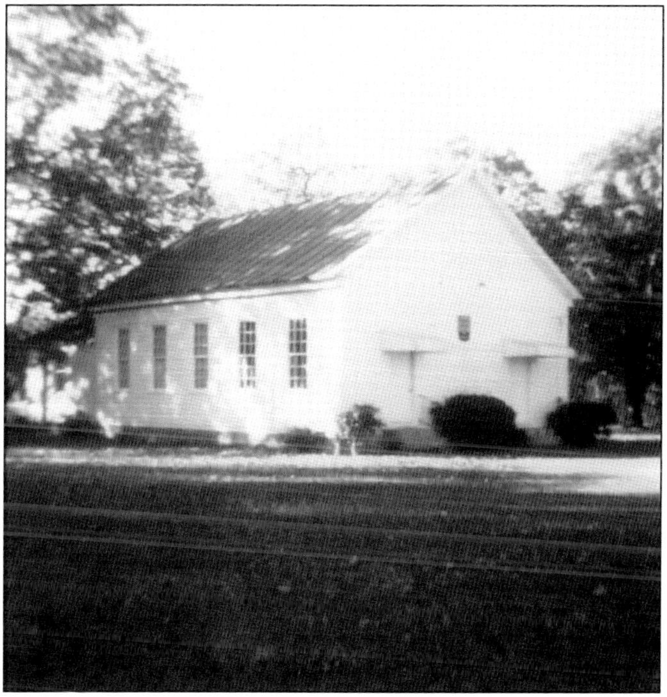

Longstreet Methodist Church developed after Native Americans ceded the lands between the Oconee and Ocmulgee Rivers in 1806. The church building is believed to have been built around 1812. Regular services are held each week. (Courtesy of Jack Lucas.)

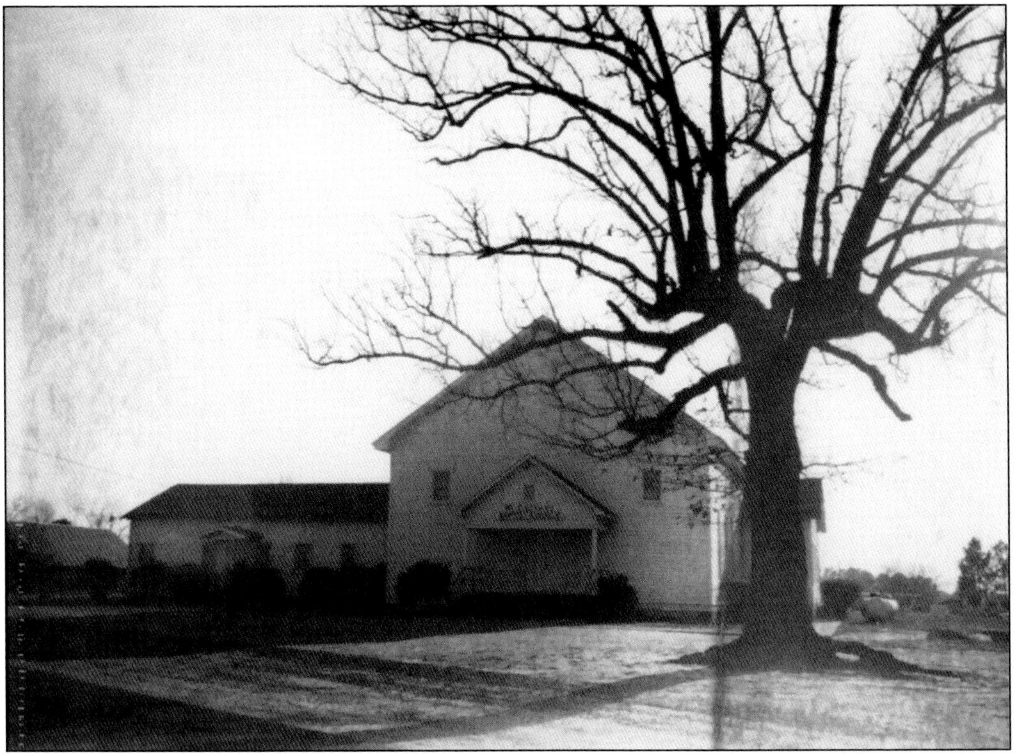

Mount Calvary Baptist Church, located in the Cary community, was established in 1840. "Cary" is said to derive its name from the first two and the last two letters of "Calvary." The church originally faced the cemetery and was later turned around to face the road. After Cary School was torn down, a new church facility was built, and the original church lands were added to the cemetery. (Courtesy of Jack Lucas.)

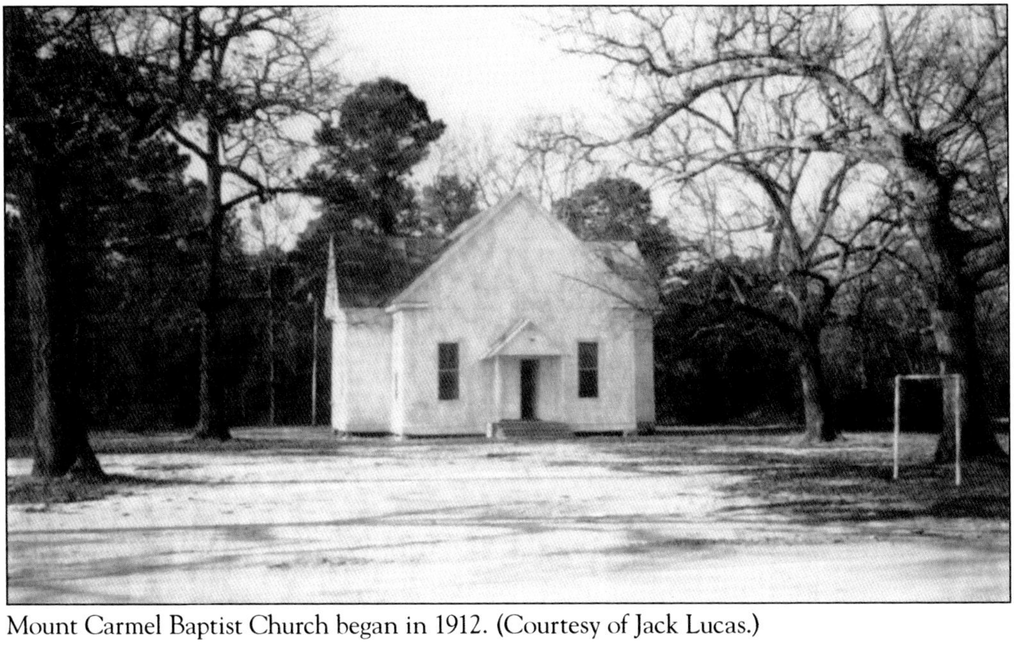

Mount Carmel Baptist Church began in 1912. (Courtesy of Jack Lucas.)

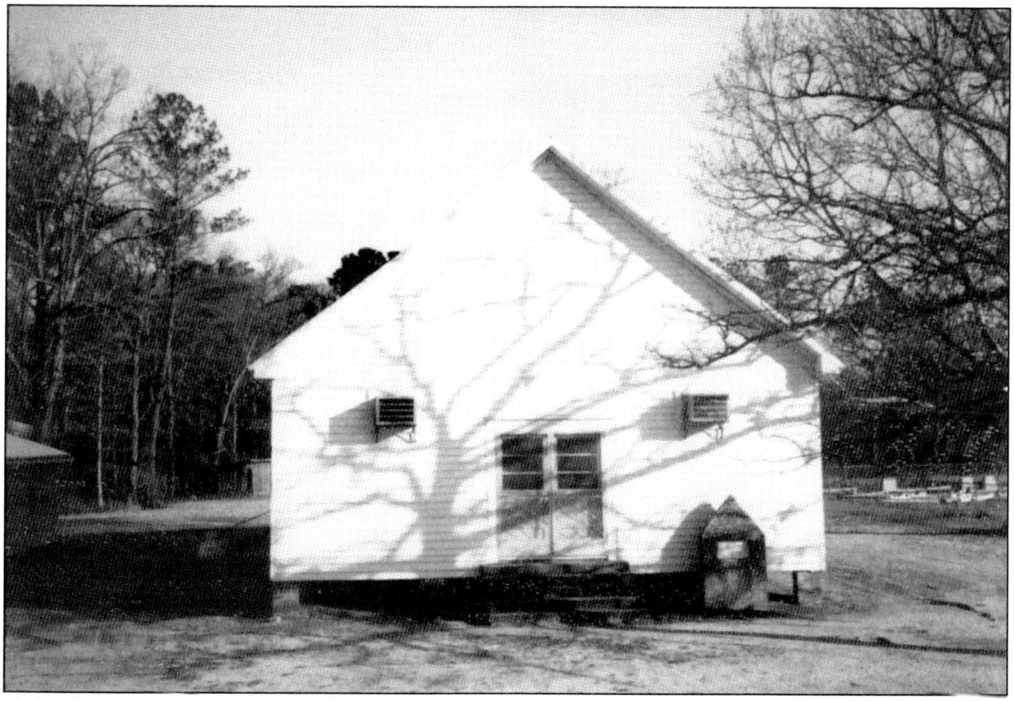

Oak Grove Primitive Baptist Church, located on the Chester Highway near Gum Swamp Creek, was formed on February 11, 1888. The church continues to have an active congregation. (Courtesy of Jack Lucas.)

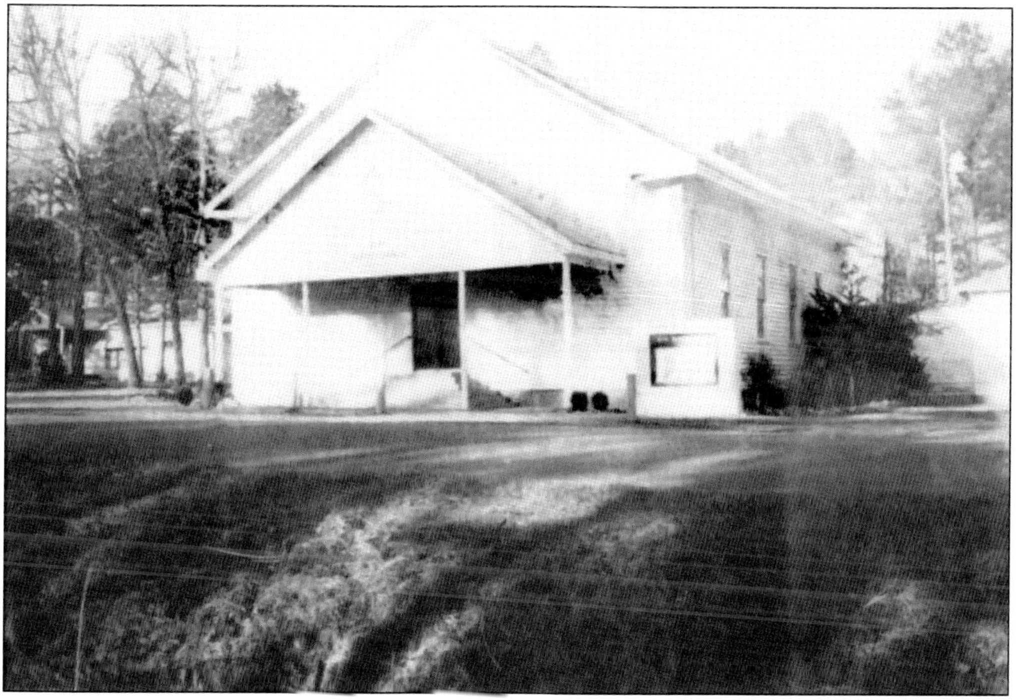

Ruth Baptist Church began in 1900. Its original frame building has been replaced with a brick facility, and a pastorium was added in 1966. (Courtesy of Jack Lucas.)

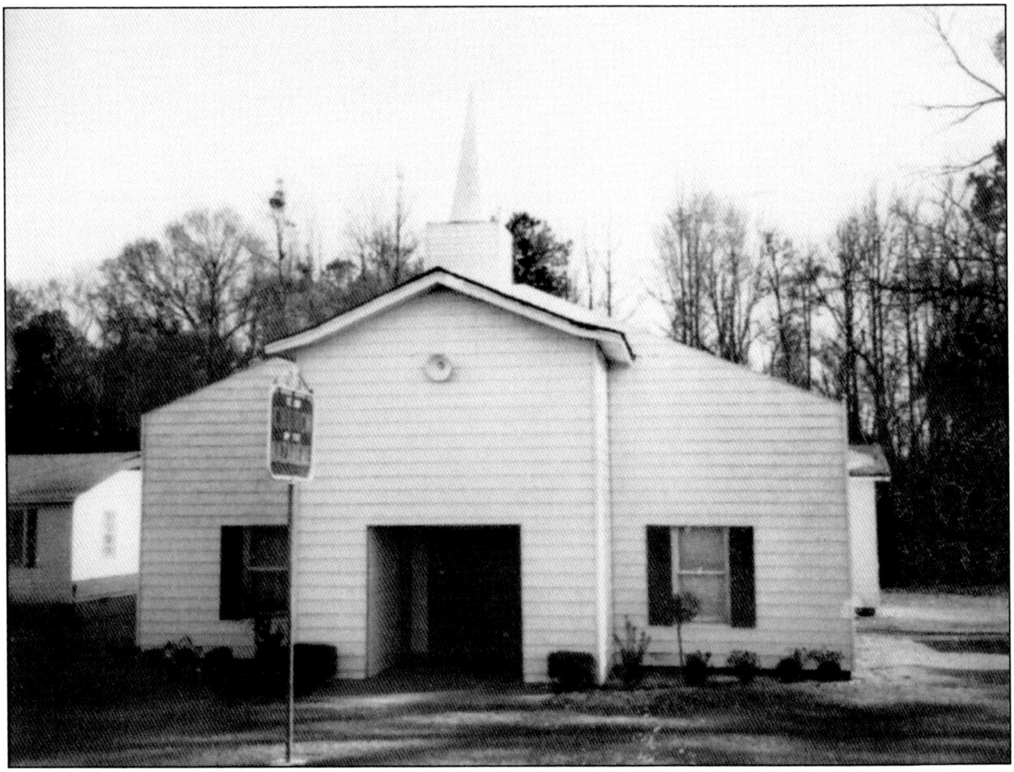

St. John Church of the Nazarene was located on the Dublin Highway. It closed in the 1970s, and most of its members moved their membership to other churches. (Courtesy of Jack Lucas.)

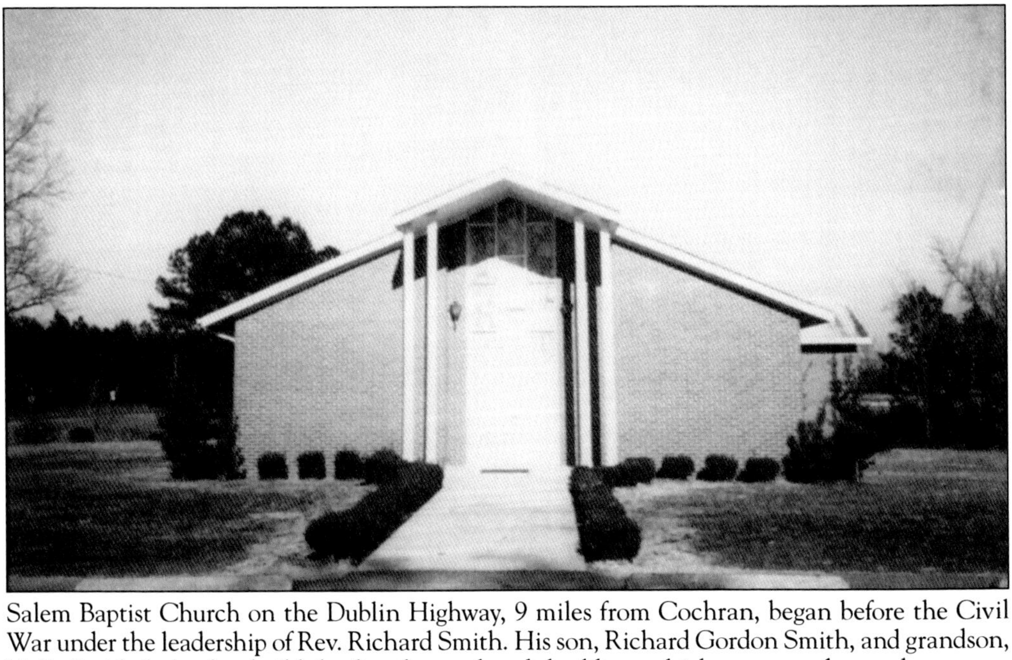

Salem Baptist Church on the Dublin Highway, 9 miles from Cochran, began before the Civil War under the leadership of Rev. Richard Smith. His son, Richard Gordon Smith, and grandson, U. R. Smith, helped to build the first frame church building, which was torn down when a new facility was dedicated in 1969. (Courtesy of Jack Lucas.)

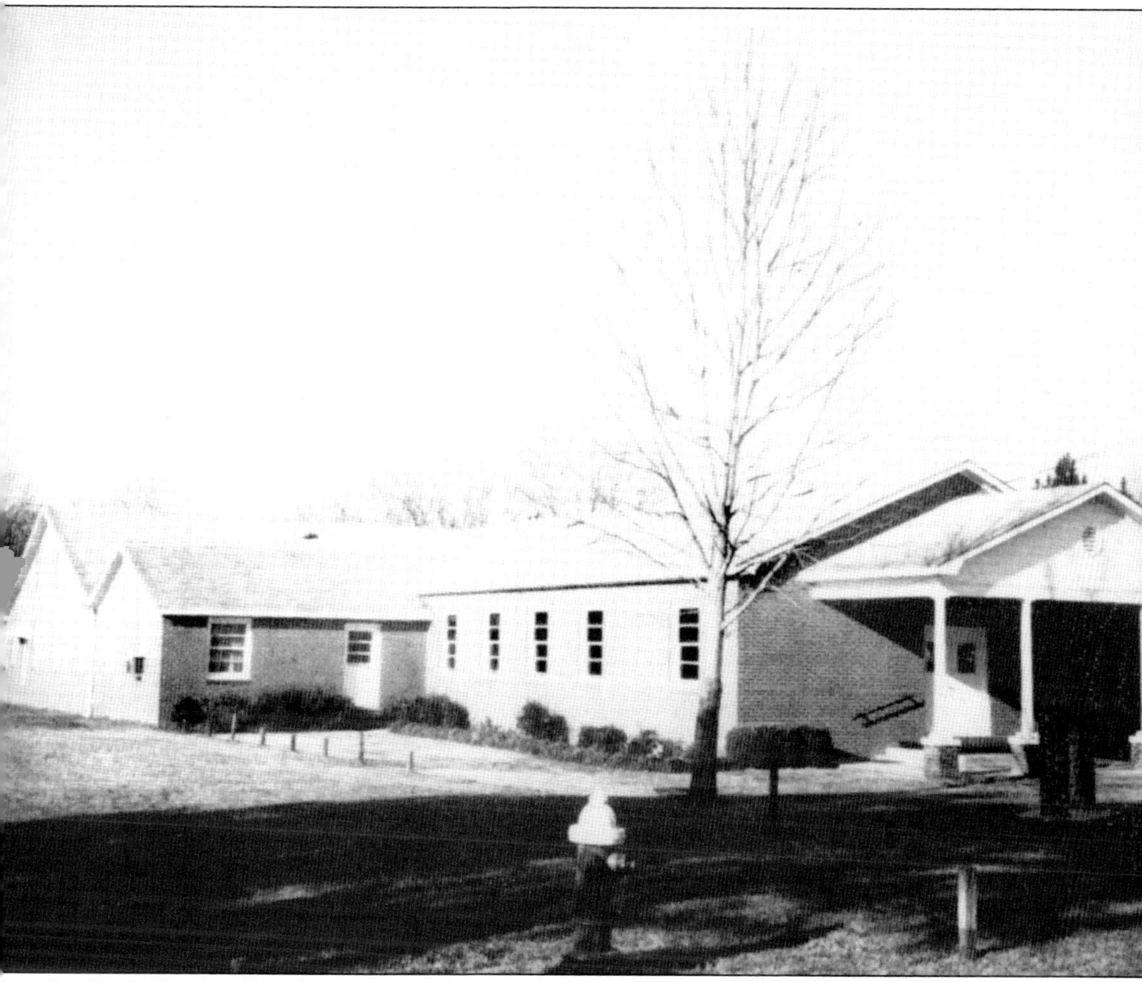

Southside Baptist Church in Cochran began in 1957 as a mission of Cochran First Baptist. J. T. Edmondson donated the land for a church meetinghouse, which despite a destructive tornado in January 1958 was completed and dedicated on June 8, 1958. (Courtesy of Jack Lucas.)

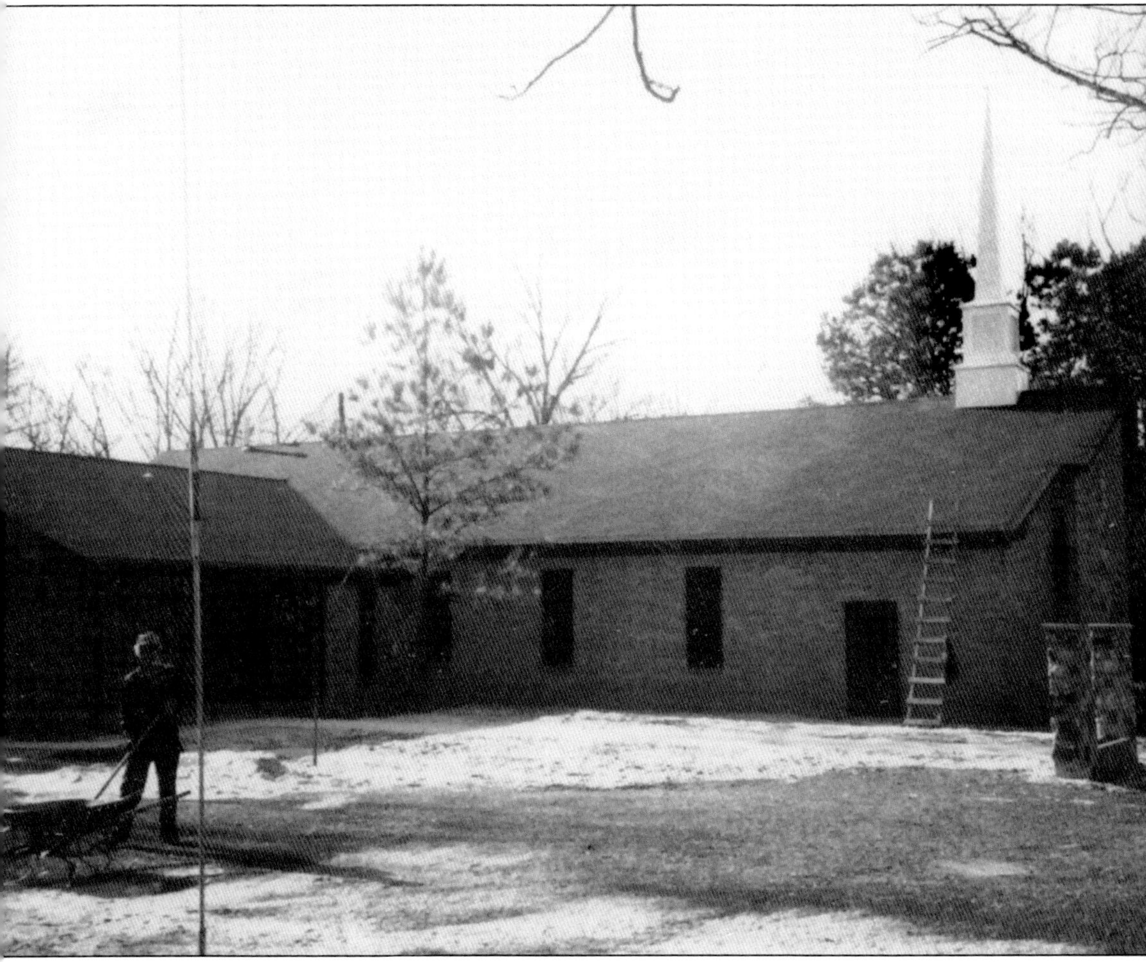

Tabernacle Baptist Church on Fifth Street in Cochran began in February 1965. A brick sanctuary seating more than 200 was built on the former home site of Annie and Ada Brown. The Brown home was used for a social hall for many years. (Courtesy of Jack Lucas.)

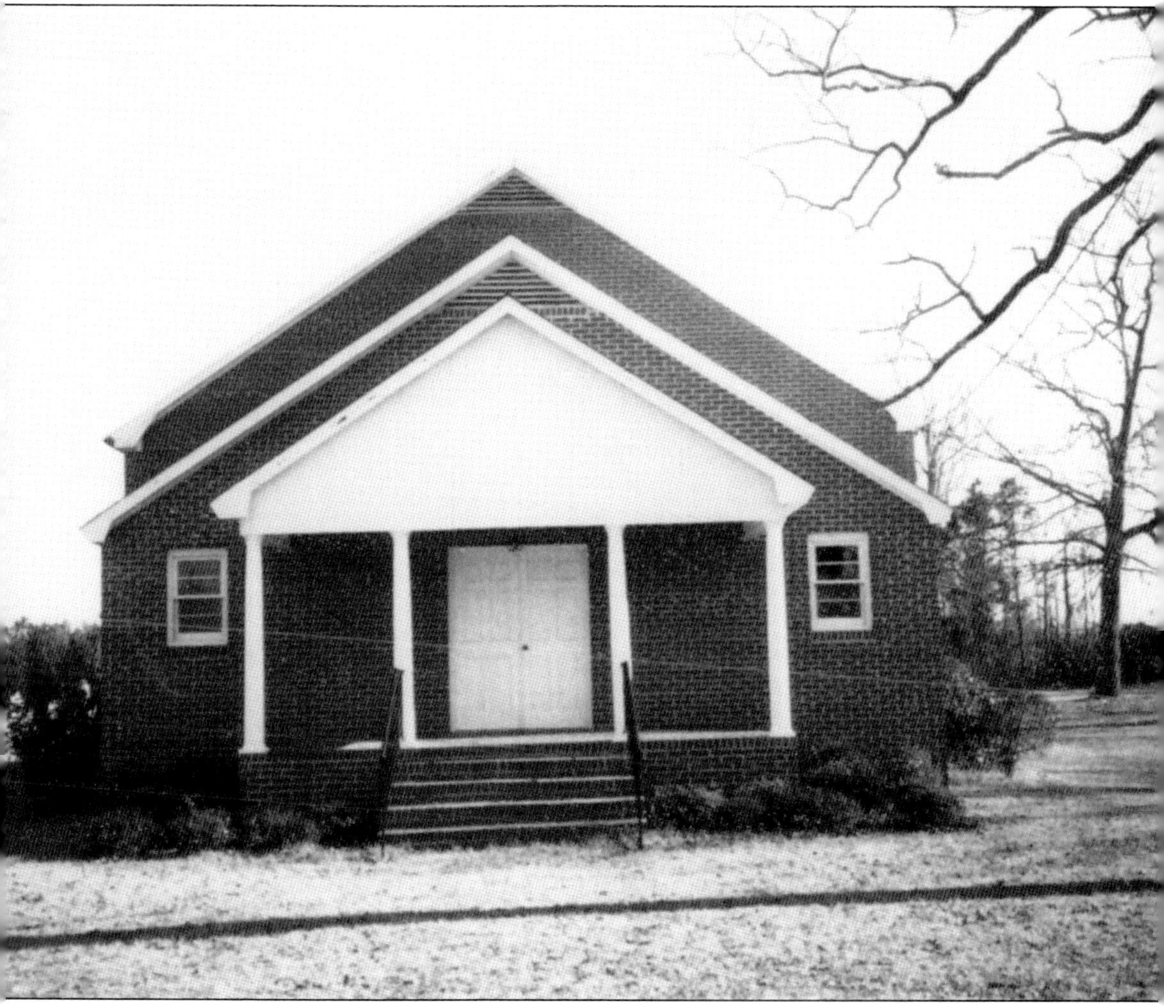

Trail Branch Primitive Baptist Church is one of Bleckley County's oldest. Organized in 1812 near Trail Branch, additional land for a church meetinghouse and cemetery was purchased in 1893, and the cemetery was enlarged in 1901. Trail Branch continues as a thriving congregation today. (Courtesy of Jack Lucas.)

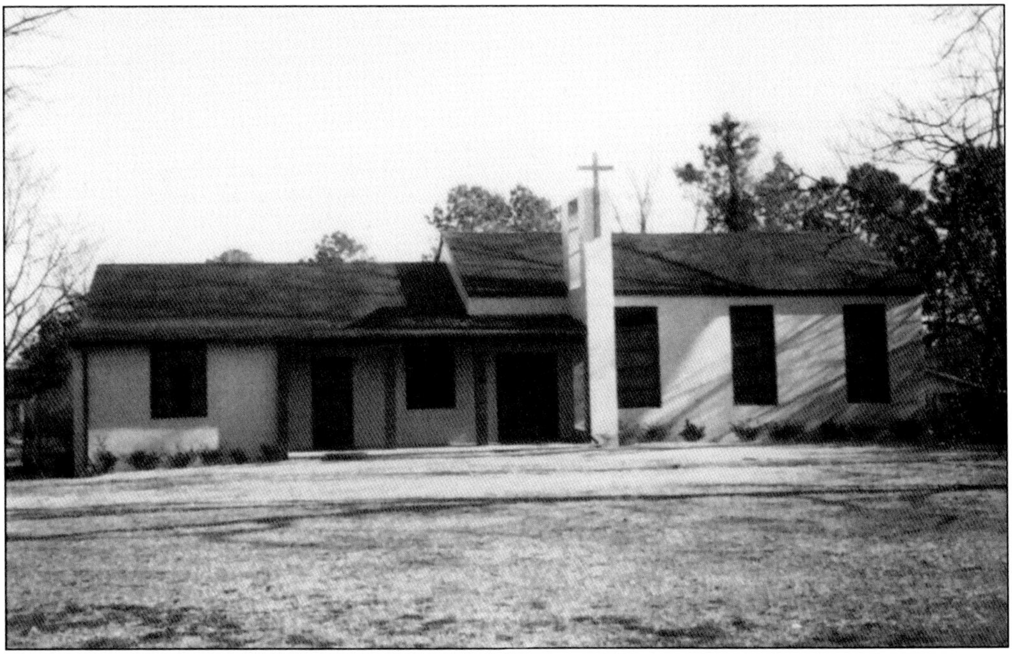

Trinity Episcopal Church began in April 1950 with communicants who previously worshiped at the Cochran Methodist Episcopal Church. The original church was built on land on Cherry Street donated by J. T. Edmondson, and today it is the parish hall. A new church building, constructed in 1980, and the Thorp House for additional meeting space completes the facilities today. (Courtesy of Jack Lucas.)

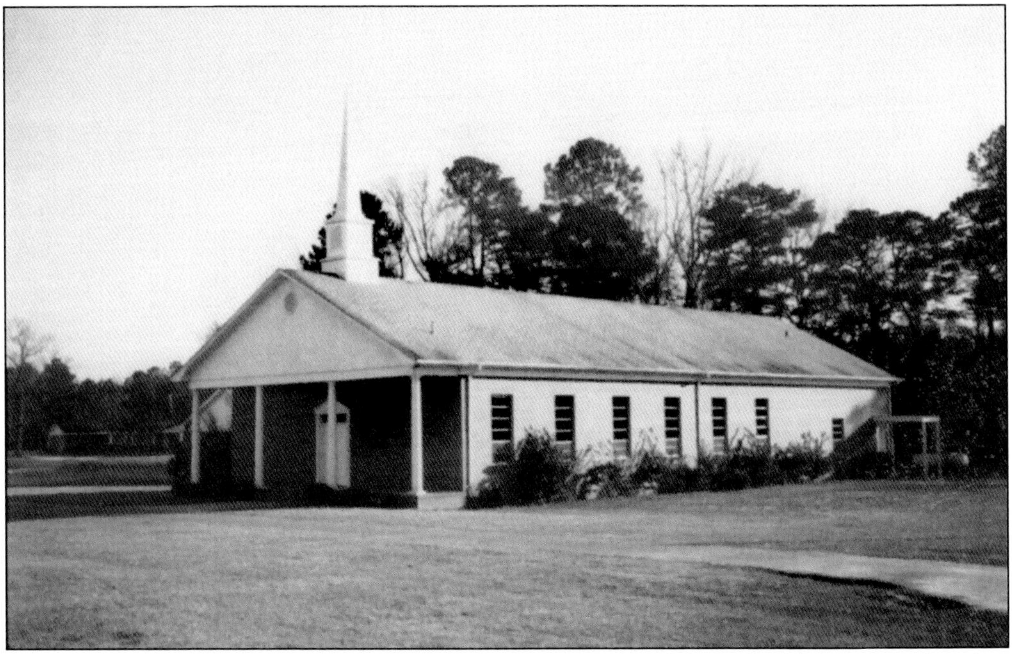

Union Hill Baptist Church was organized in 1895. An original frame building was replaced in 1963 with a brick facility, which continues to serve the needs of church members. (Courtesy of Jack Lucas.)

Four

HOMES

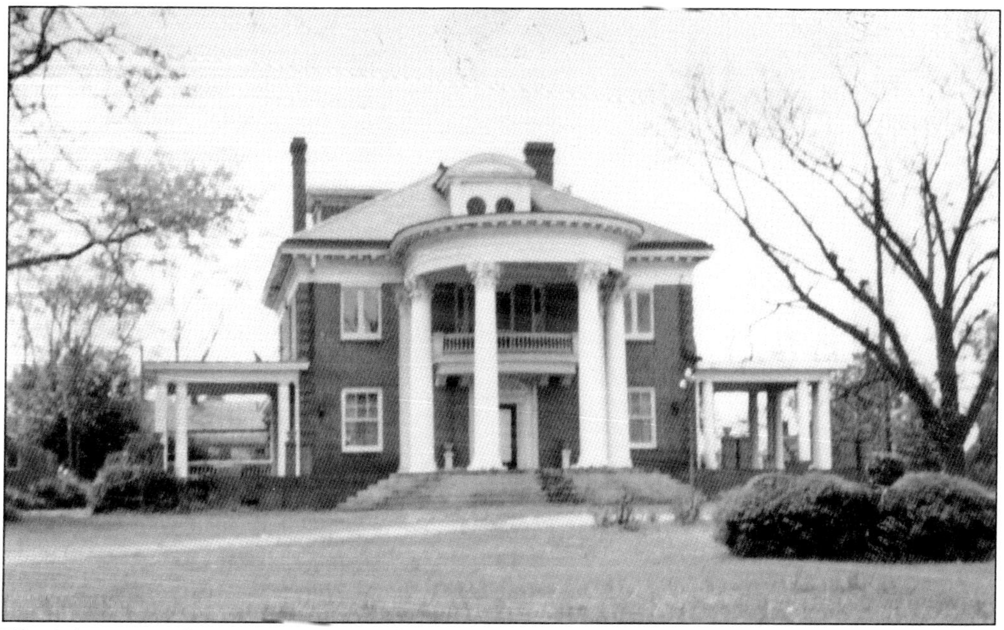

The John H. Mullis–Anderson Lee Howard house on Second Street was built in 1910 by John H. Mullis. Known as "Big John," he was chairman of the Building Committee when First Baptist Church was built directly across the street. The front door of his home was in perfect alignment with the Good Samaritan window of the church. When he walked out the front door of his home, he looked directly into the church window. Similarly when he stood in front of the window on the church porch, it looked directly into the glass front door of his home. He hoped that on equinox days in March and September the sun would rise in the glass door of his home and set in the Good Samaritan window of the church given in memory of his parents, William Jacob Mullis and Elizabeth Horne Mullis.

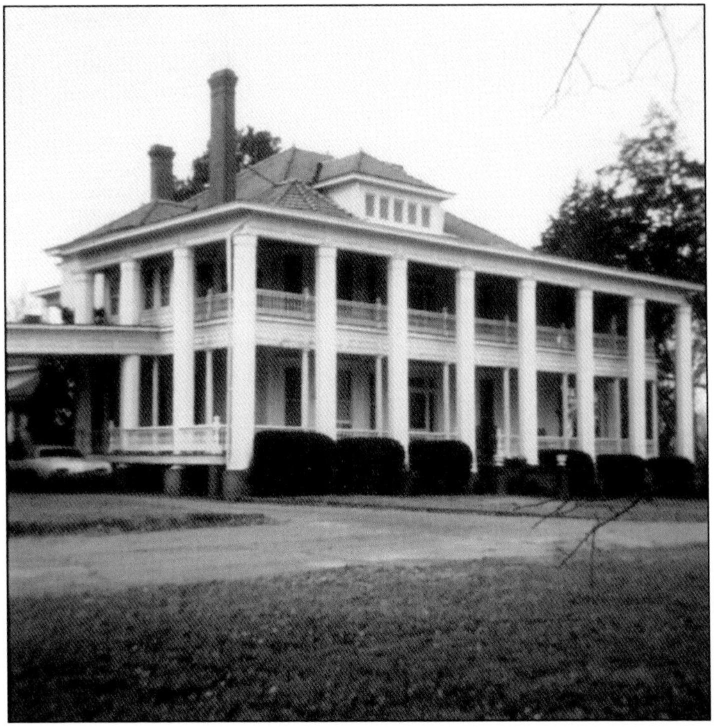

The home of Peter Lewis Peacock and Sarah Anne O'Berry Peacock was built in 1907; it became the home of Andrew J. Thompson and Kemper Peacock Thompson in 1913. When the Thompsons died, it was the home of their son, Andrew Lewis Thompson, and Elizabeth Proctor until 1944. It was purchased by James Marion Dykes and Kathryn Crooms Dykes Cheshire in 1944. In 1998, it became the home of Jerry Van Dykes and Jan Barber Dykes.

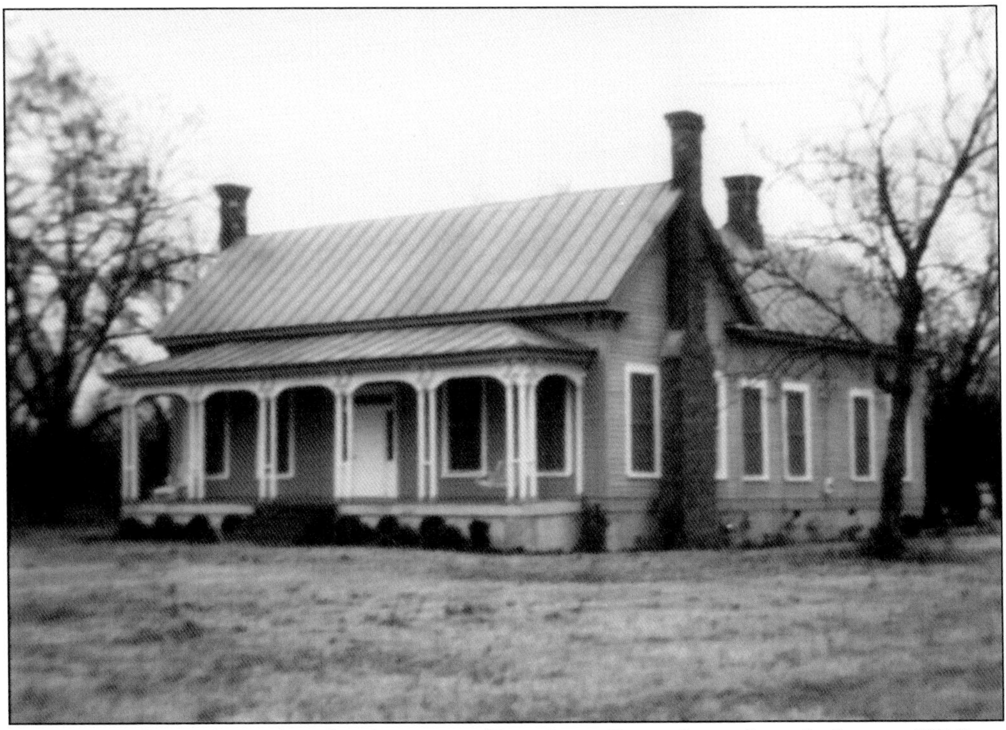

The O'Berry home, located on the plantation of Peter Lewis Peacock, was later the home of Wallace and Linda Dykes Padgett on Limestone Road. Presently it is the home of Donnie Thompson and Mary Turner Thompson.

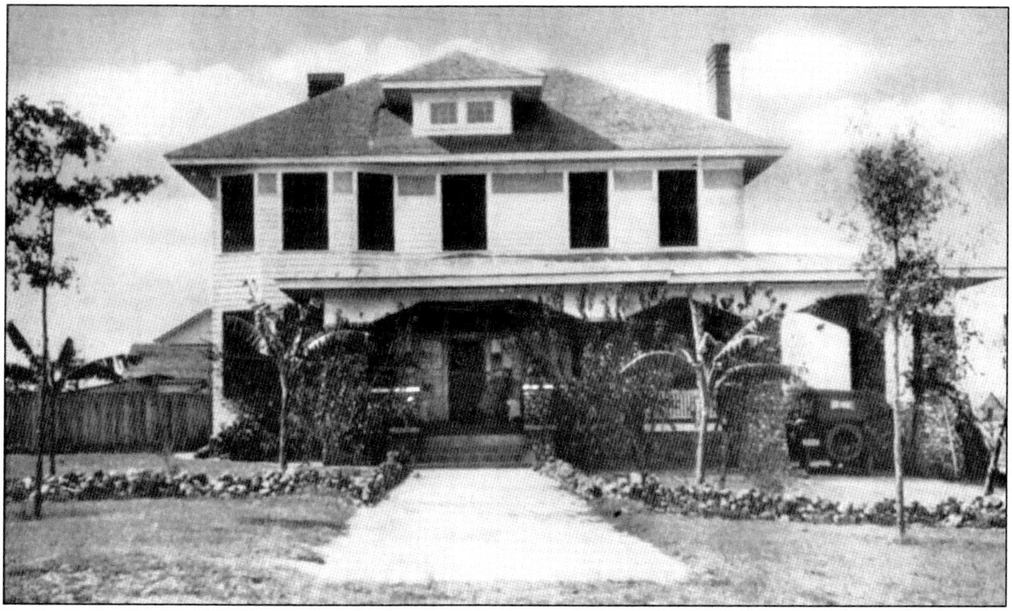

Built around 1919 for Tendall Harris and Vance Peacock Harris, this Second Street home near Middle Georgia College was the residence of Robert Emmett Dykes and Lillie Carden Dykes. It was later the home of their daughter, Jeynell Dykes, and today it is the home of Malcom G. McPhaul and Sandra Dykes McPhaul. (Courtesy of Deborah L. Ellis.)

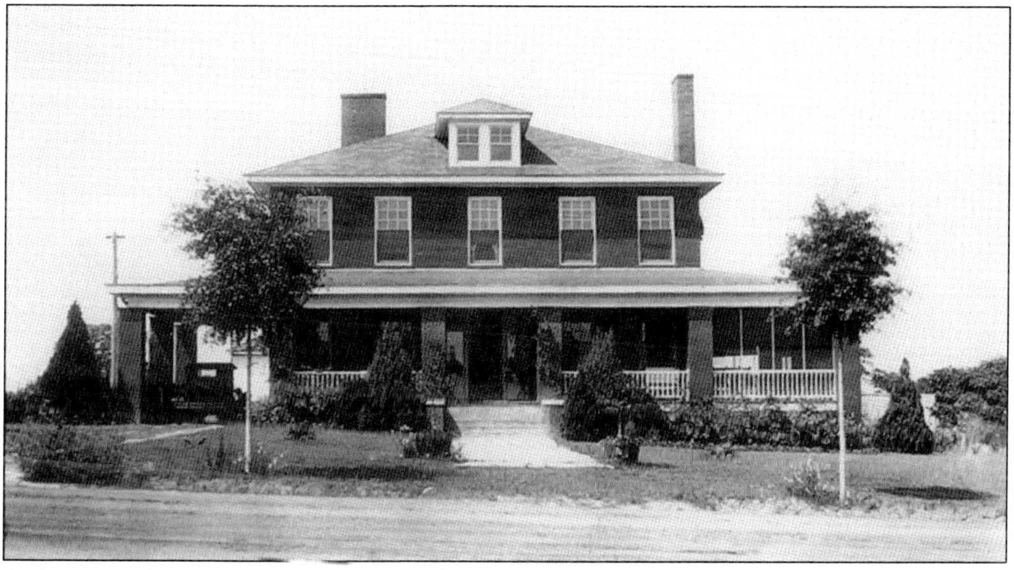

Built in 1921 for Wallace Leigh Harris and Virginia Speer Harris, this Second Street home is the residence of their daughter, Mrs. Early A. Ellis (Lola), and her daughter, Deborah Louise Ellis. Lola Harris Ellis is the great-granddaughter of Peter Lewis Peacock. This photograph was taken in 1926 by Virginia Speer Harris. (Courtesy of Deborah L. Ellis.)

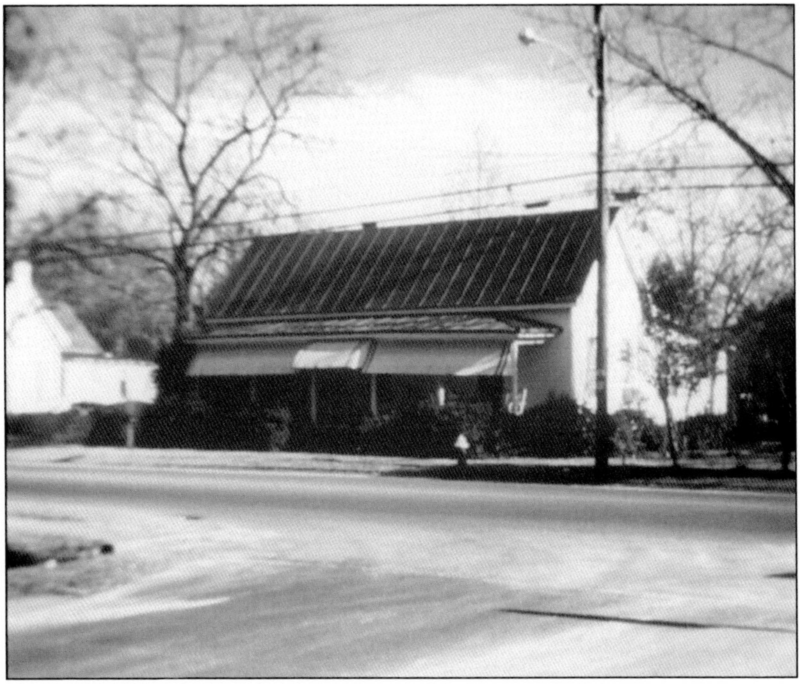

On Dykes Street, there were once three homes side by side belonging to J. T. Dykes, M. H. Dykes, and Tom Watson Dykes. The home of J. T. Dykes and Dora Dykes was near the "Big Ditch" (the present location of Subway).

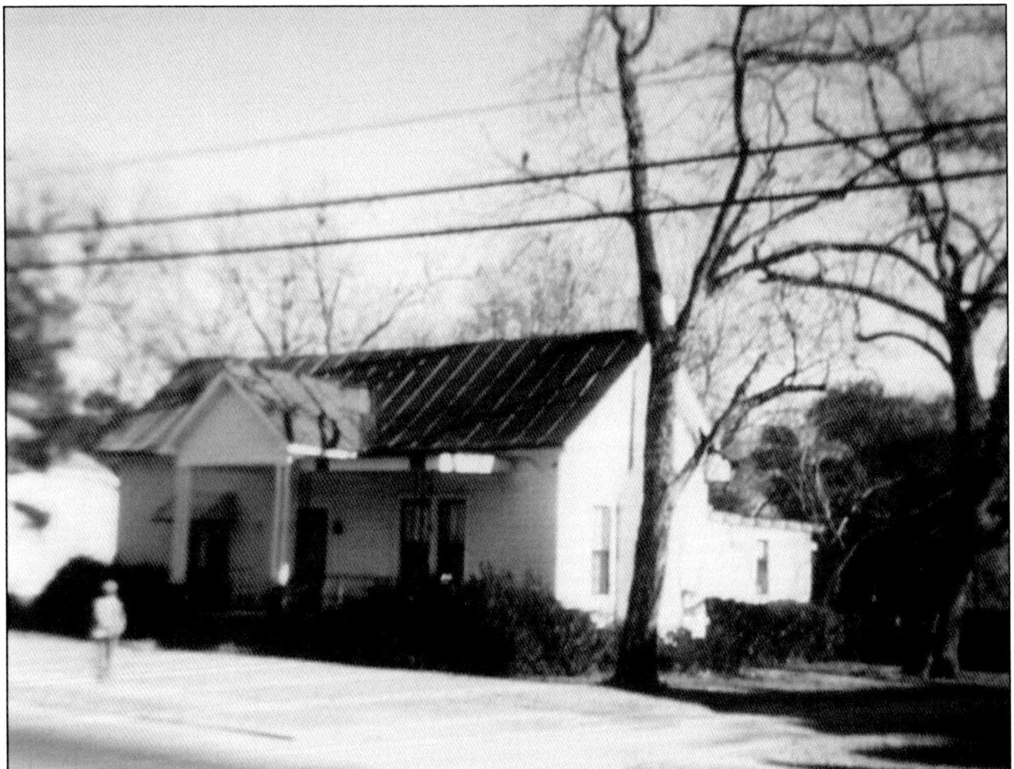

The home of Mr. and Mrs. Robert Emmett Dykes was later the home of M. H. "Buddy" Dykes, and Mae Meadows Dykes, and Kate Meadows, then it became the location of the Huddle House.

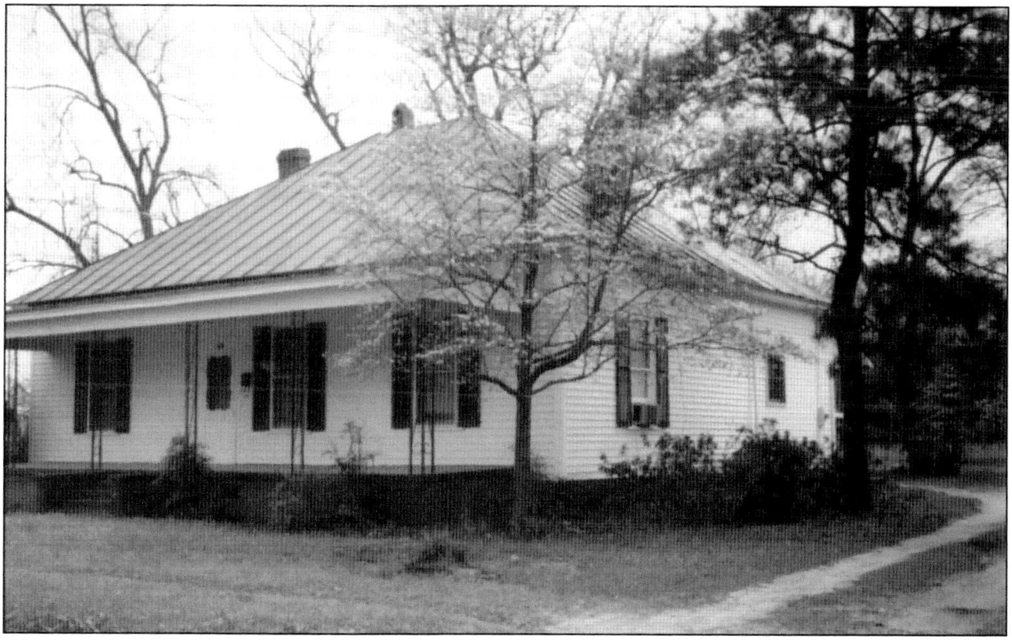

The home of Dr. Rufus Soloman Forehand and Retta Wilkinson Forehand became the home of Tom Watson Dykes and Aline Lewis Dykes. After the previous owners, it was the home of Ruth Johnson and is the present location of Royal Inn.

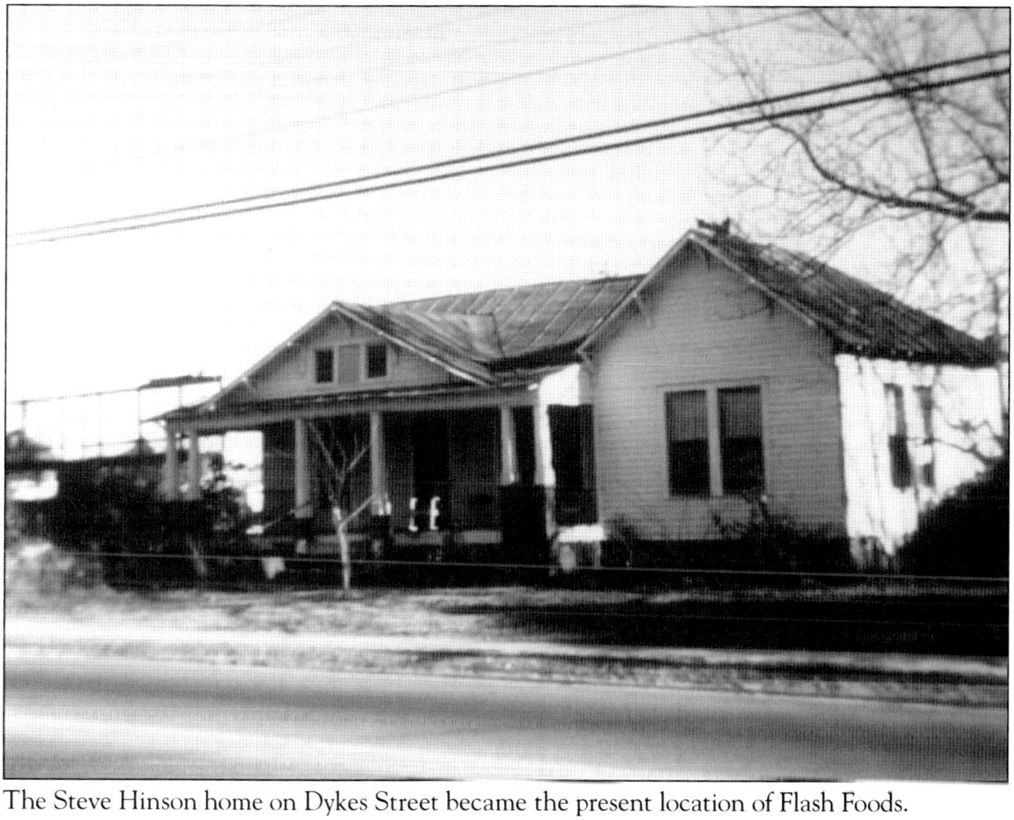

The Steve Hinson home on Dykes Street became the present location of Flash Foods.

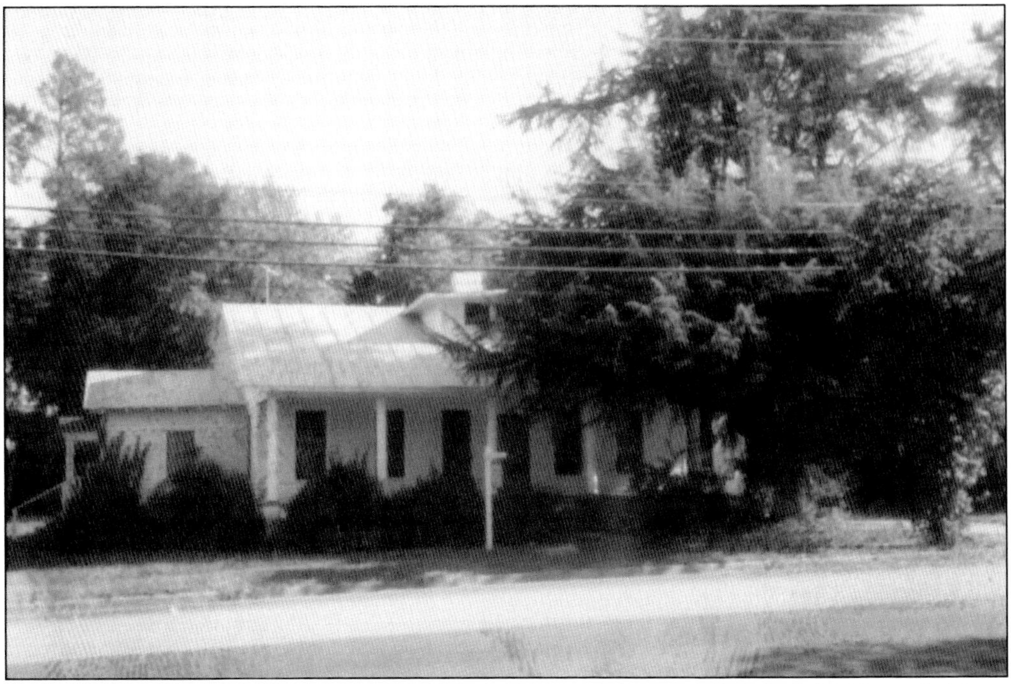

The Dykes Street home of George and Ruby S. McVay and their sons, Birch G. McVay and Robert Harrell McVay, became the location of Citizens Bank of Cochran.

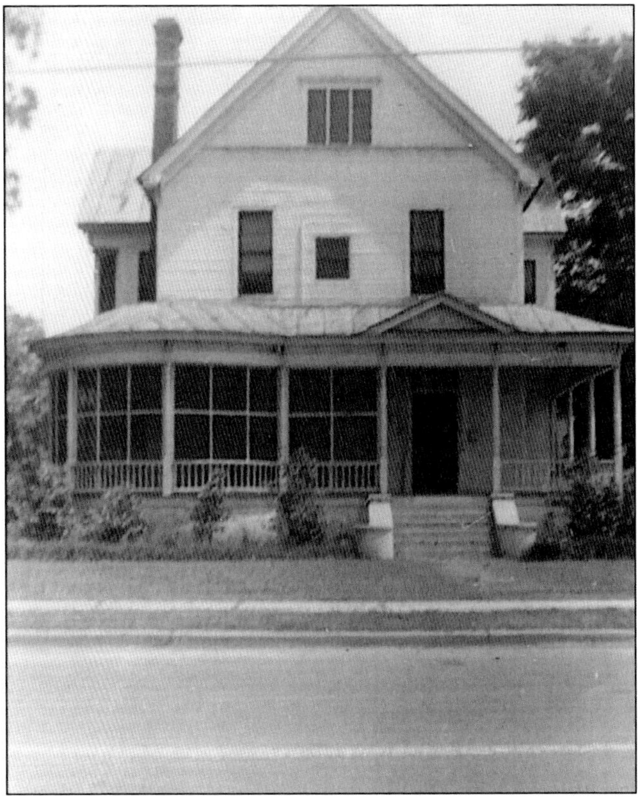

Built by Dr. Charles E. Taylor and his wife, Ida (daughter of Andrew Jackson Thompson Sr. and Frances Parten Thompson), in 1944, this home was purchased by Ruth J. Johnson, who operated a boardinghouse for Cochran High School teachers until 1965, when the property was purchased by First Baptist Church. Today it is part of the Dykes Street building. (Courtesy of Jane Durham Johnson.)

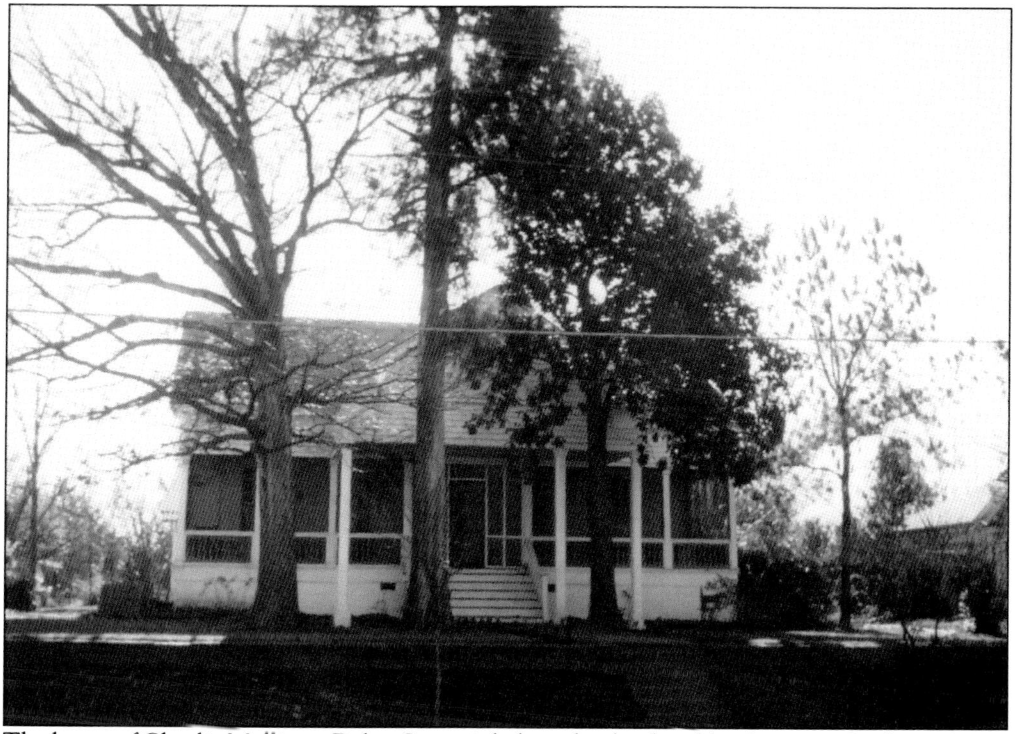

The home of Charlie Mullis on Dykes Street is believed to be the oldest house in Cochran. It was later the home of Leo H. Browning, president of Middle Georgia College. Today it is the home of F. D. "Freddy" Wimberly and Juanita Curington Wimberly.

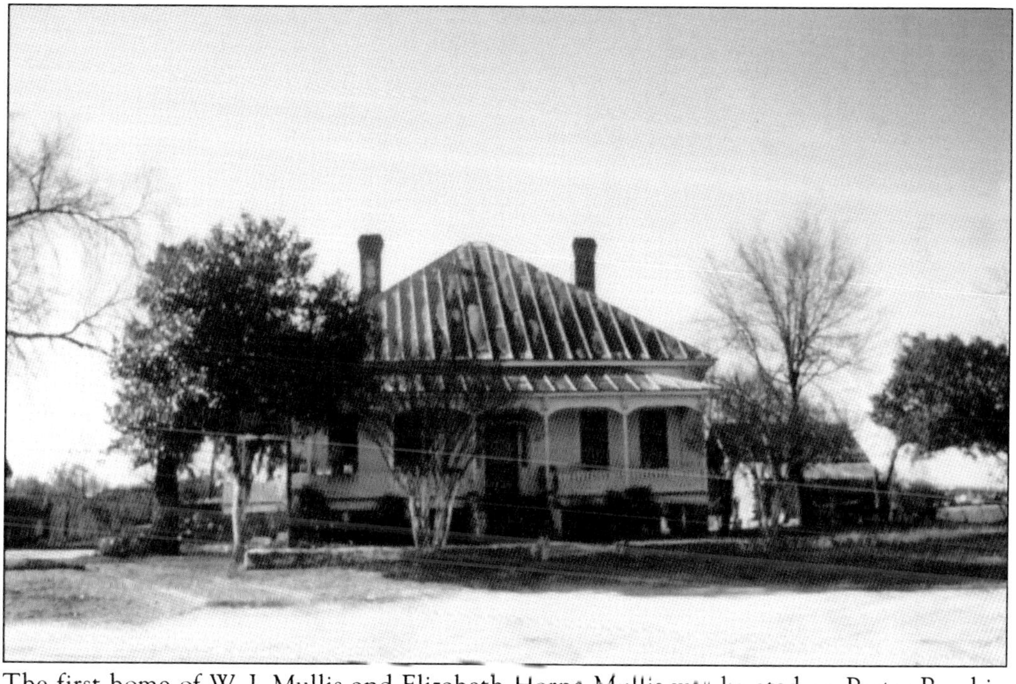

The first home of W. J. Mullis and Elizabeth Horne Mullis was located on Porter Road in Cochran, Georgia.

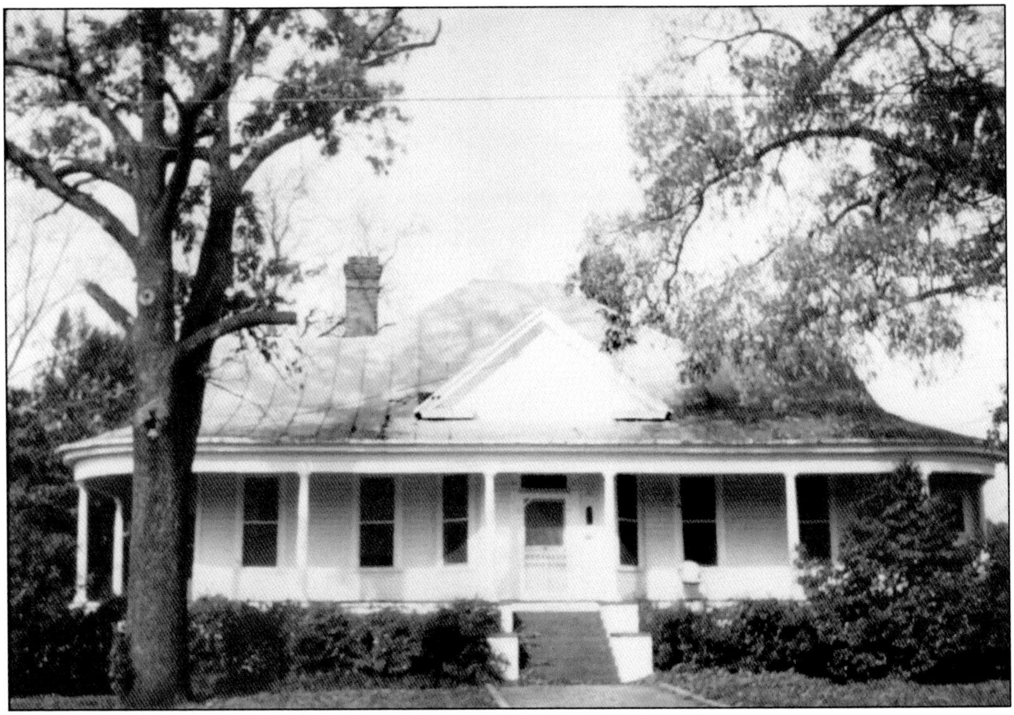

The Beech Street home of W. J. Mullis and his daughter, Sara Mullis, was built in Cochran after the death of his wife; later it was the home of Harry Daniel and Florence Crum Daniel and their three sons, Harry Jr., David, and Remer, before being torn down for a grocery store parking lot.

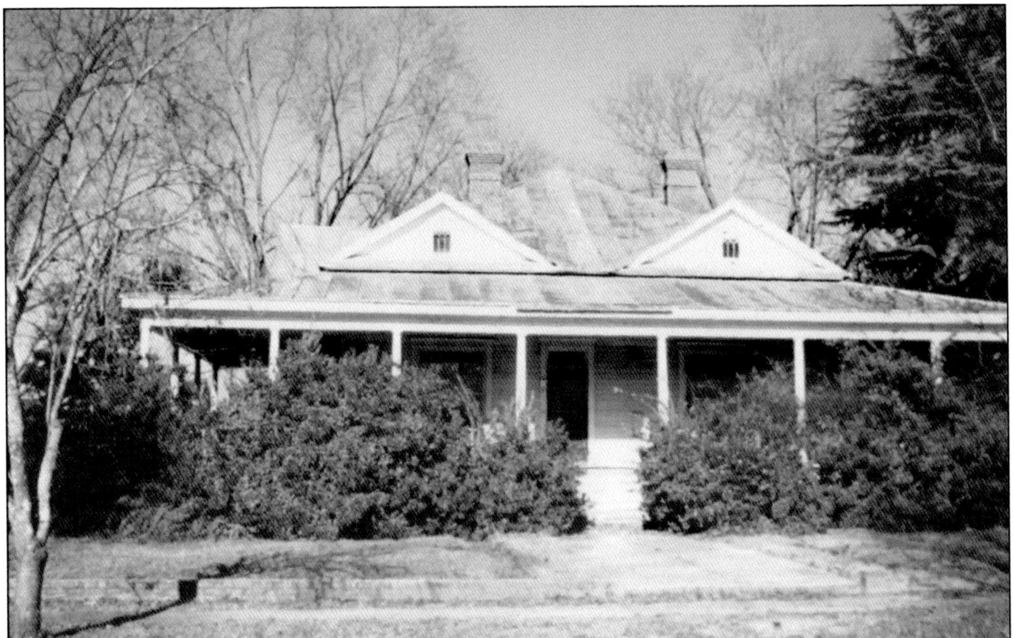

The Beech Street home of Charles Mullis and Mattie Lee Dunham Mullis was sold to H. Augustine. Later it was the home of Dr. A. L. Smith and Irene Smith until it was torn down to build a grocery store.

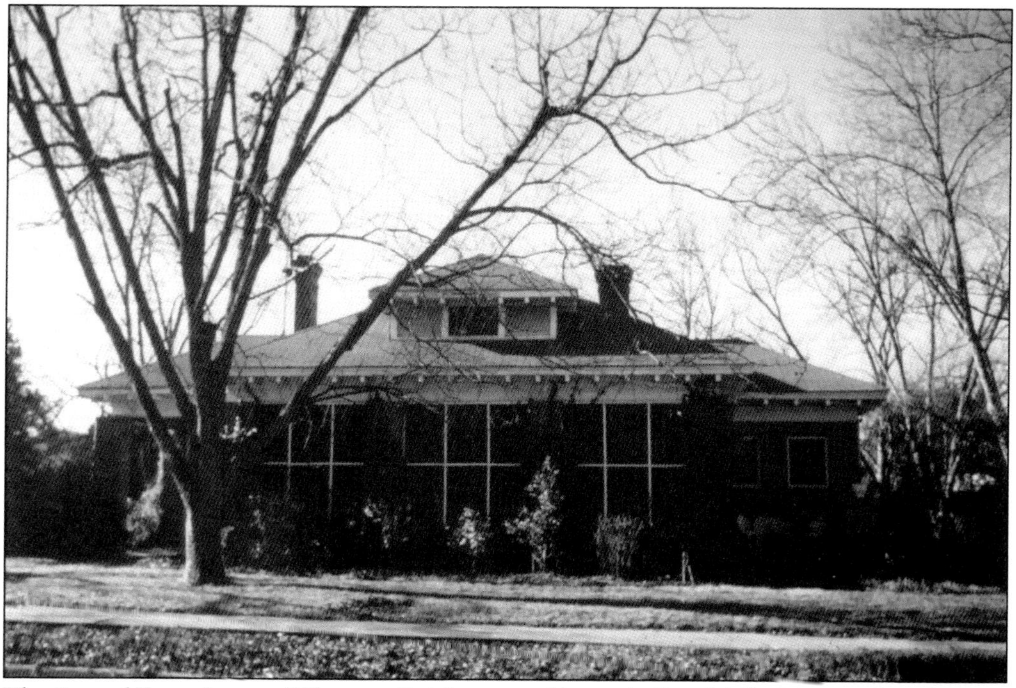

The Second Street home of Cheatam B. Morgan and his wife, Sara Mullis Morgan, later became the home of Leroy Hamrick.

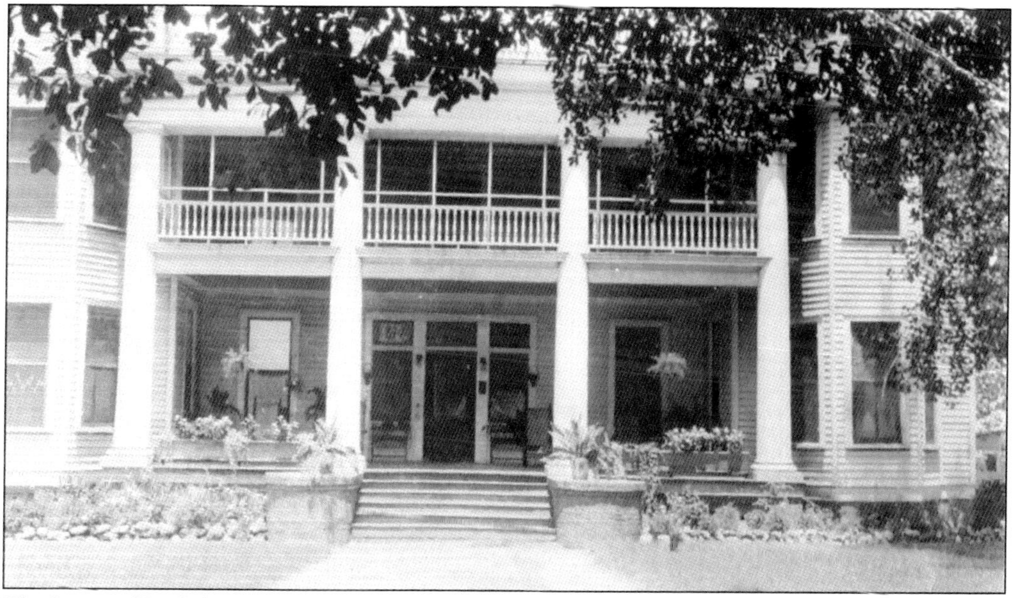

The home of Dr. John B. Peacock and Pauline Whippo Peacock was built around 1908. After the death of Dr. Peacock, it was the home of Charles Mullis and Mattie Lee Dunham Mullis until 1929. During the Depression, the house was rented by Middle Georgia College for the college football team, coached by Jake Morris and later Jody Matt. In the 1940s, it became an apartment house known as the Georgian Apartments and was home to Jody and Ruby Bullard Matt; John T. and Marcelle Morris; and Martha Bullard and Florene Jones Greene. Today it is the home of Roger Parks.

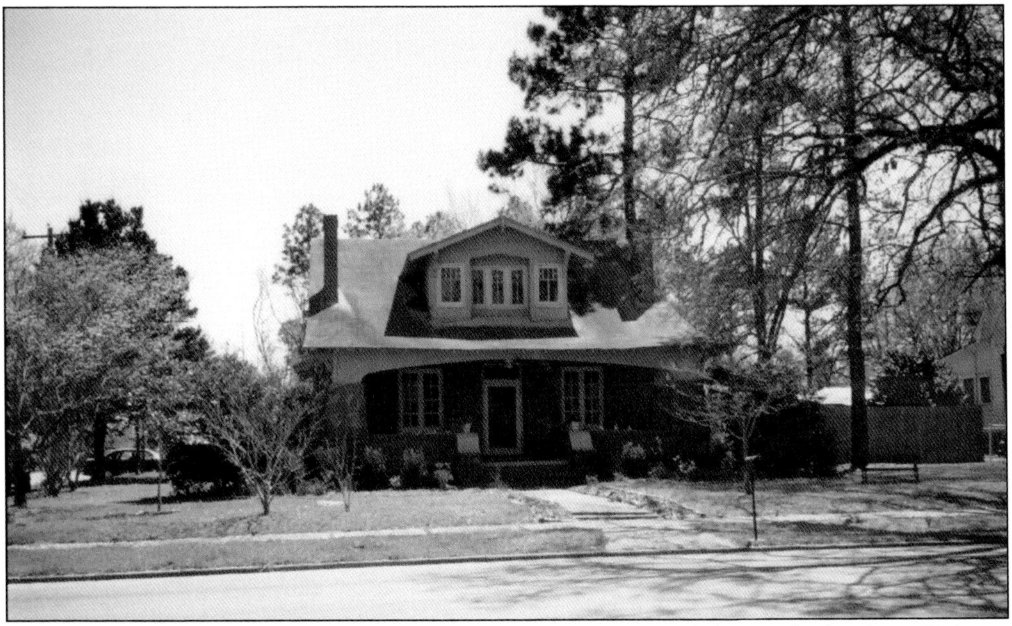

The home of Ralph Harris Peacock, Mae Urguhart Peacock, and their only daughter, Dolores, was built on Beech Street. Ralph Peacock was county commissioner for 26 years (longer than any other commissioner). Later the house was the home of James L. and Frances Keeney and their children, Randall and Anne Graves. (Courtesy of Jerri Tuck.)

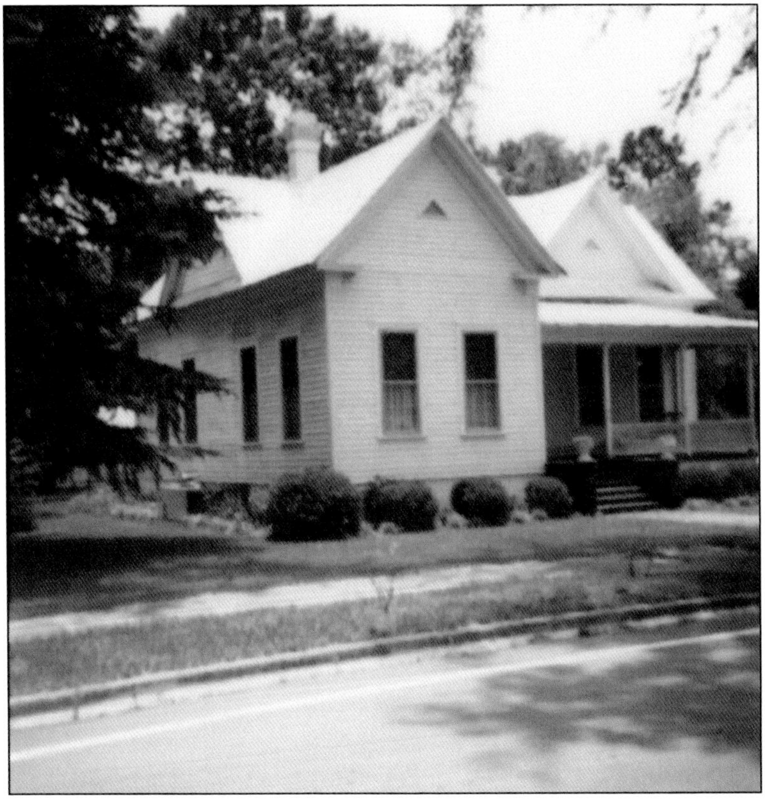

The home of Thomas S. Vinson and Kate Grimsley Vinson was on Beech Street. Mr. Vinson was clerk of the City of Cochran until his death in 1937. Later the home of Jordan and Arrie Fisher, Guyton and Dollie Skipper, and Lonnie Barlow, it is today owned by James and Christy Collins.

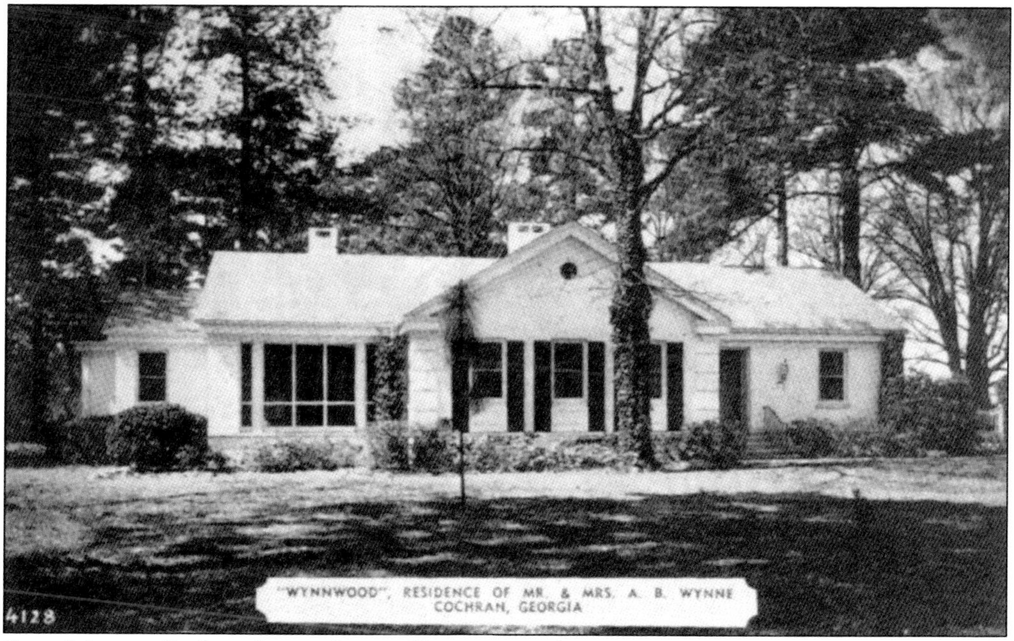

One of the two Cochran homes designed by Macon architect Ella Mae Ellis League was Wynnwood, which was built on Second Street by Andrew Brown Wynn, Jesse Ellis Wynn, and their son, Jack. It is today the home of Joe and Kathryn Fisher. (Courtesy of Kathryn Davis Fisher.)

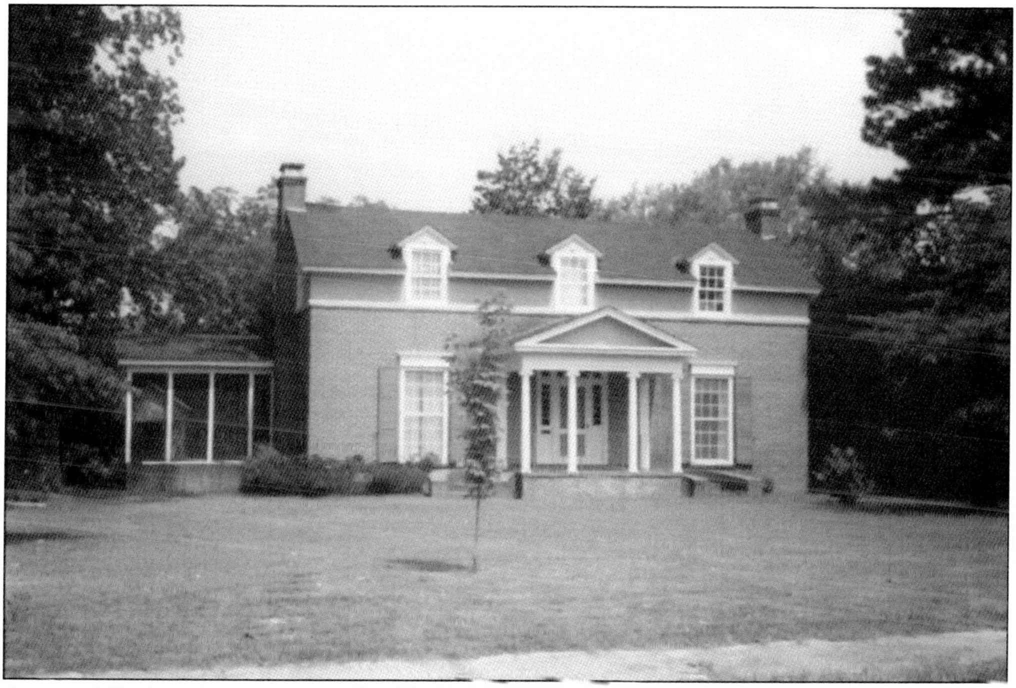

A second Cochran home designed by Ella Mae Ellis League is the Lewis Sullivan Leach and Maude Nutting Leach home on Beech Street. It was later a law office but is now a private residence.

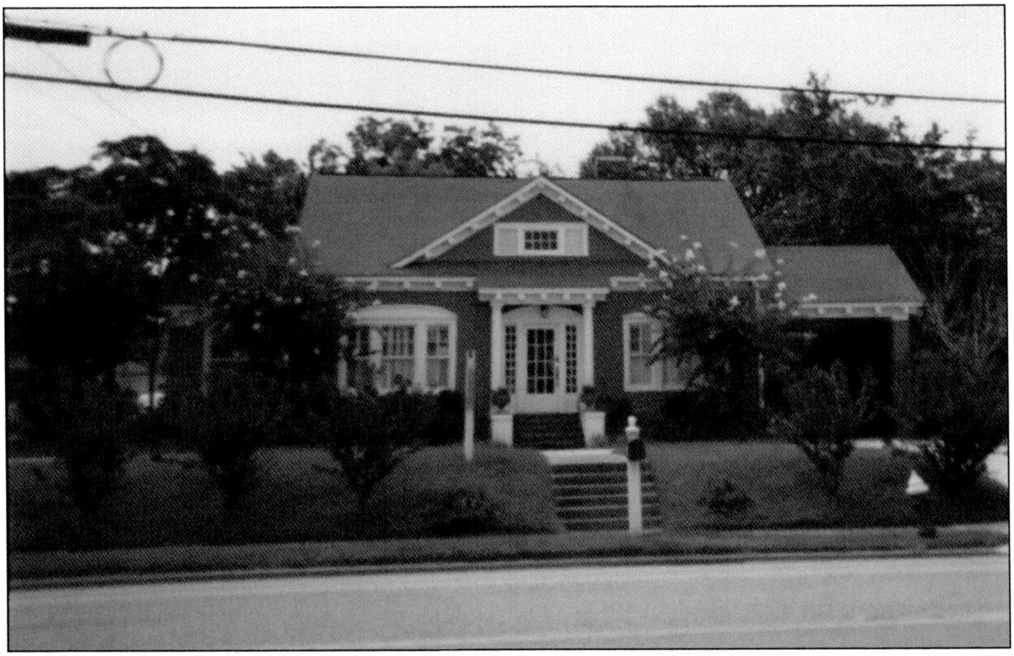

Built by John H. Mullis for his son, Howell Mullis, and Howell's wife, Lucille Horton Mullis, this Dykes Street home became the home of John Anderson and Jewell Wynn Anderson; later it was the home of Richmond Calvin Manning. Today it is the home of Irma Lucas Greene.

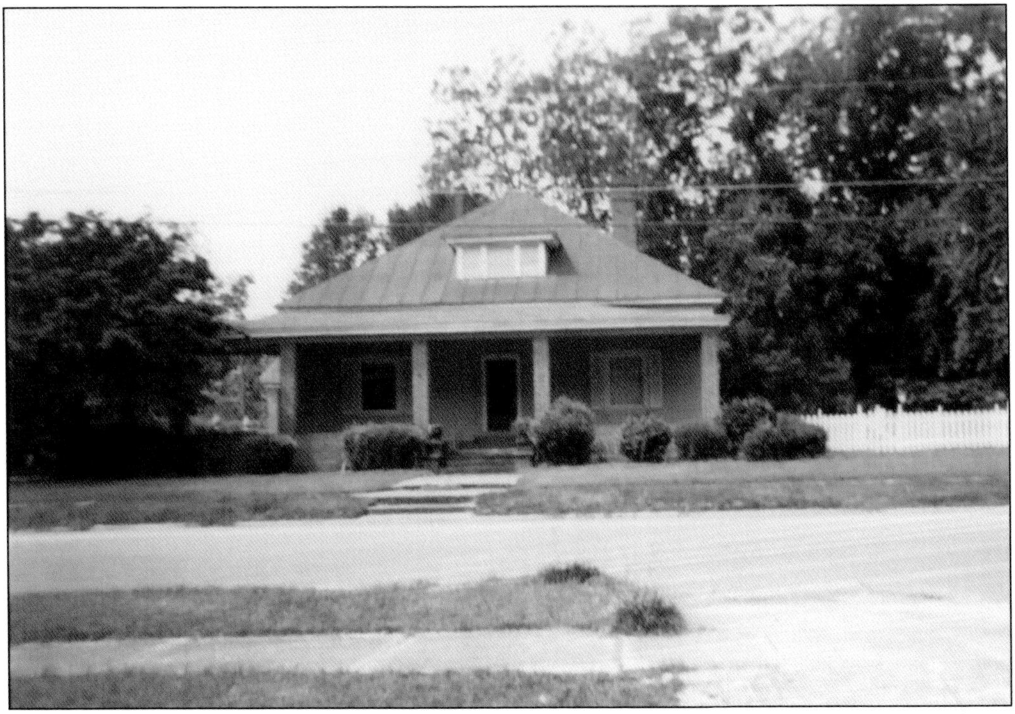

Built by Guy Jackson Sr. and Marie Walker Jackson, this Second Street home became the residence of Henry and Sarah Griffin. Later purchased by Jeff and Jill Fisher, it is today the home of Eric and Allison Bisher. (Courtesy of Jerri Tuck.)

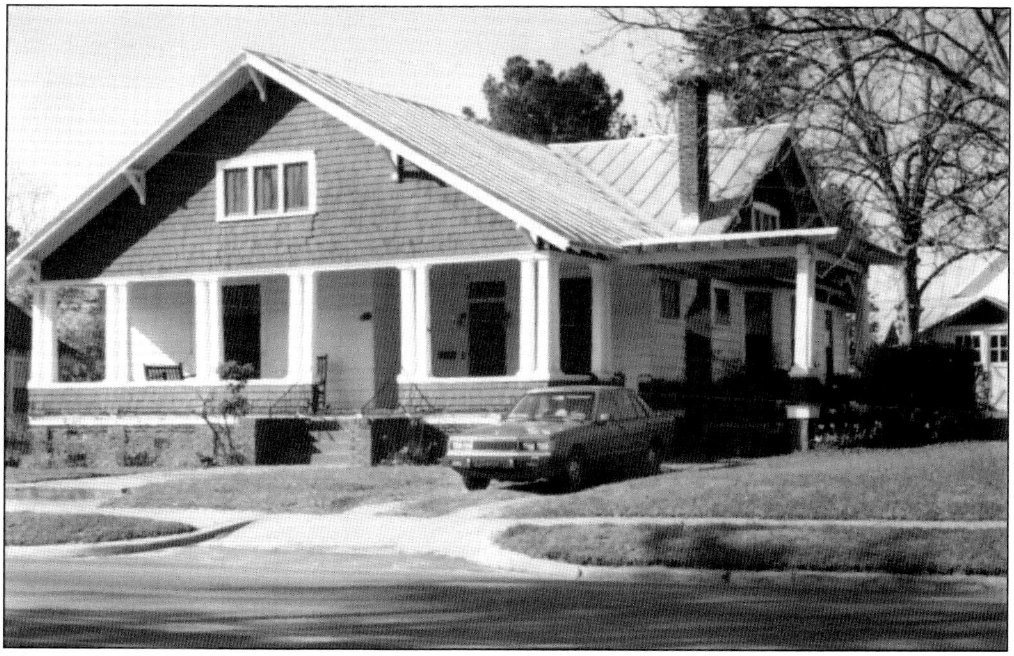

This Second Street home was built by Uriah Patrick. In 1919, it was purchased by Dr. William Homer Pirkle and Lacy Banks Pirkle. After Mrs. Pirkle passed away in 1976, it was purchased by L. A. Whipple and Lilla Dillard Whipple. Later it was owned by Robert and Lynda Schuman. Today it is the home of William W. Davis and Deborah M. Davis.

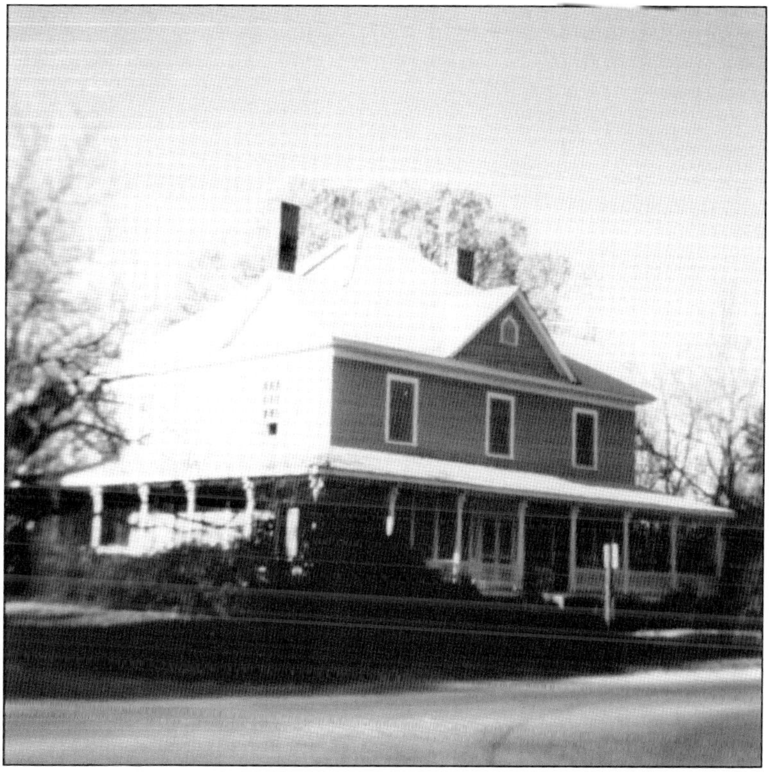

Built by Steve Whipple on Dykes Street, this home was the residence of Dr. J. M. and Anna Smith; later it was the home of Dr. Reid and Margie Gullatt, who remodeled the house and sold it to Willie Brantley and Elizabeth Zellner Brantley. It is the present location of the Auto Zone Parts Store. (Courtesy of Jerri Tuck.)

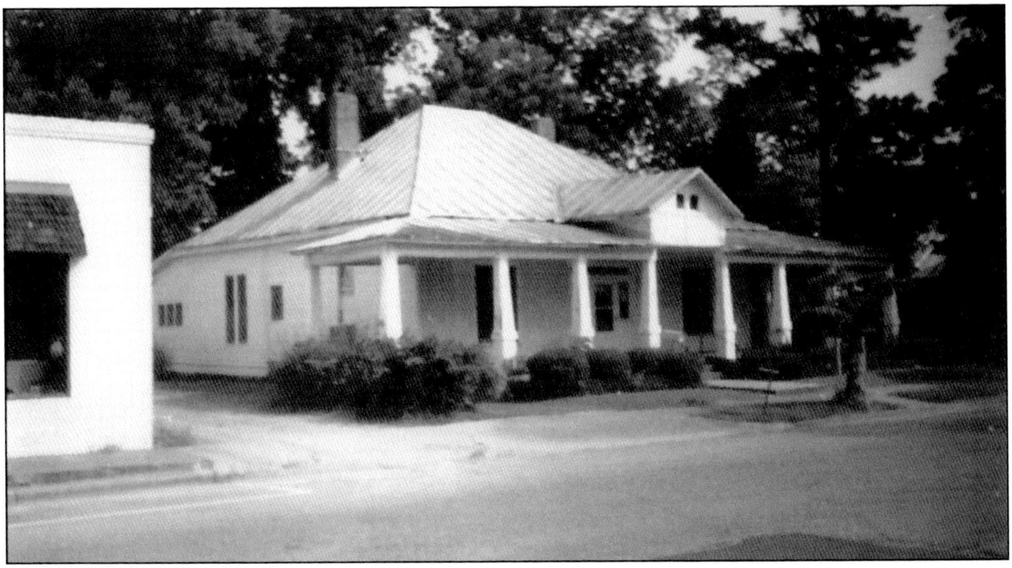

The home of Barney Wilson Hendricks Sr. and Margaret Cook Hendricks on Cherry Street from 1921 to 1995 was located near downtown. Mrs. Hendricks thought the property would be good for commercial use someday. It became a commercial building in 1996. (Courtesy of Barney W. Hendricks Jr.)

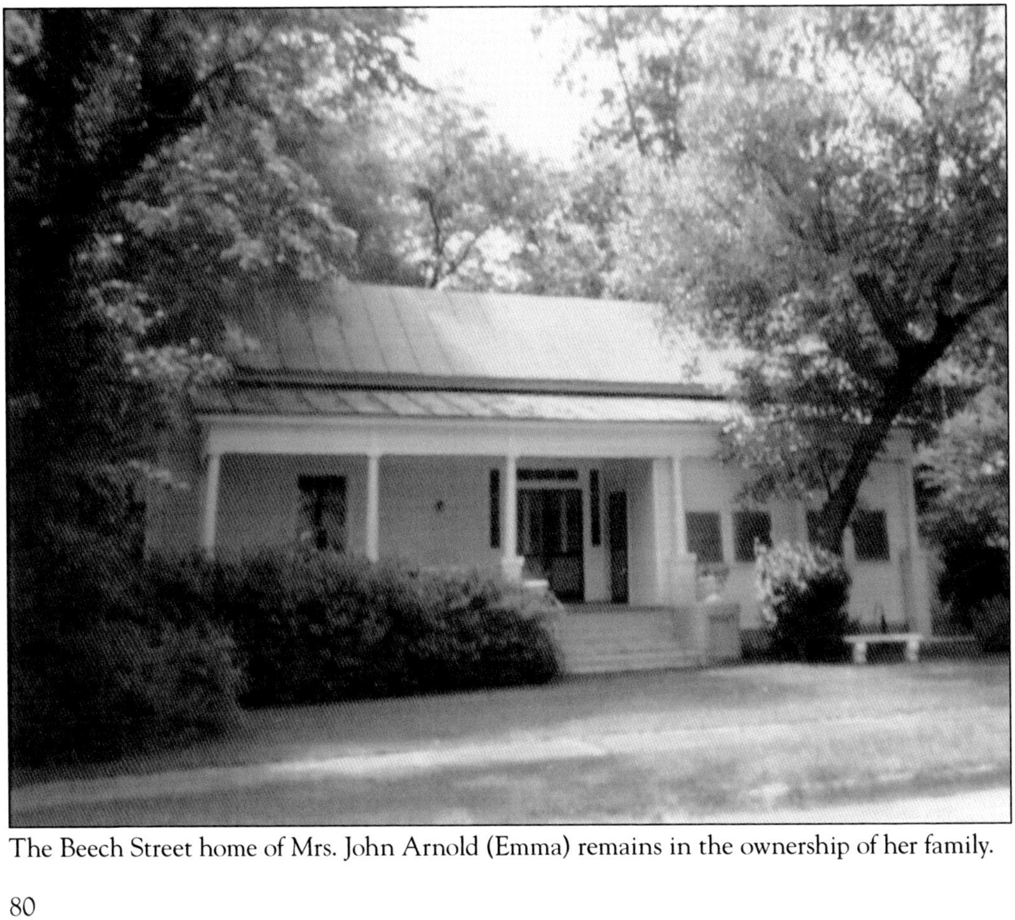

The Beech Street home of Mrs. John Arnold (Emma) remains in the ownership of her family.

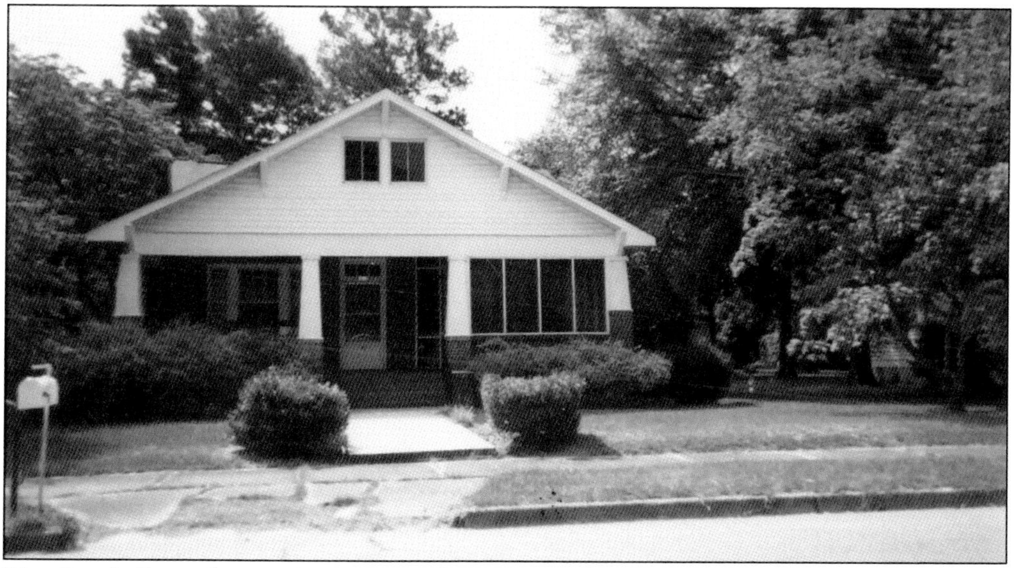

The Beech Street home of attorney-at-law H. McWhorter and Mary Durham McWhorter and their beloved bulldog, "Bob," was later the home of Willie Marion Dykes and Mary Estes McWhorter Dykes.

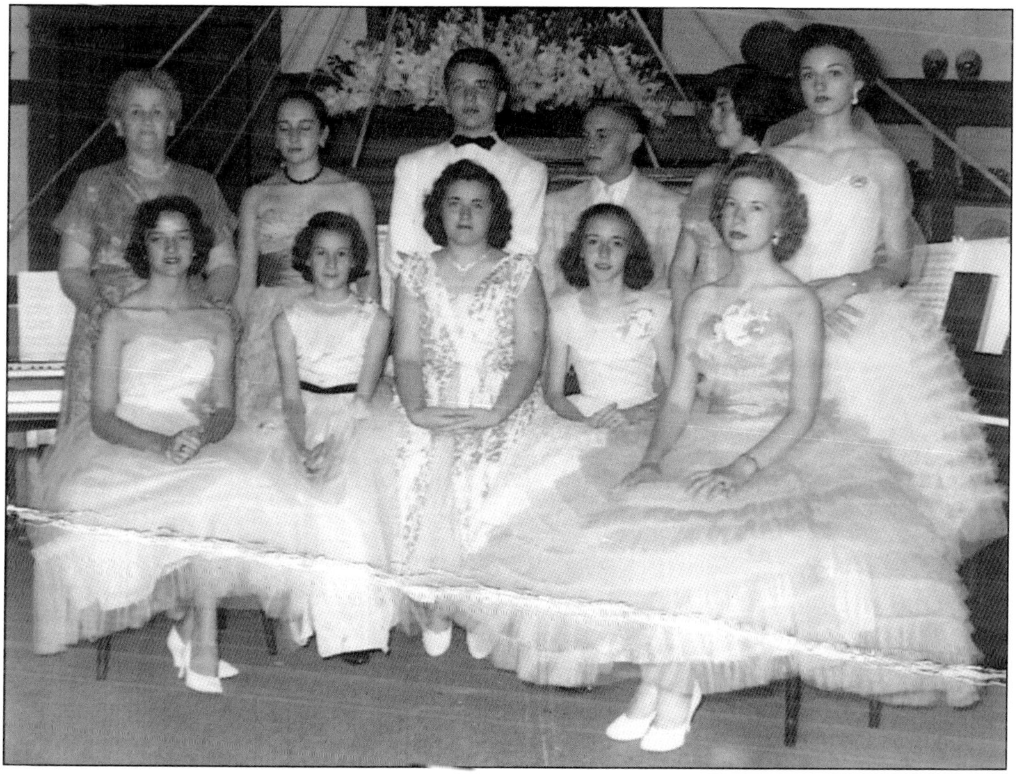

A piano recital given by Mary McWhorter was held in her Beech Street home in 1954. From left to right are (seated) Ouida Newby Williams, Sandra Jones Ricks, Shirley Sanders, Judy King Southerland, and Freida Faulk Yearty; (standing) Mrs. H. McWhorter, Linda Dykes Padgett, Monty Wilson, Lonnie Barlow, Billie Ann Willingham Barnett, and Barbara Cook.

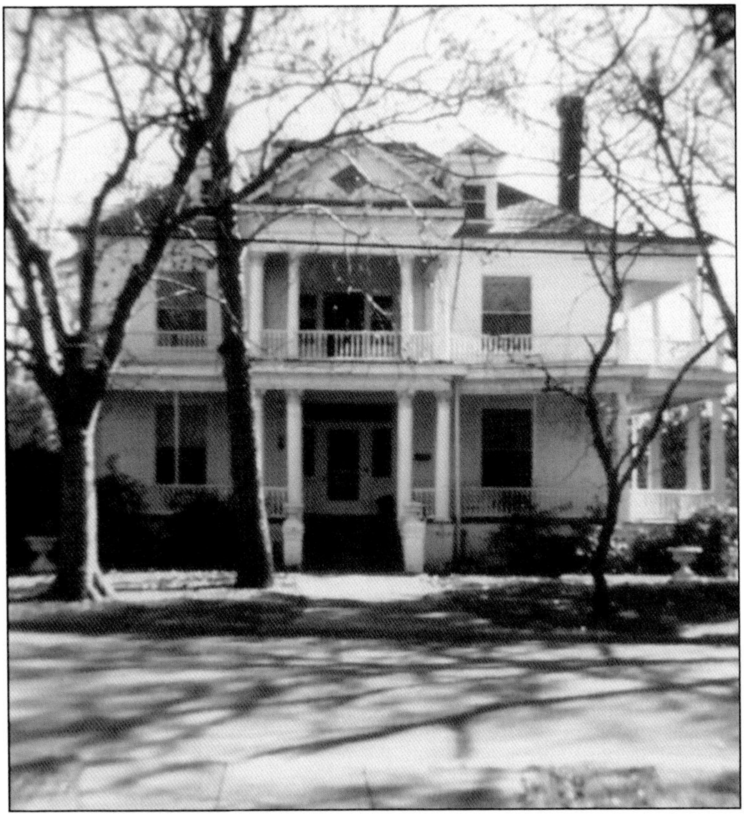

Built in 1906 by Wilmer O'Berry Peacock, this stately residence on Cherry Street was the home of Thomas Malcom Purcell and his wife, Myrtle, during the period that he was superintendent of Cochran Public Schools, until 1948. Later it was purchased by George E. Greene and Mary Jane Greene. Remodeled in 1985, it is today the home of Crystal Samulowicz. (Courtesy of Clyde Hill.)

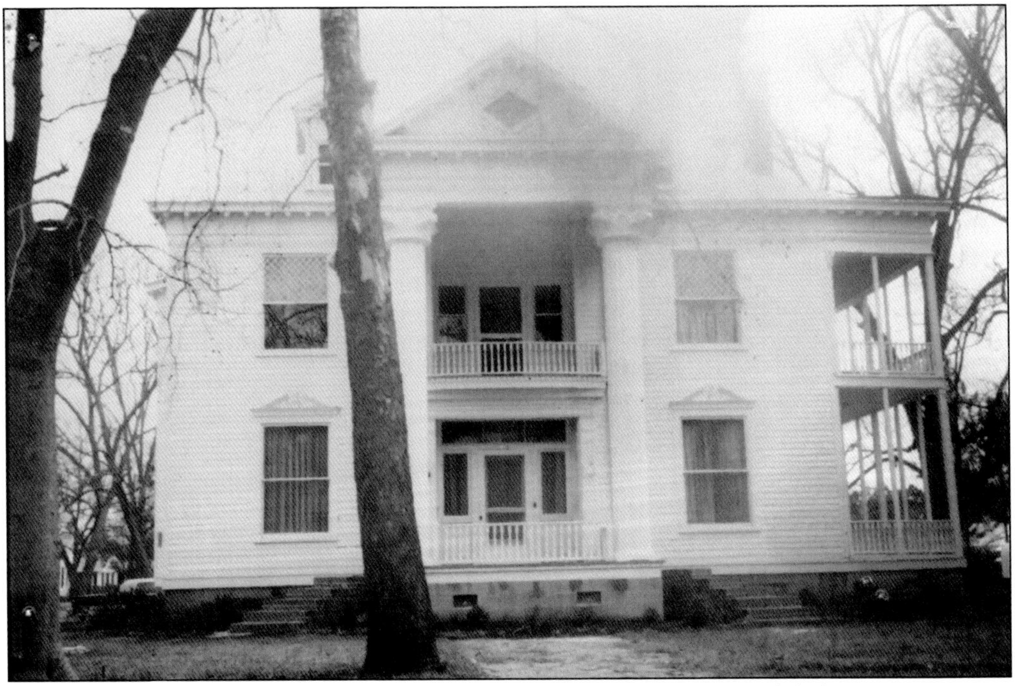

The Peacock-Greene home was known as Greenewood after it was remodeled in 1984.

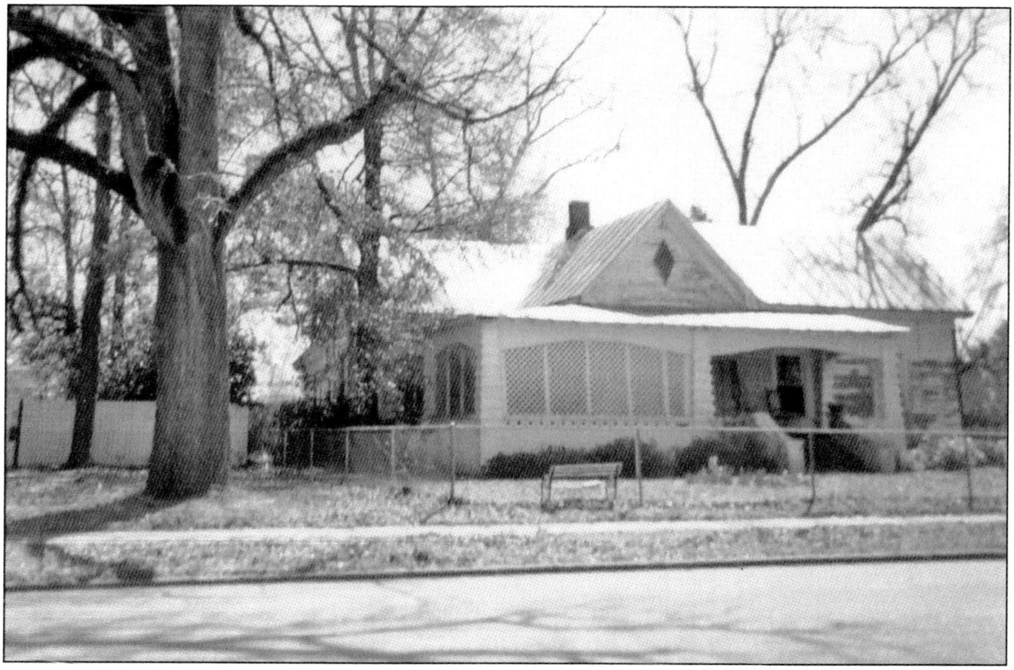

Beech Street, known as "Silk Stocking Street" was home to mayors of Cochran, the county commissioner of Bleckley County, doctors, lawyers, and merchants through the years. Frazier and Lassie Smith lived in this Beech Street home, which was later the residence of the Monroe Curington family and their daughter, Nell.

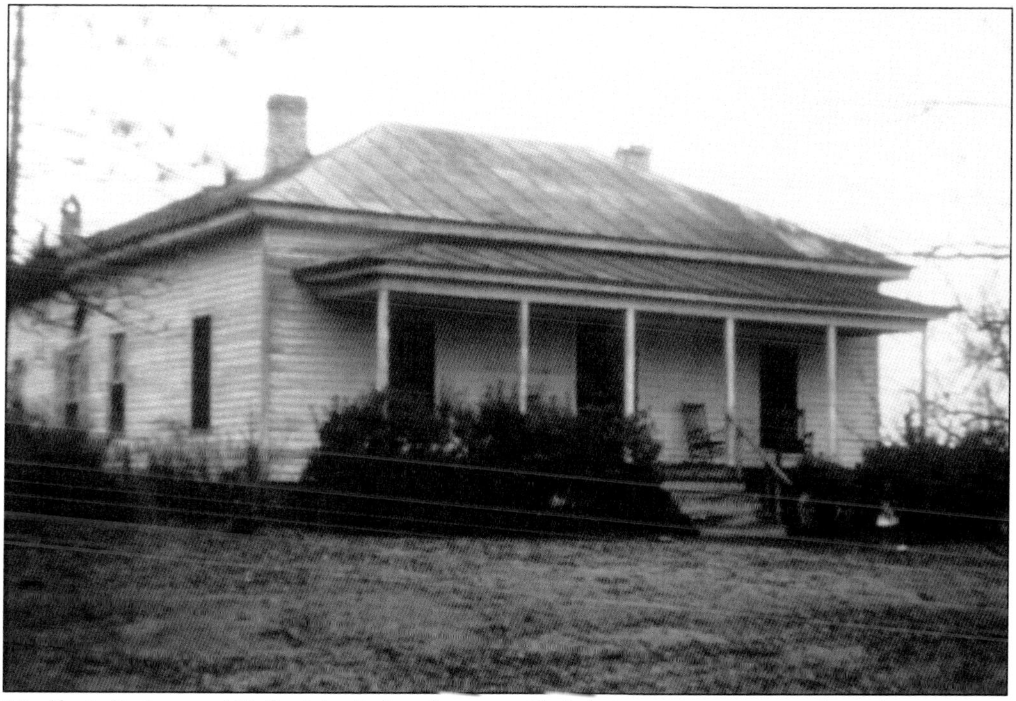

The B. A. Bishop and Vallie Mae Bishop home on Eighth Street Crescent was later the residence of David Q. Roland Sr. and his wife, Nadine, before being torn down to build a motel.

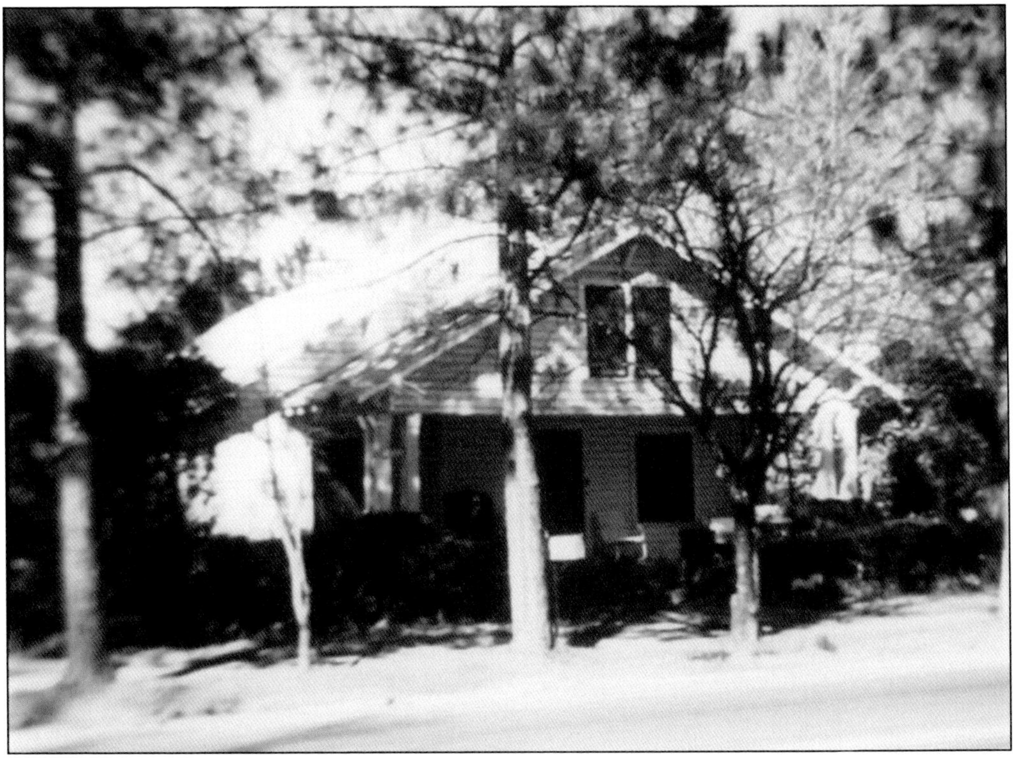

The Dykes Street home of James Benjamin Elliott Sr. and Nettie Legg Elliott is the present location of Edgewater Media.

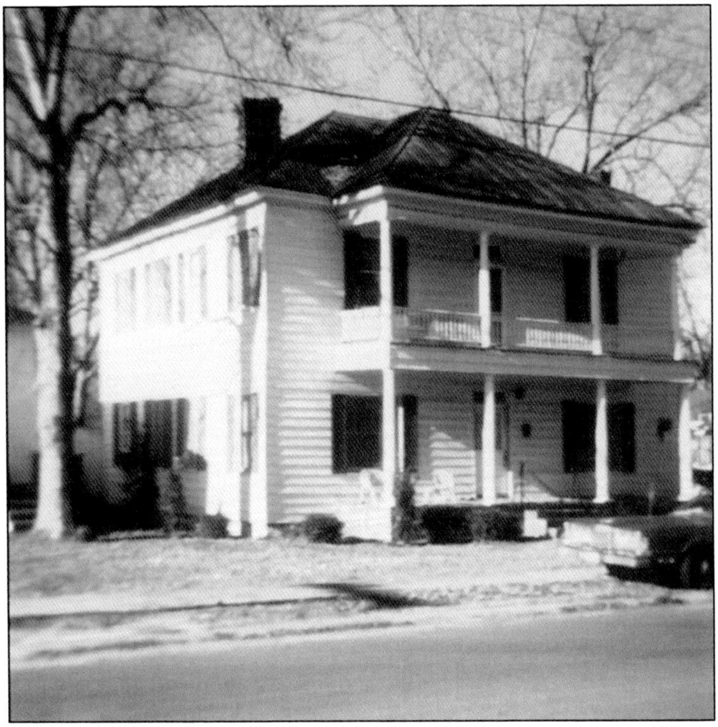

The Beech Street rental house of Toombs and Madge Kimbrough was known as "Honeymoon Heaven" due to the high number of just-married couples who rented apartments there. The home was later remodeled by Beatrice Griffin Waters as a private residence. The house later burned.

The home of John Rawls Taylor and Minnie Cook Taylor on Dykes Street was later the home of their daughter, Carry Mae Fulton. It is the present location of Needle in a Haystack.

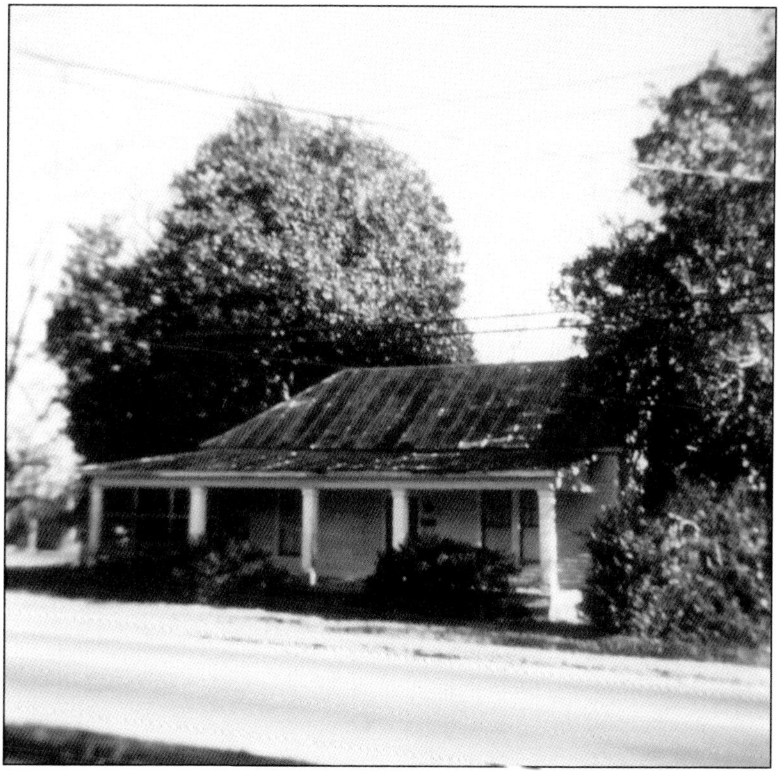

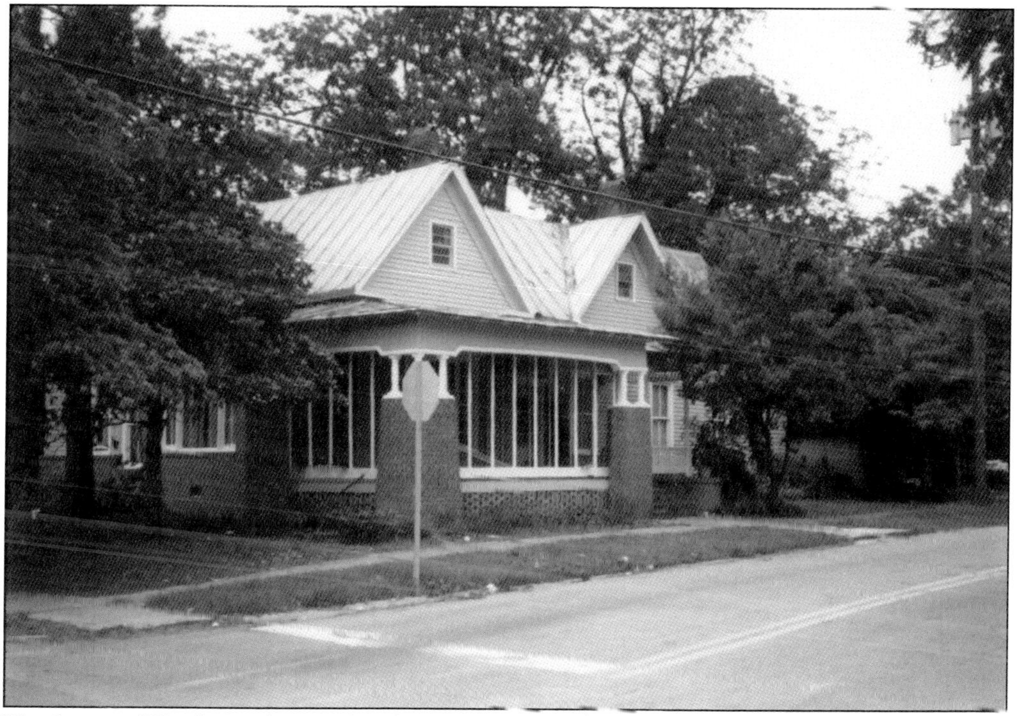

The home of Elijah Cook Jr. and Leila Hendricks Cook on Dykes Street was torn down and is the present location of Hong Kong Restaurant.

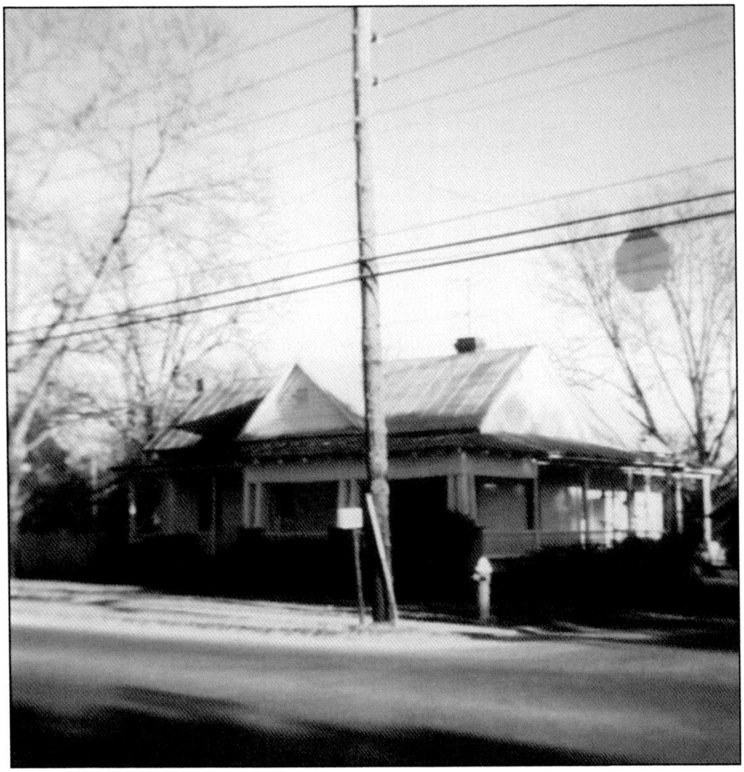

The Dykes Street home of Clerk of Bleckley Superior Court James A. Floyd and Willie Simpson Floyd was later the home of their son, John F. Floyd, and his wife, Ruby H. Floyd. The house was sold to Cecil and Anne Marie Layton and later became the home of Alton and Carolyn Young.

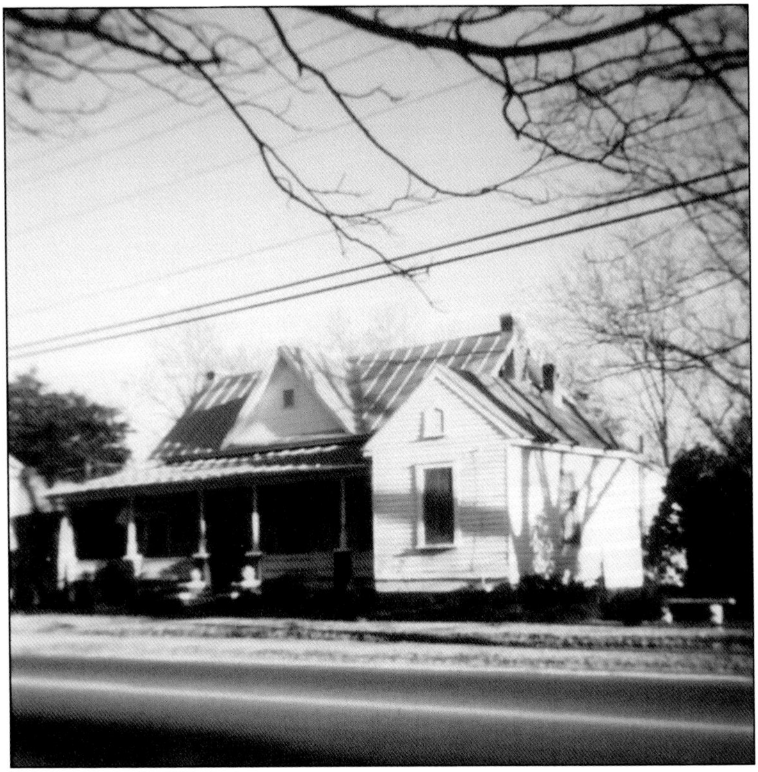

The home of Charles Edward Martin and Cornelia Burns Martin on Dykes Street contained a store, which is today an insurance office.

The Dykes Street home of Darnell and Callie Glisson is the present location of B. J.'s Beauty Shop.

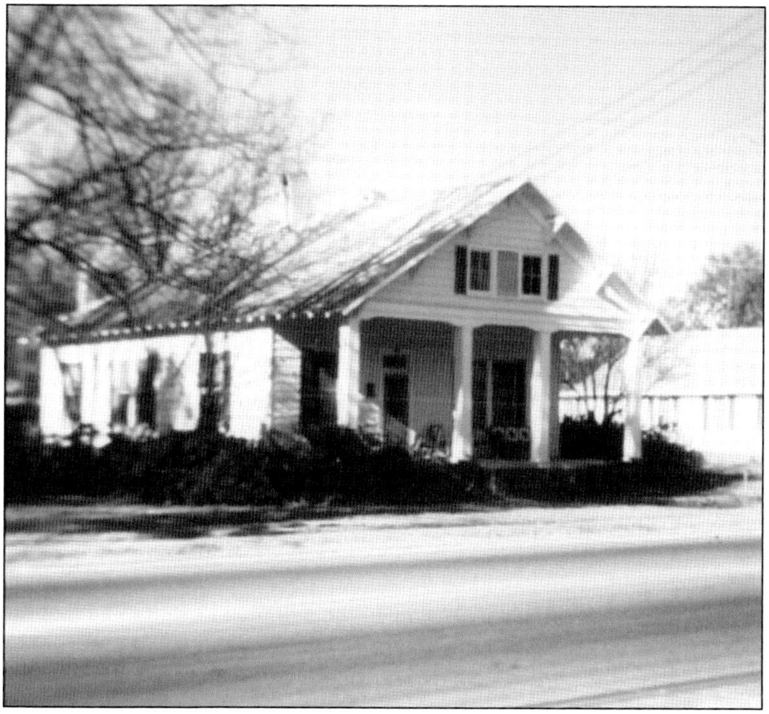

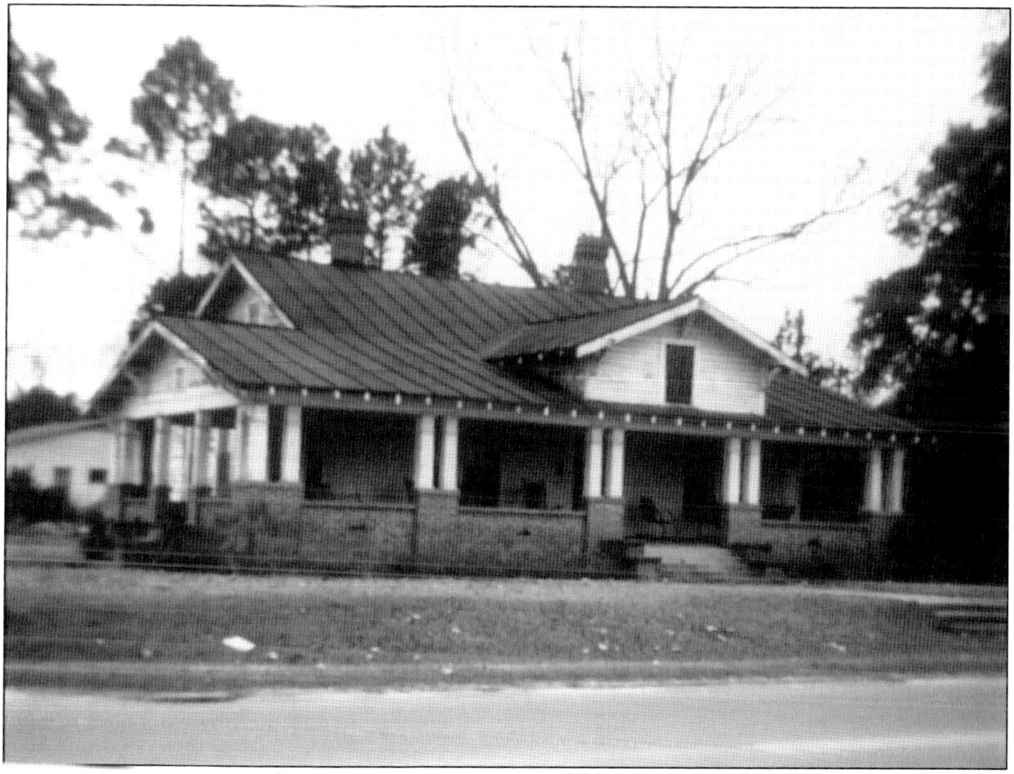

The Dykes Street home of Minnie Lee Dykes is today the home of Faustine Lister Bates and her son, Earl Lister Bates.

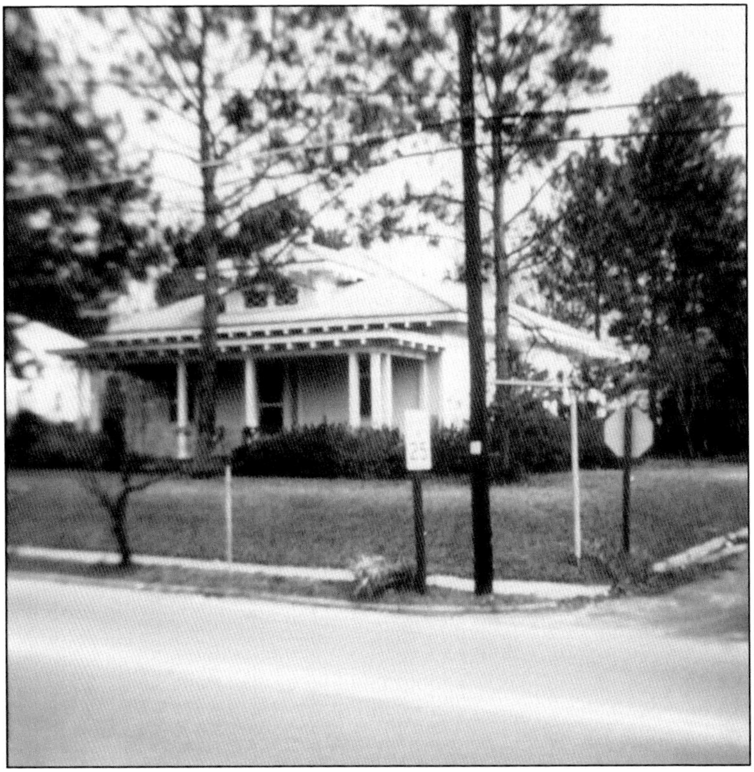

The Dykes Street home of J. Philip Taylor and Louise Thompson Taylor is today the home of Layne Wimberly Purser.

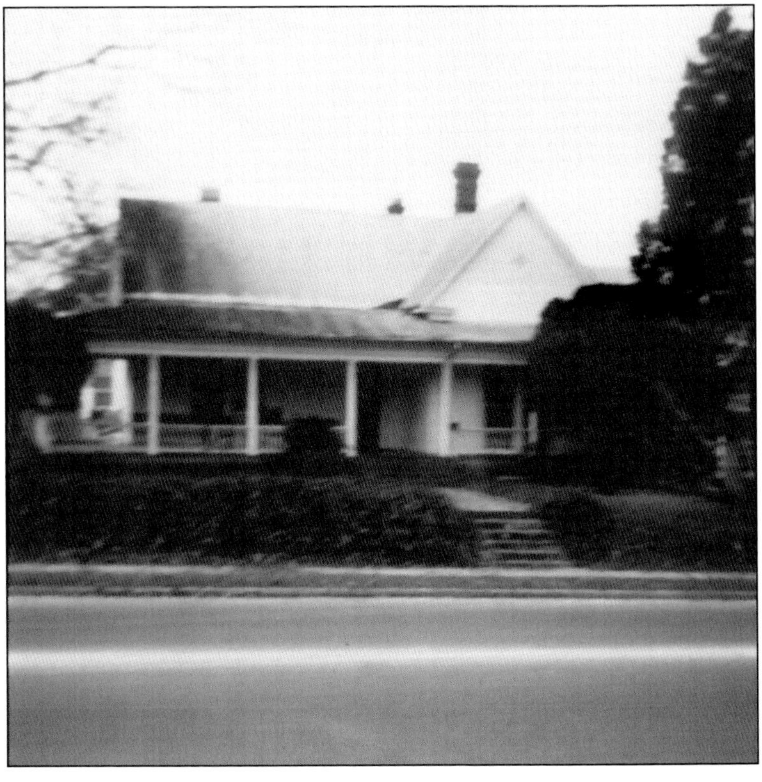

The town home of Dr. Thomas Duhart Walker Sr. and his wife, Jemima Edith, later became the home of John G. Purser and Beatrice Nobles Purser. It was later a restaurant known as Lila Jane's on Dykes Street.

The home of James E. "Jim" Cook and Charlotte "Lottie" Taylor Cook was located on Dykes Street.

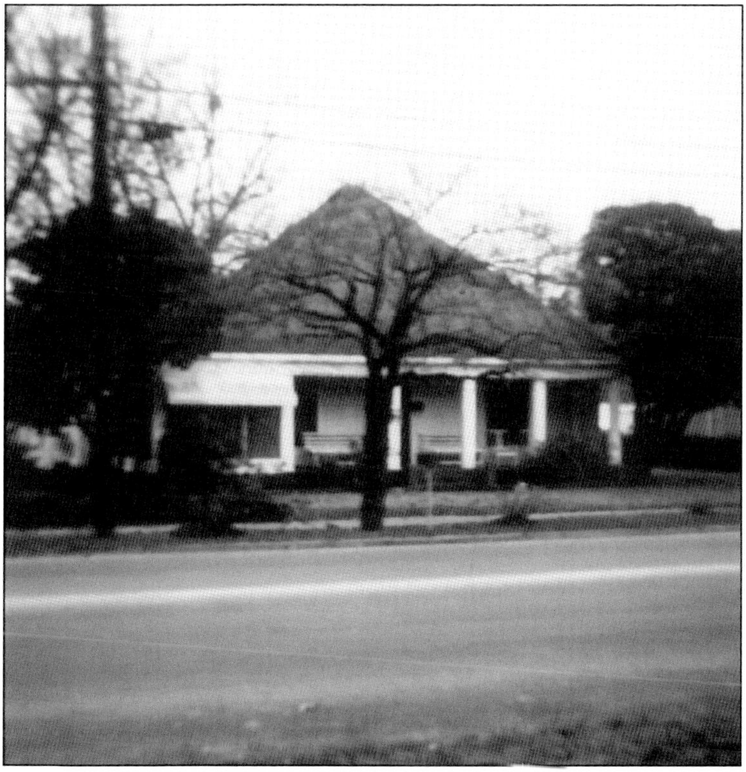

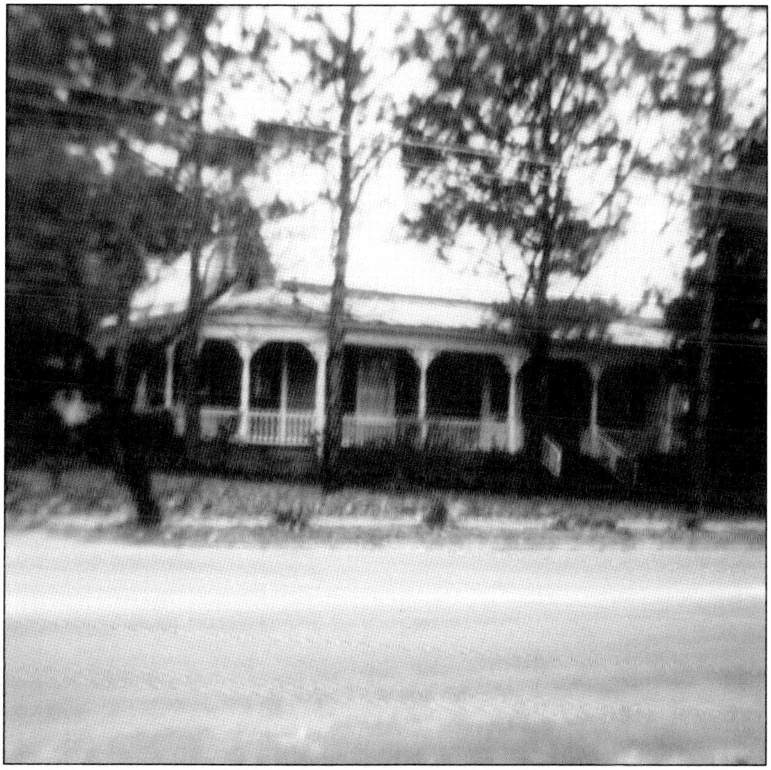

The home of Morgan Taylor and Eva Taylor was located on Dykes Street.

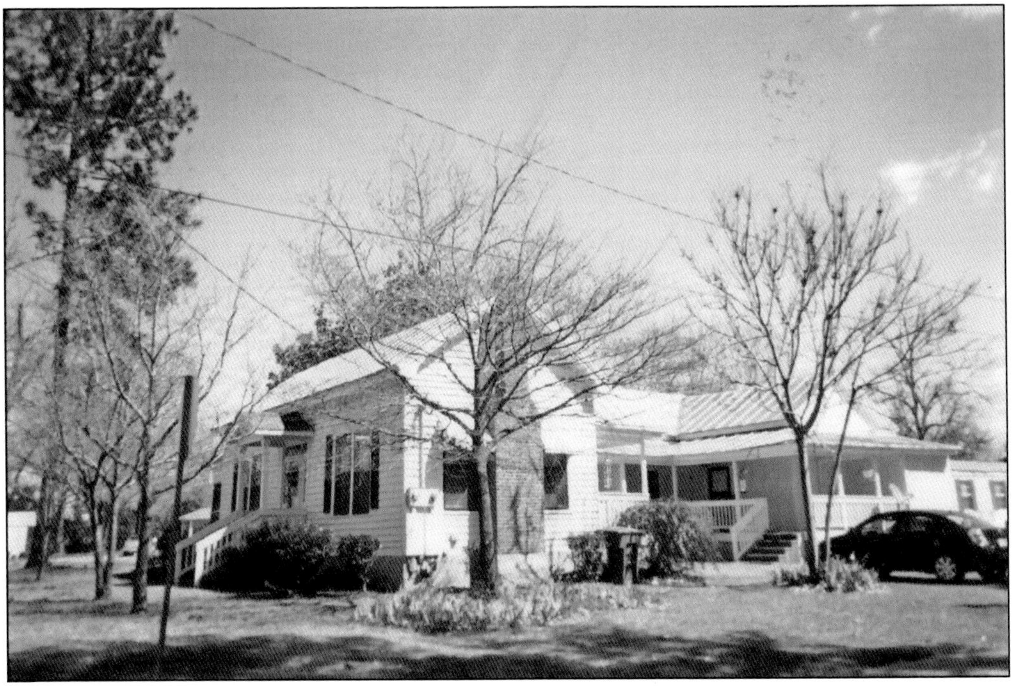

The home of the Harry Williams family was located on Dykes Street.

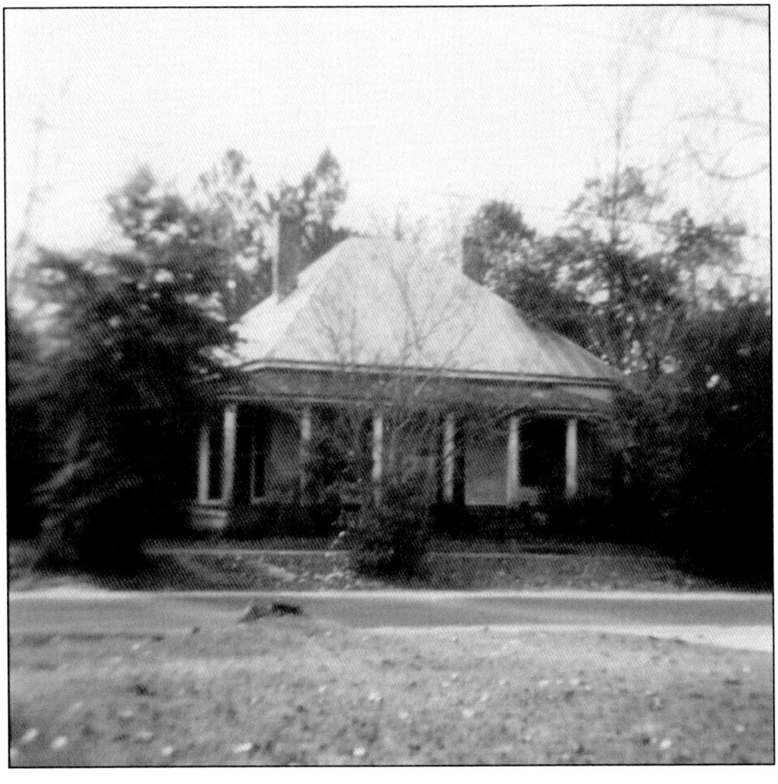

Built by the McVay family, this Fourth Street home was the residence of Jamie and Pearl Taylor Vaughan.

The Bill Livingston family lived in this Dykes Street home, which is today the residence of their son.

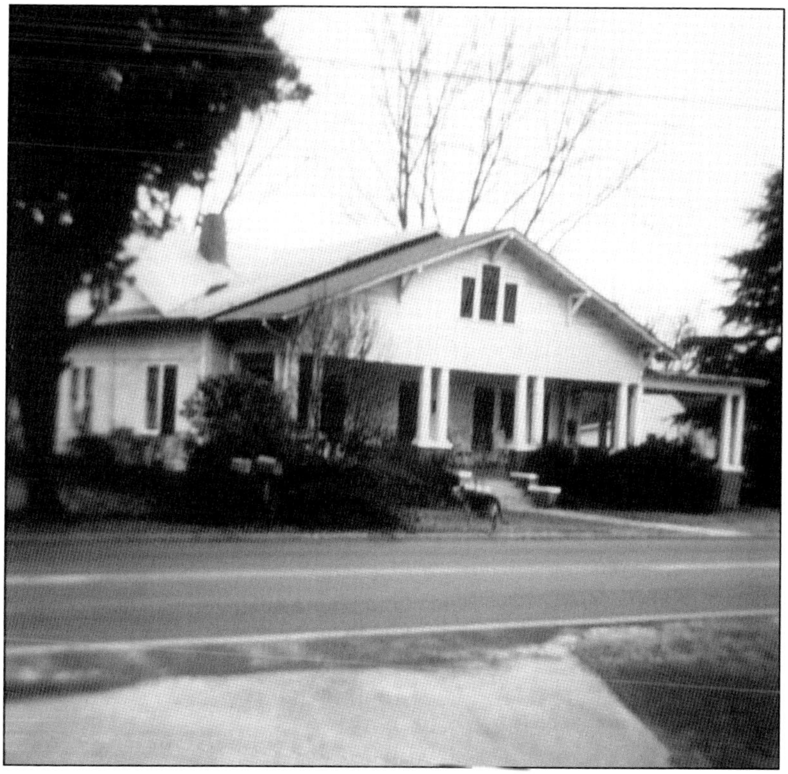

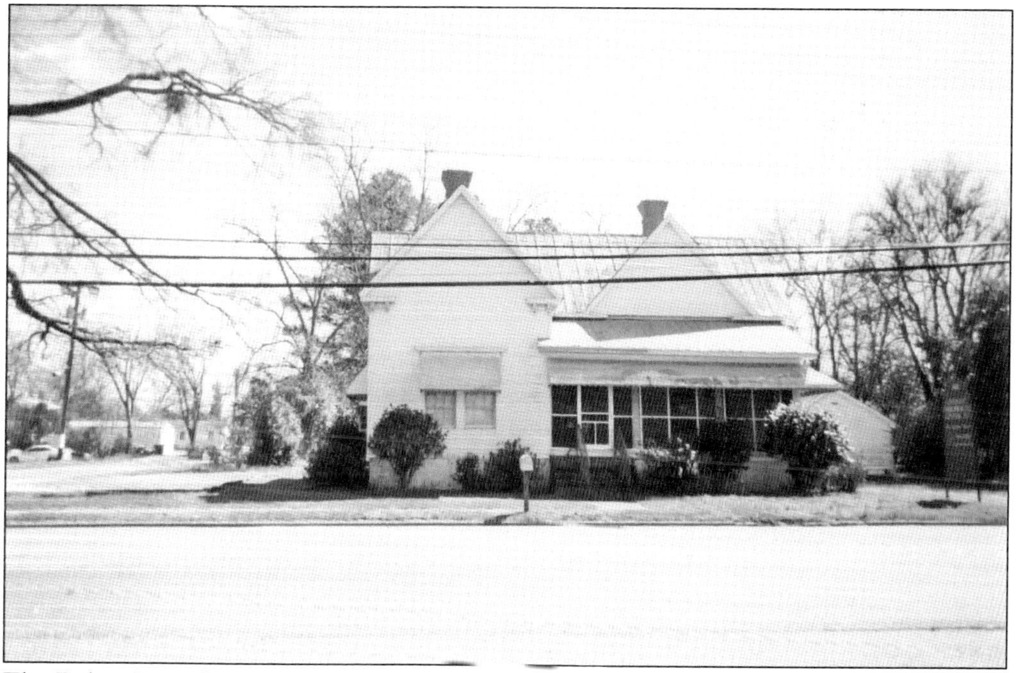

The Dykes Street home of the J. J. Johnson family was later the residence of Neal and Alice Arrowood. It is the present location of chiropractor Dr. Kathy Wood's office.

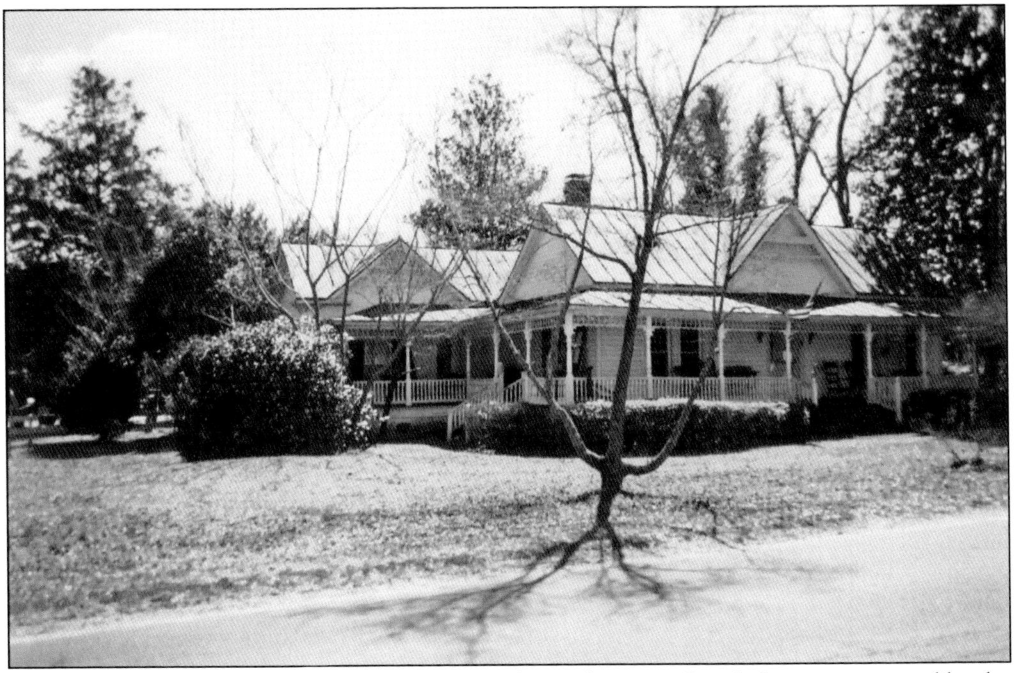

James Soloman Abney and Martha Jane Jones Abney's home on Beech Street was owned by the Abney family for 90 years.

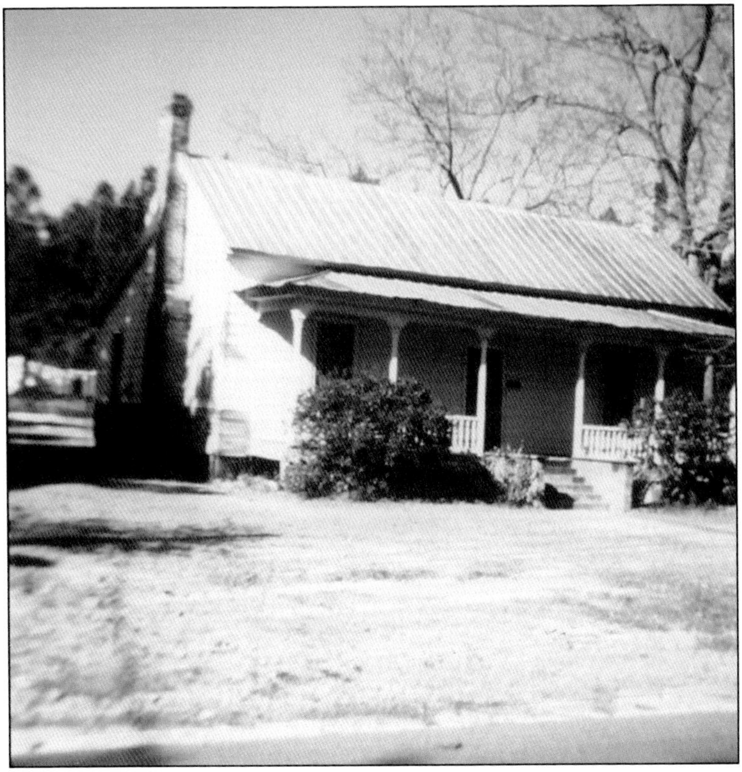

The Elmer S. Chapman home is on Beech Street.

Dr. Phillip Lemle Hudson and Julia Belle Hendricks Hudson built their home on the corner of Beech and Sixth Streets.

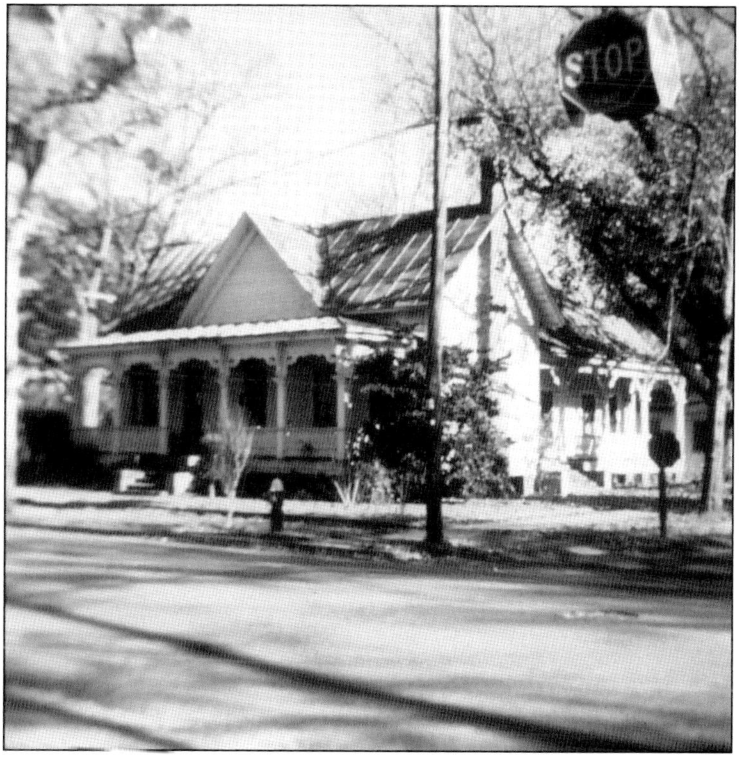

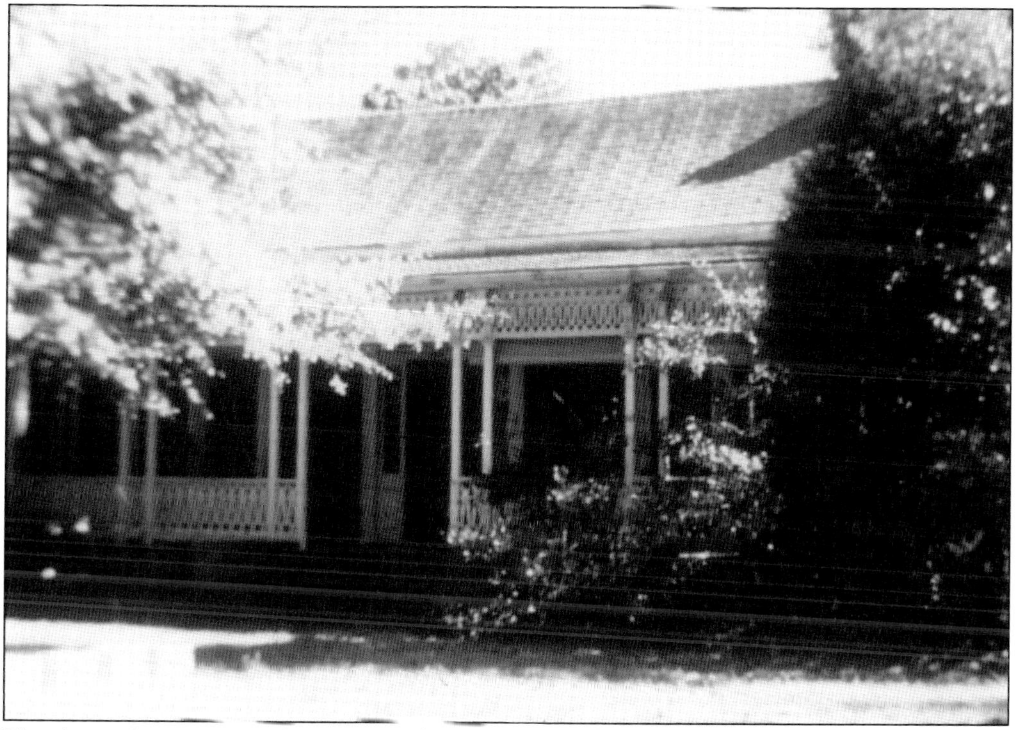

The Austin home on Beech Street was later the home of Herman Maloy Godfrey Sr. and Sarah Austin Godfrey.

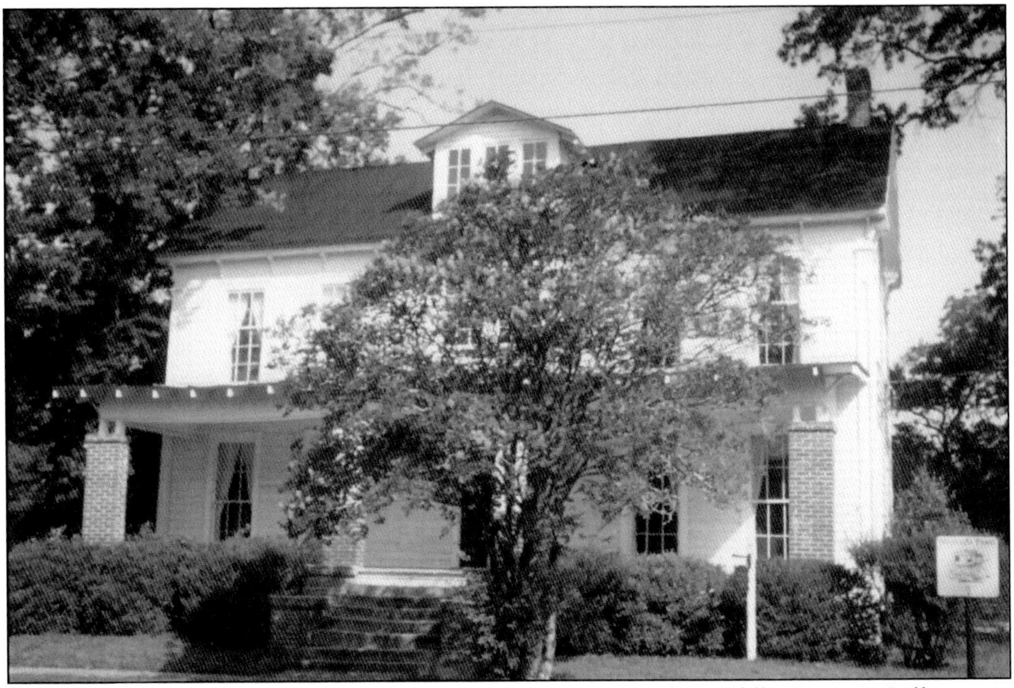

The Pace House on Beech Street was owned for many years by Middle Georgia College as a historical center for an early college official, Thomas B. Pace. It is today a private residence.

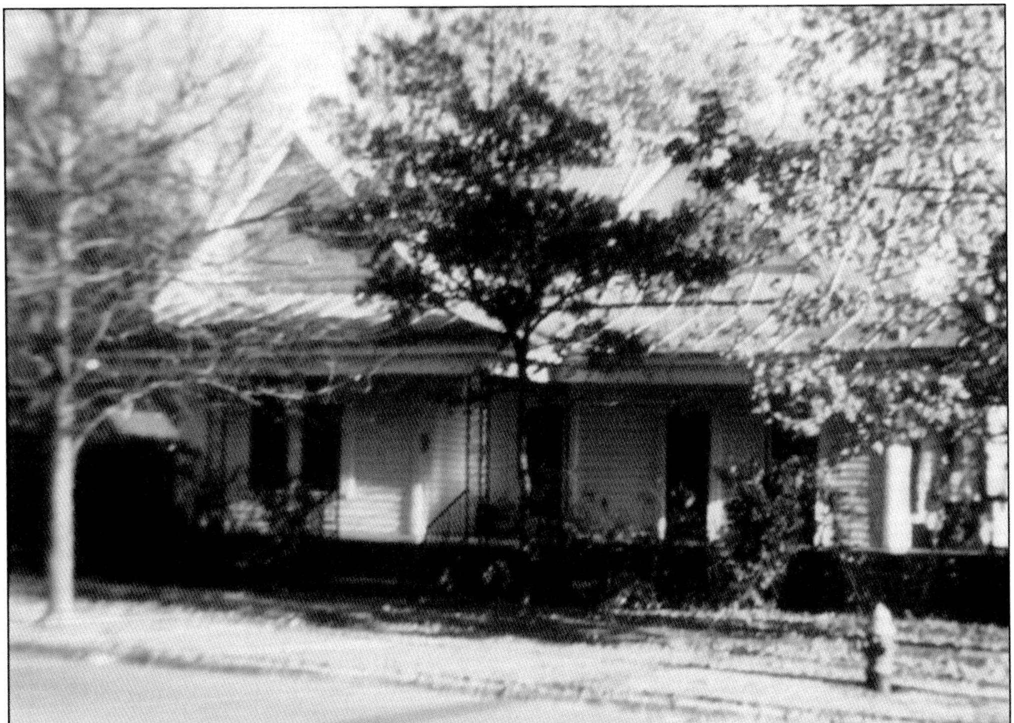

The Beech Street home of Nathaniel and Bessie Bulloch was located on the corner at Fourth Street. The Bullocks drove Lincoln sedans; his was yellow, and hers was pink.

The Beech Street home of Henry and Ruby Morgan Bullard was later the apartment house of Eloise C. Taylor and, after her, of Lamar Rutland. The structure is today owned by Dr. Richard Anderson.

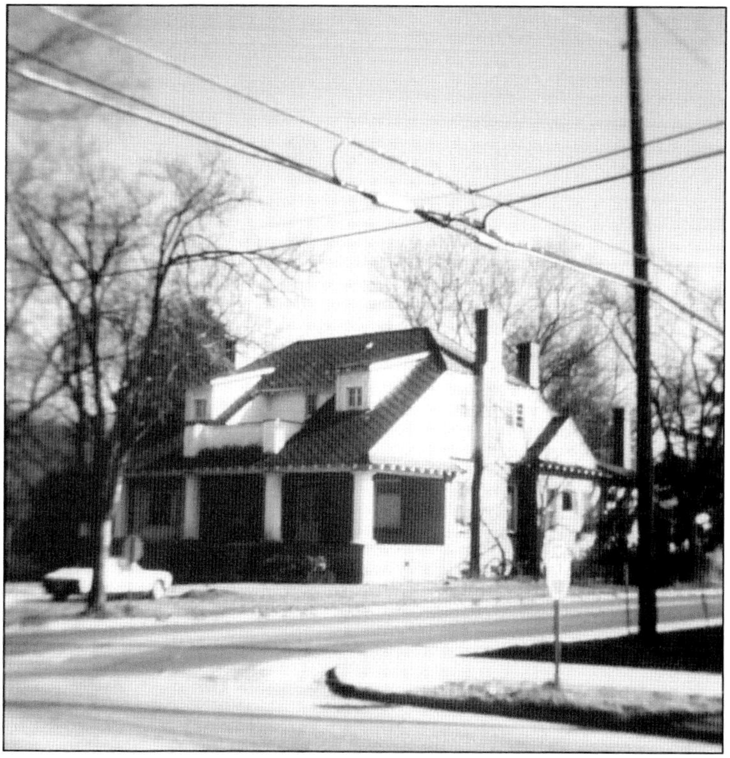

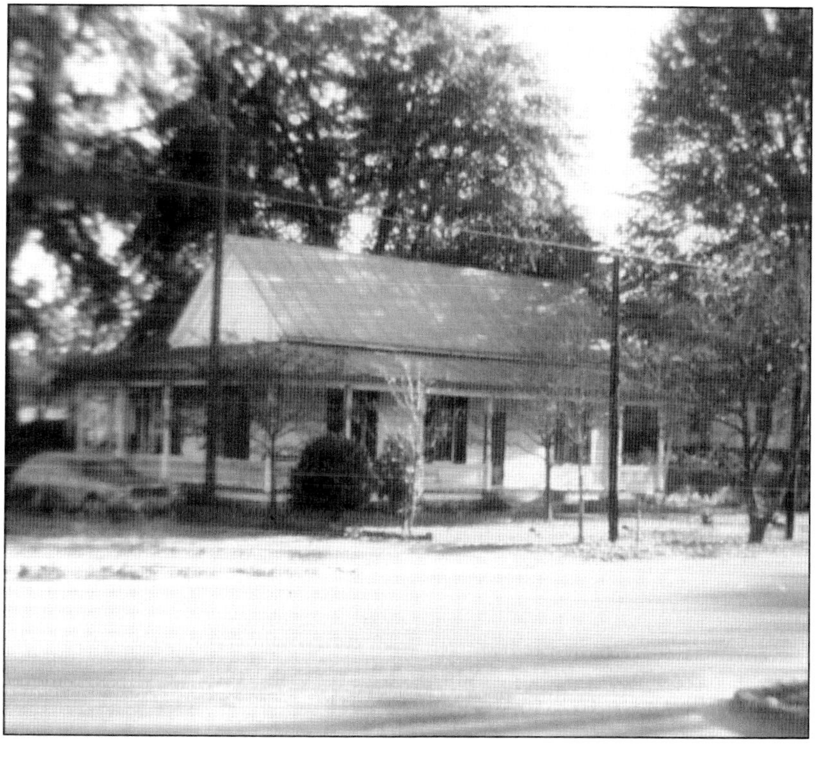

The Beech Street home of Julia Killen later became the residence of Mel Ray and Dorothy Bland.

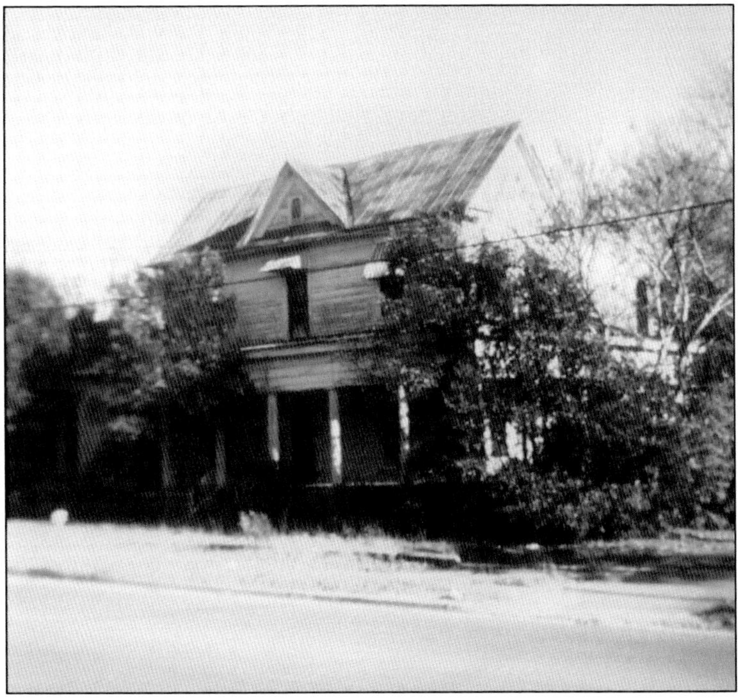

The Beech Street home that belonged to Emma Storey King for many years is today the apartment house of Danielle Smith.

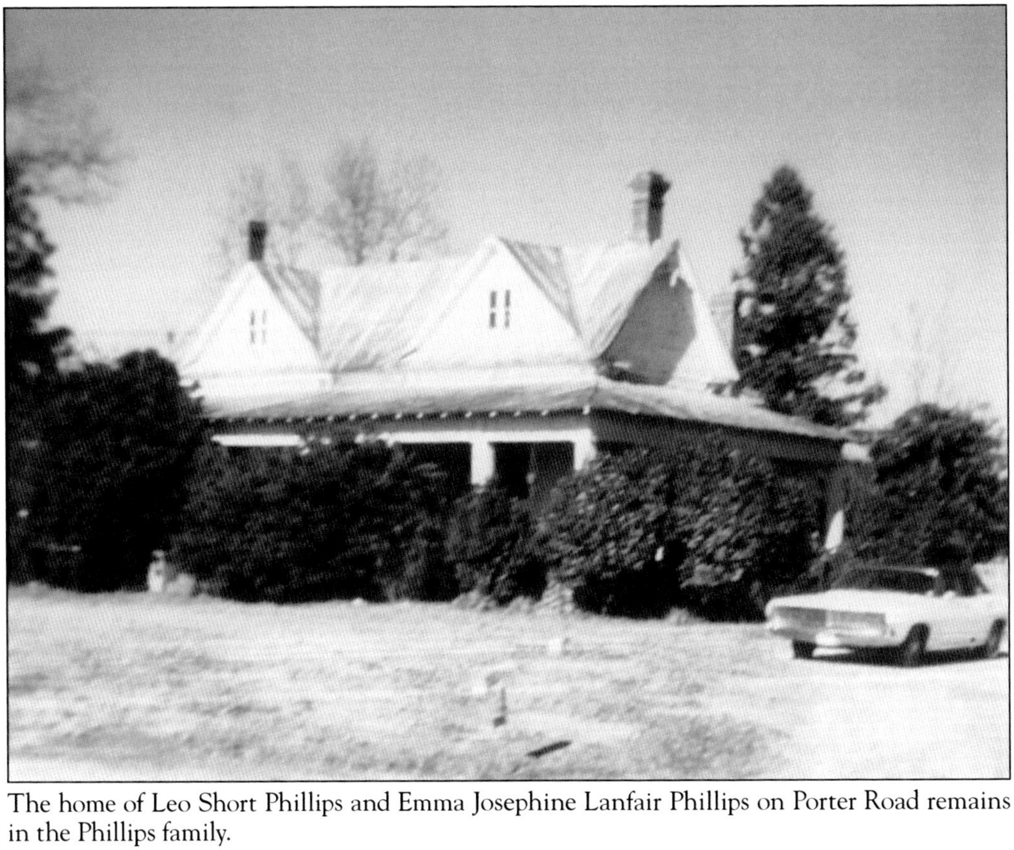

The home of Leo Short Phillips and Emma Josephine Lanfair Phillips on Porter Road remains in the Phillips family.

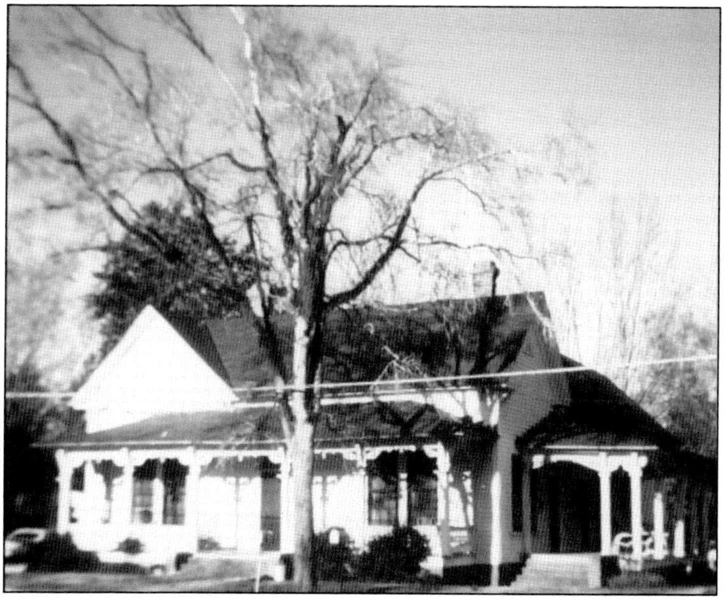

The Second Street home of Irvin A. Willis and Martha Clements Willis was later the home of their daughter, Merle Willis Barwick.

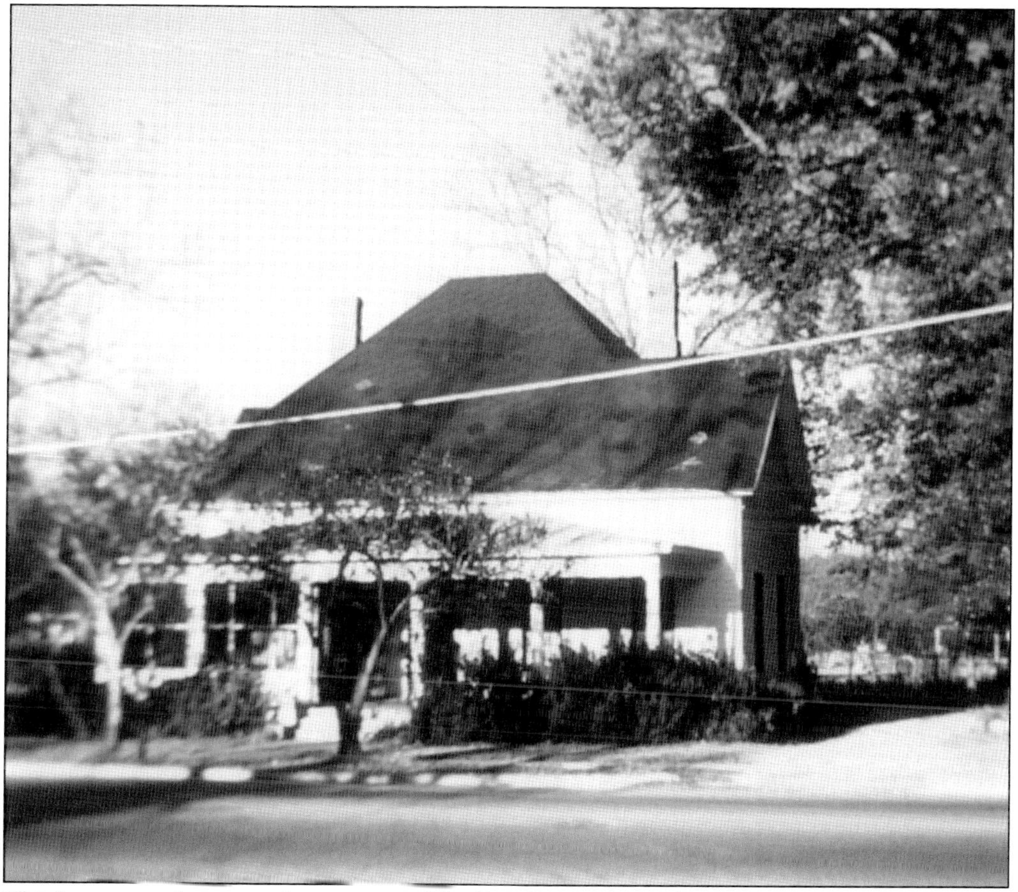

This home was the original pastorium of the First Baptist Church of Cochran. The last pastor to occupy the house was Roy O. Peyton, who lived here with his wife, Dorothy.

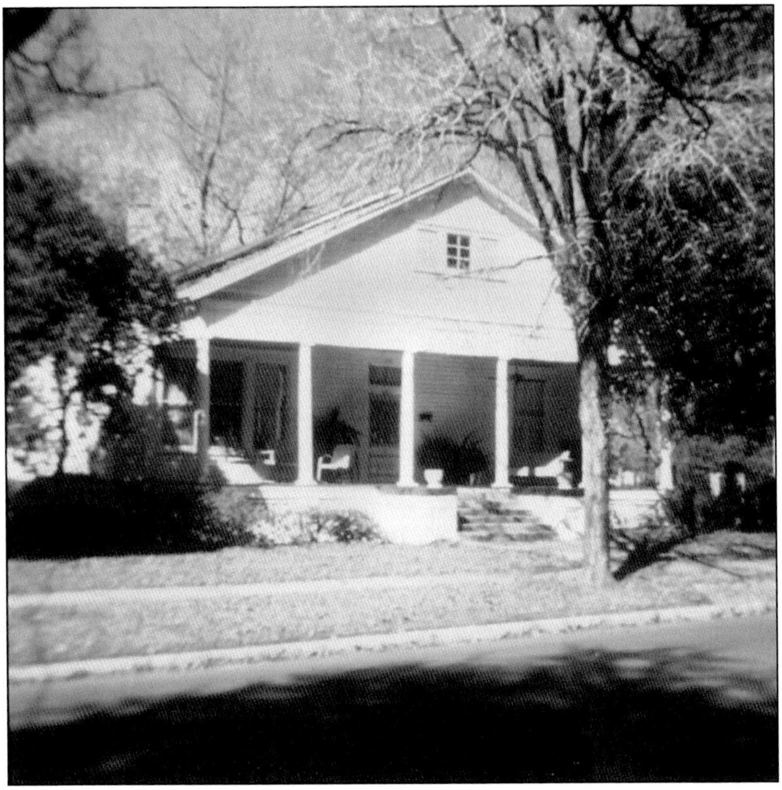

Beverly John Wynne built his home on Cherry Street. Originally a two-story residence, it was remodeled with a single story after a fire and is today the home of A. Lester Dykes and Dorothy Mullis Dykes.

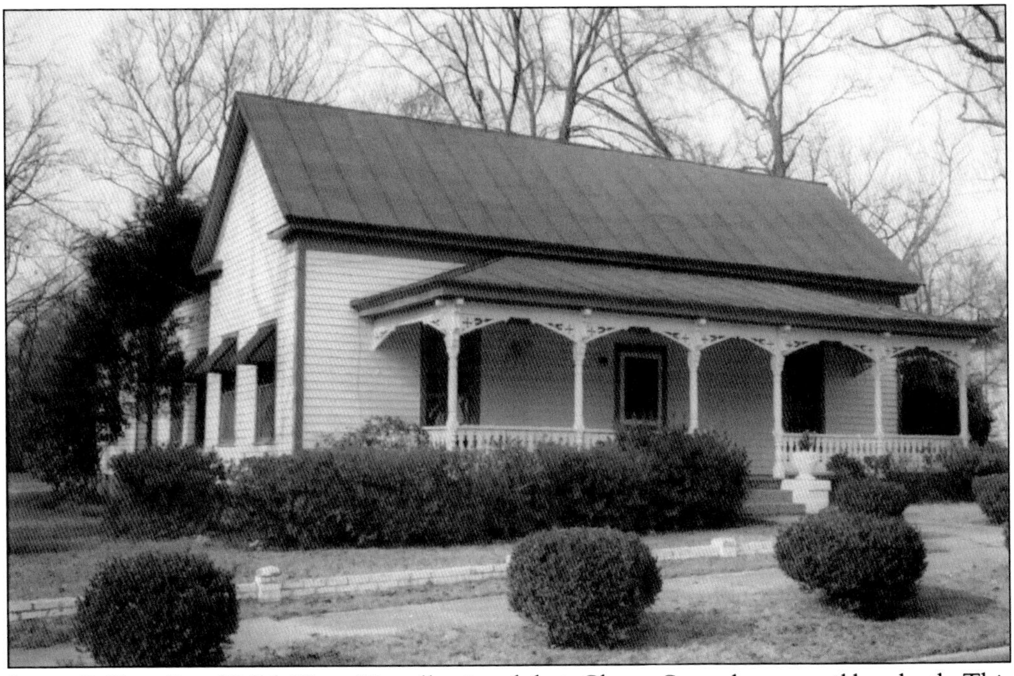

Lovett S. Harrell and Edith Tison Harrell enjoyed their Cherry Street home until her death. This house was later the home of Doris Martin.

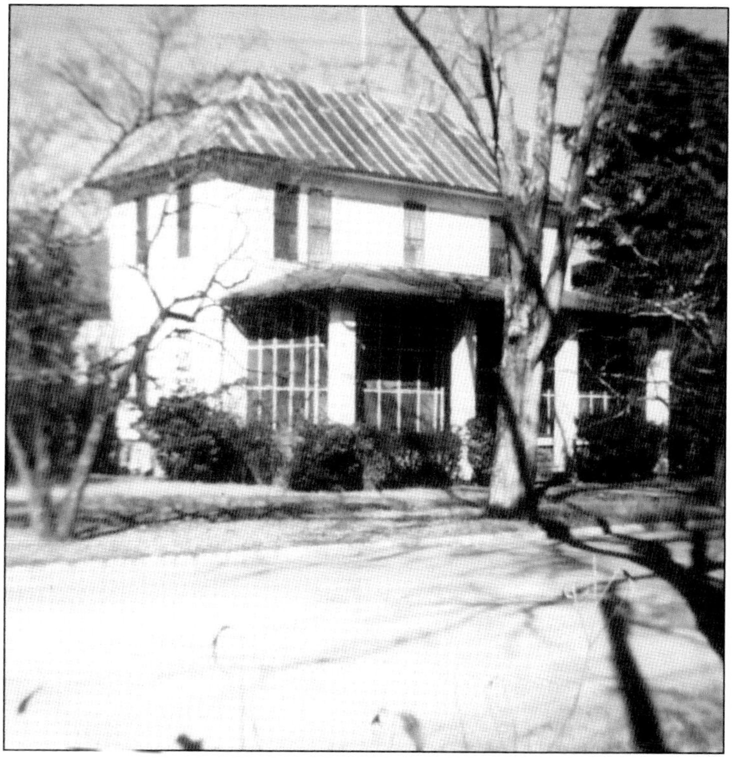

The Allen Parks Urquhart home on Cherry Street was the home of his daughter, Marguerite Smith, and her husband, Hal Smith, for many years. Mrs. Smith taught piano. The house was later a rental unit of Ben and Lillie Mae Barrow Jessup. The apartment on the right was occupied for many years by Lucy Coley Dyer.

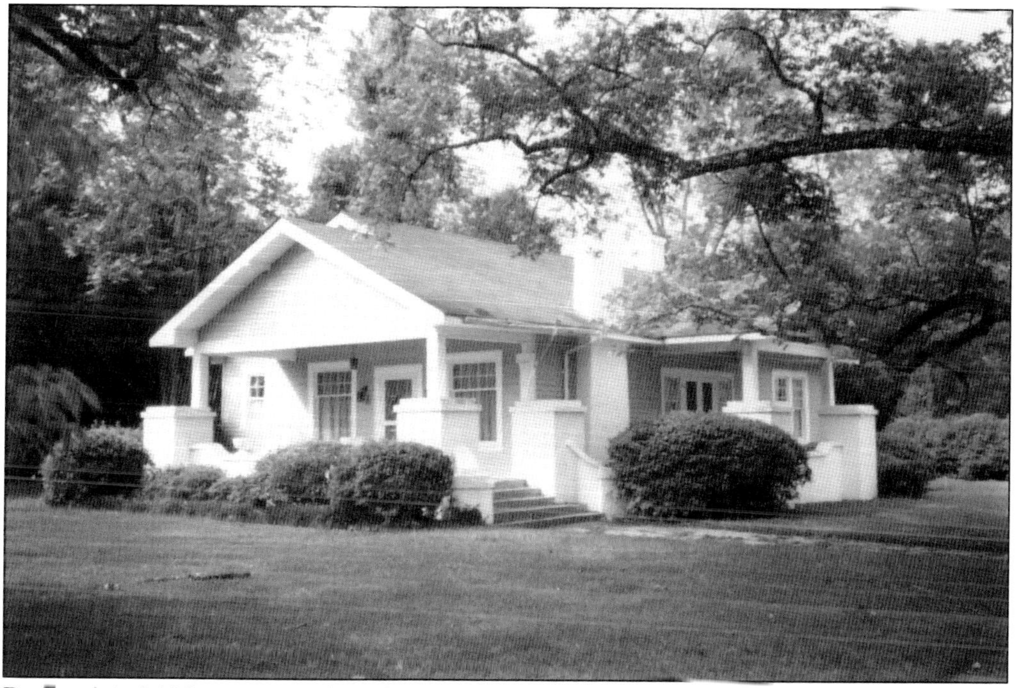

Dr. Frank L. McVay was considered by many to be the most prominent man in Cochran in the 20th century. He built his home on Cherry Street for himself and his wife, Rubye Taylor McVay. The home is today the residence of James and Regina Sanders.

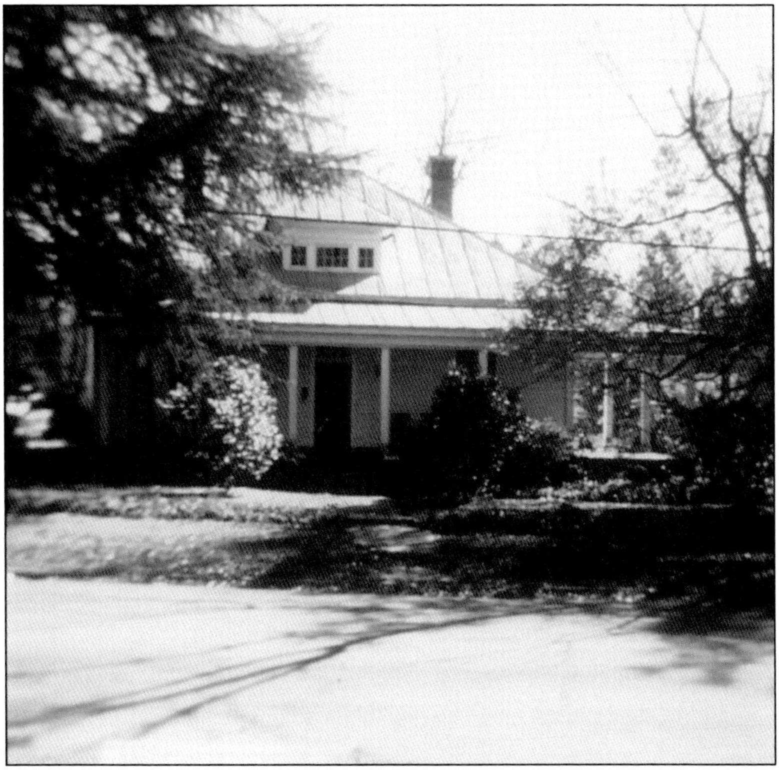

This Cherry Street residence was the home of W. T. and Leila McVay. W. T. McVay was manager of the Roxy and later the Vogue Theatre in Cochran. The home was later the residence of Alton and Carolyn Young and is today the home of Joel Hart.

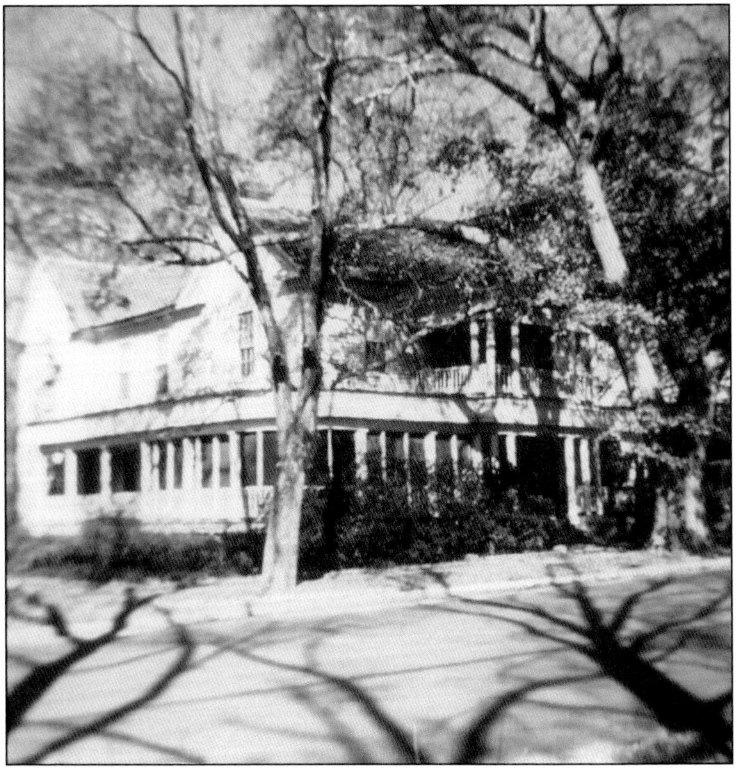

The *Cochran Journal* was edited for many years by Thomas Lee Bailey. He and his wife, Kittie Blevins Bailey, lived on Beech Street in this two-story home. It was later the home of Emma Noegel. The vacant lot is today owned by Joel Hart.

This Beech Street house was built by John J. Taylor and Alice Grimsley Taylor. It was later the home of James Perry Dykes (county commissioner) and Susie Petty Dykes. John and Susan Turner extensively remodeled the house, which is today the home of John and Elaine Ricks.

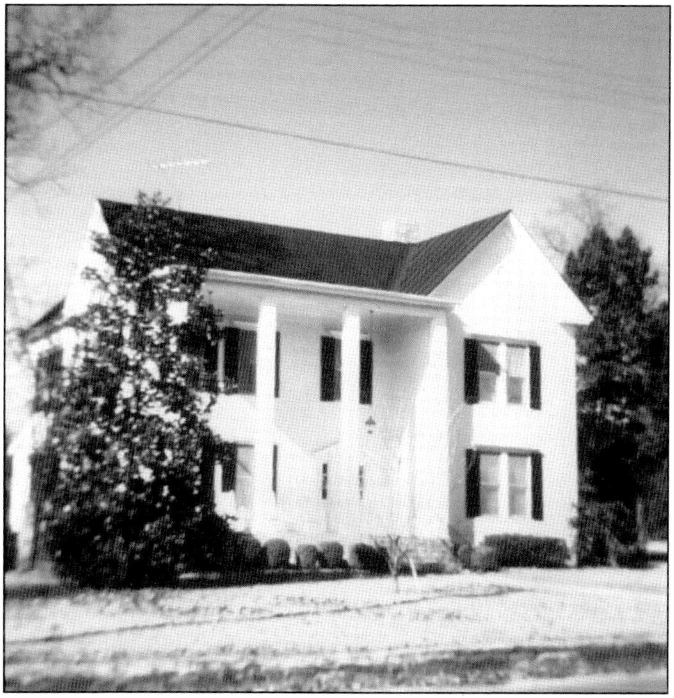

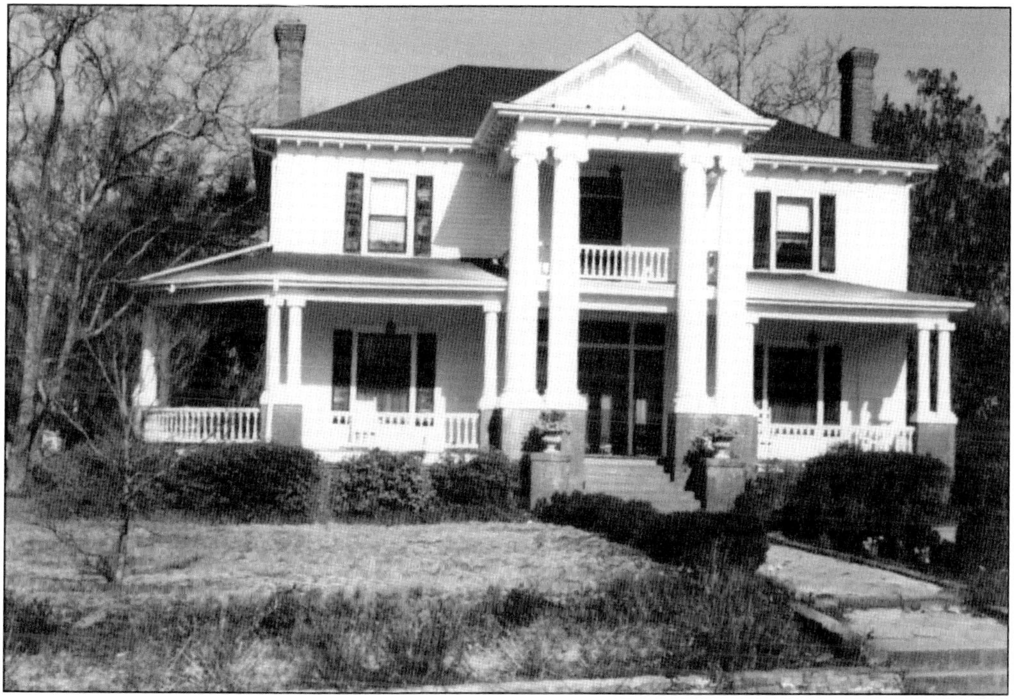

Built by John J. Taylor as a wedding present in 1910 for his daughter, Alice Taylor, upon her marriage to John A. Walker, this Beech Street home was later owned by Bennie and Gynelle Moore Stokes. Rev. Virlon H. Griner and JoAnne Williams Griner extensively remodeled the house while it was their home. Jim C. Usry owned the house for several years before selling it to John C. and Karen I. Adams. It is today the home of Charles Minnick.

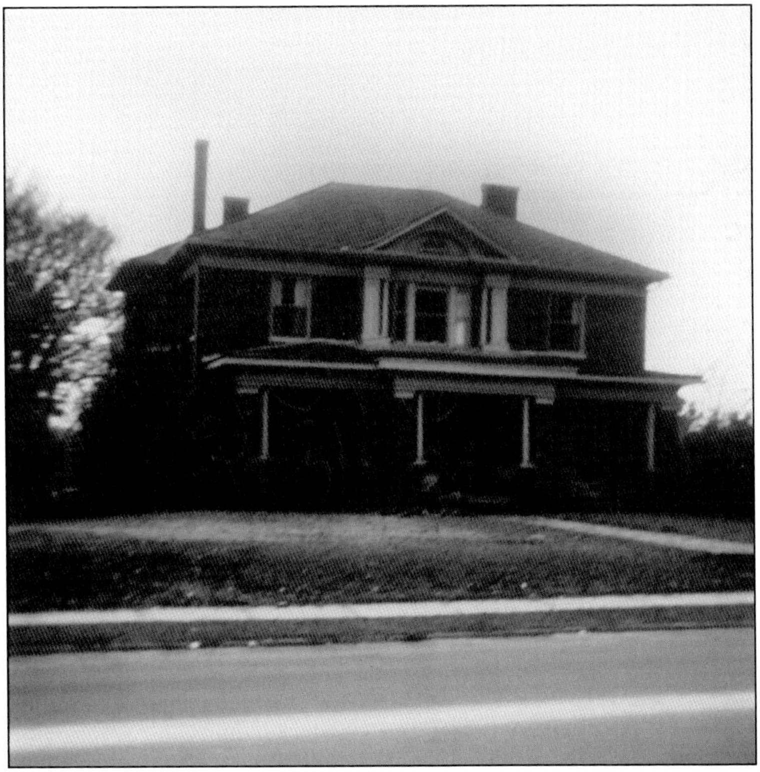

Thomas Wilmore Fisher Sr. and Jeffy Jordan Fisher built their two-story home in 1916. It was later the home of Tommy and Freida Fisher and of Tom and Joy Fisher before becoming the present location of Fisher Funeral Home at Dykes and First Streets.

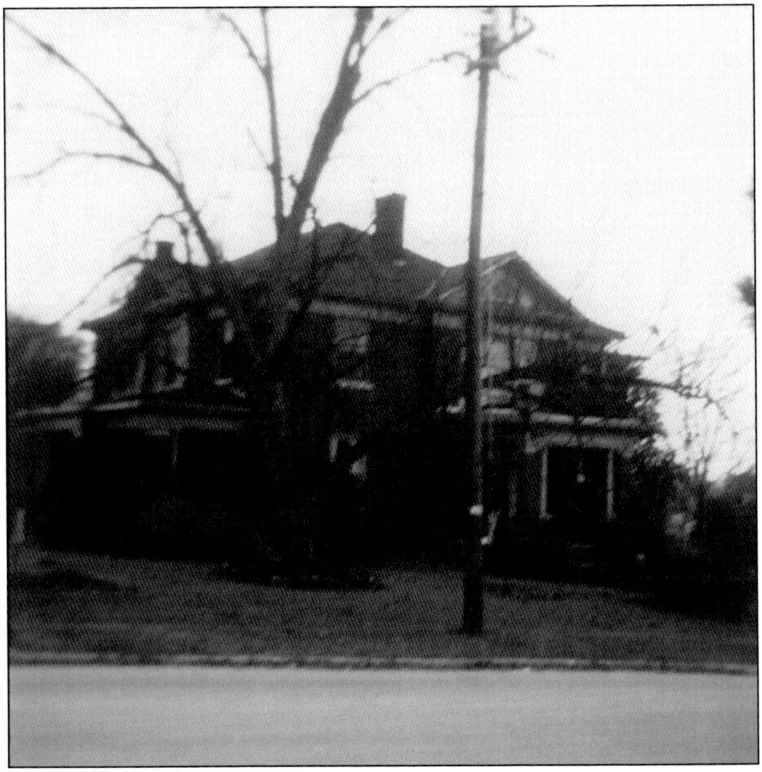

The Fisher home had a side porch facing First Street.

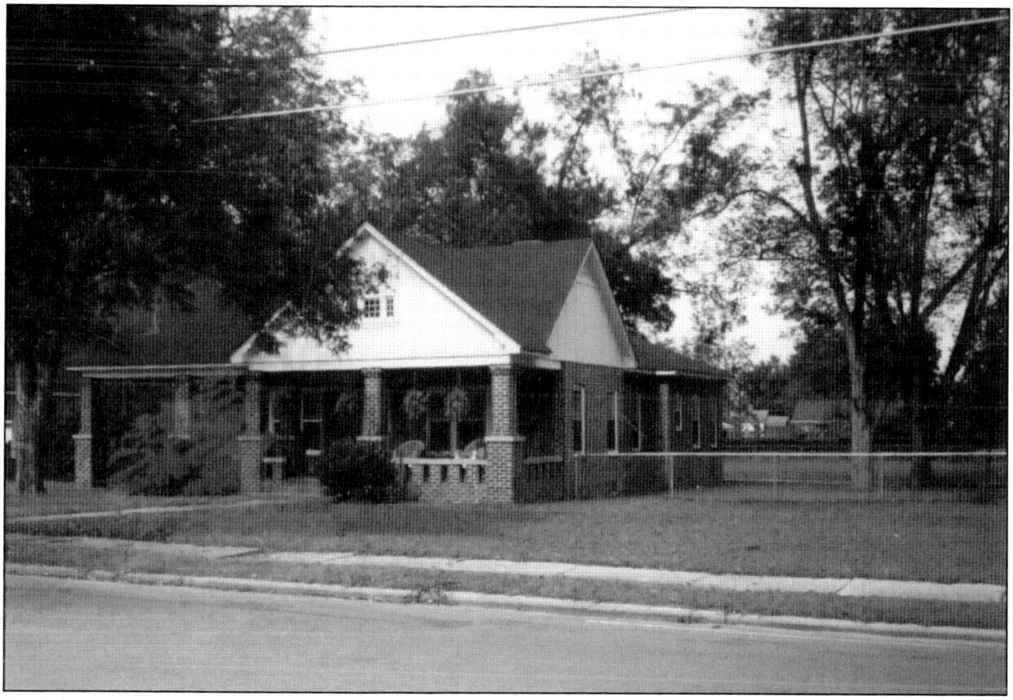

Built by Ross and Willie Phillips Hammack (owners of the *Cochran Journal* for many years), this Second Street home was later the residence of Clayton Crabbe and Evelyn Graham Crabbe. It is today the home of Tom and Joy Fisher.

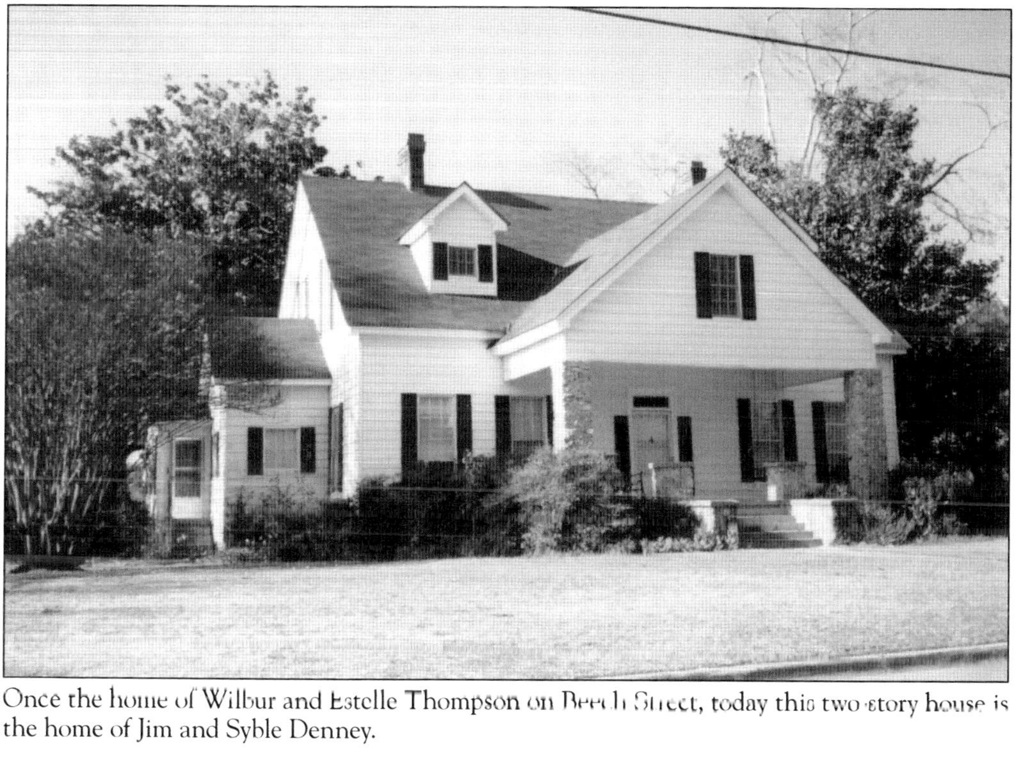

Once the home of Wilbur and Estelle Thompson on Beech Street, today this two-story house is the home of Jim and Syble Denney.

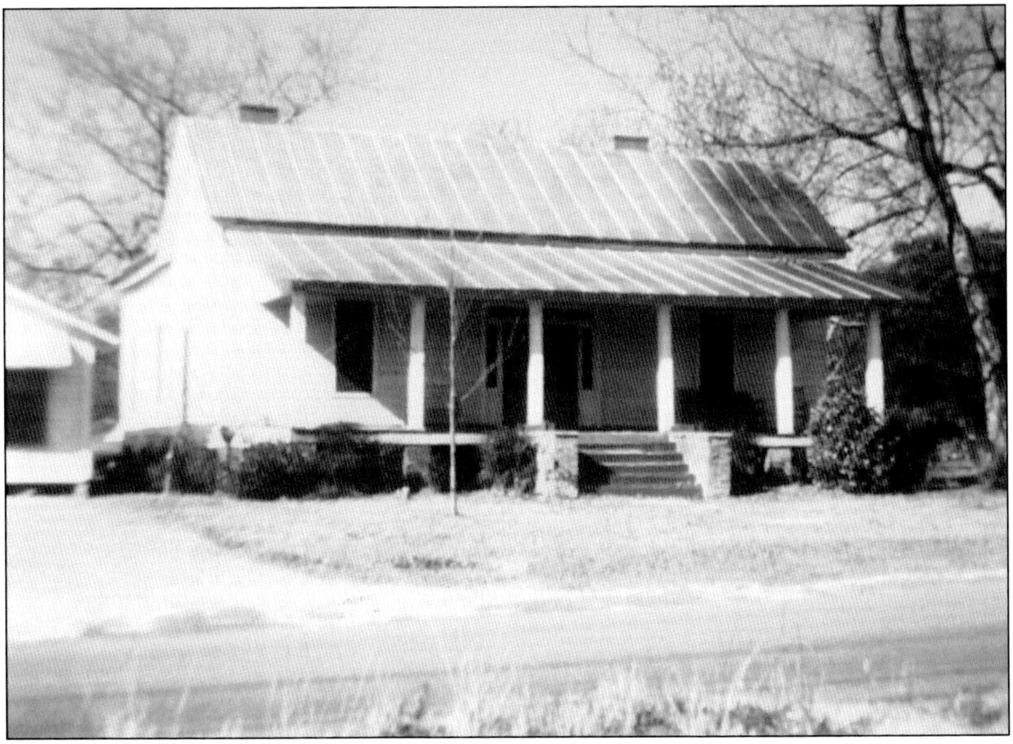

The home of William Lonnie Berryhill and Amanda Jane Nobles Berryhill was located on Ash Street at Seventh Street.

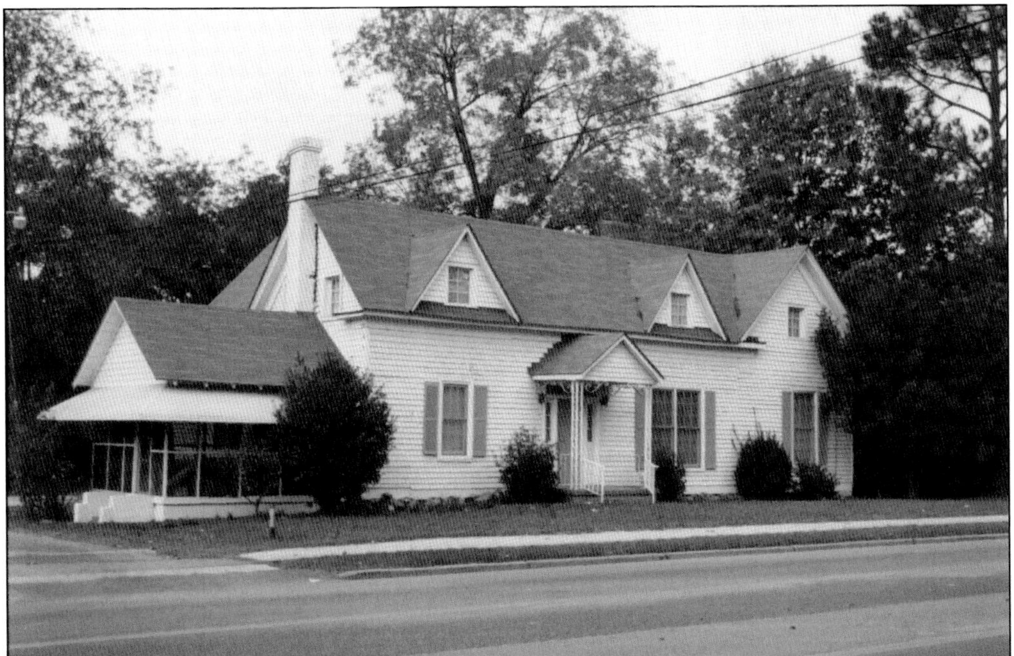

This Dykes Street residence was the home of George Travis Legg and Pearl Storey Legg. It is today the home of Dennis and Eva Jane Garrett.

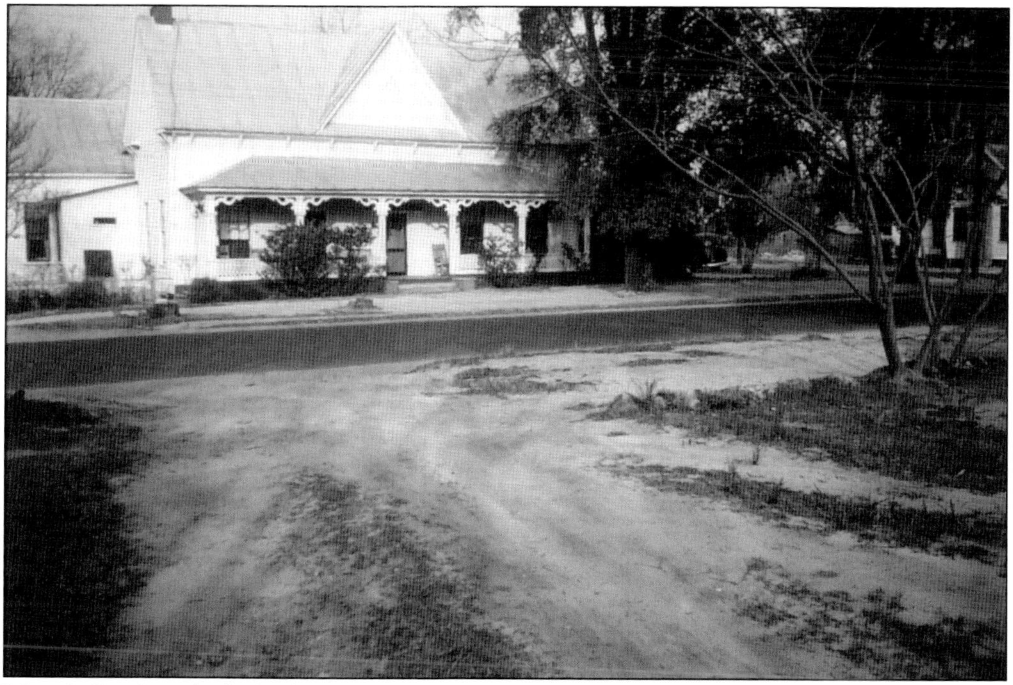

John C. Dunham built this home on Third and Cherry Streets for himself and his wife, Augusta Josephine Evans Dunham. The Horne family later lived in the house, and the last occupant was Cora Defore. It is presently the location of AT&T.

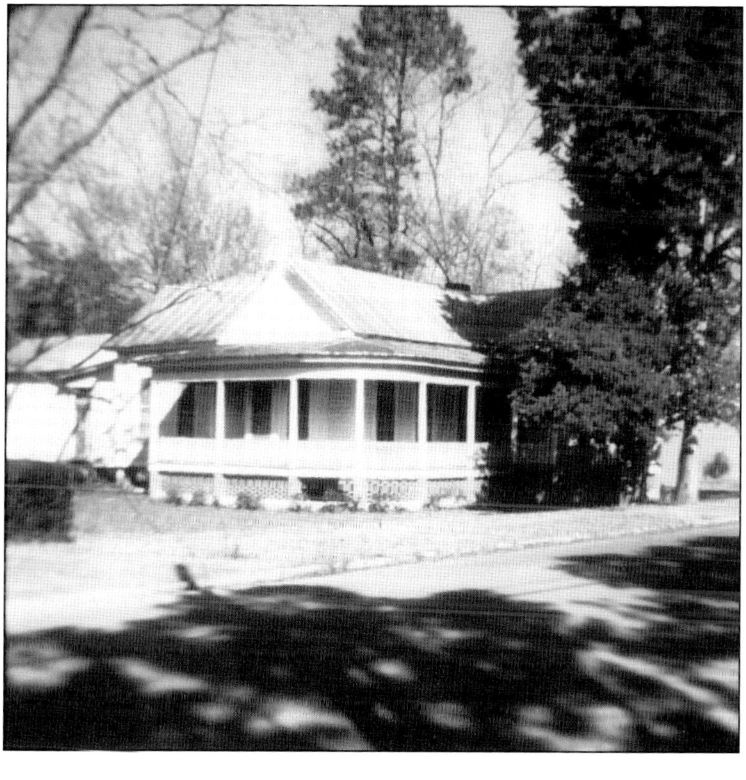

Built by Jesse Wynne, this Cherry Street home was later occupied by his daughter, Laurie Wynne Garner, and John Garner. Their two children were Robert "Bobby" Garner and Henrietta Garner Schacherbauer.

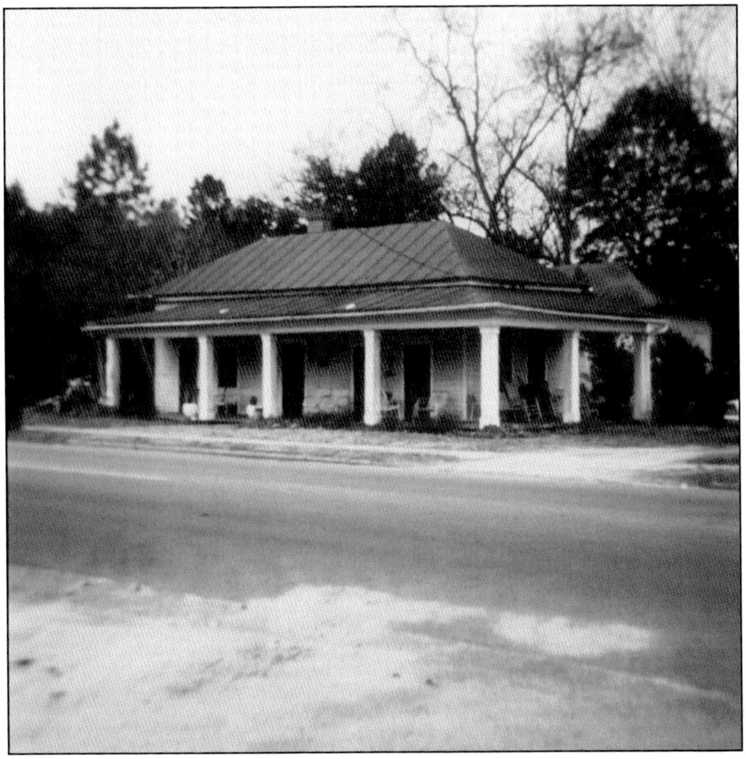

The home of George Franklin Hendricks and Emma Schilling Hendricks was later the home of their daughter, Henny May Hendricks, and of Thomas Howard Reeves and Emmie Hendricks Reeves. It was torn down to build a grocery store and car wash.

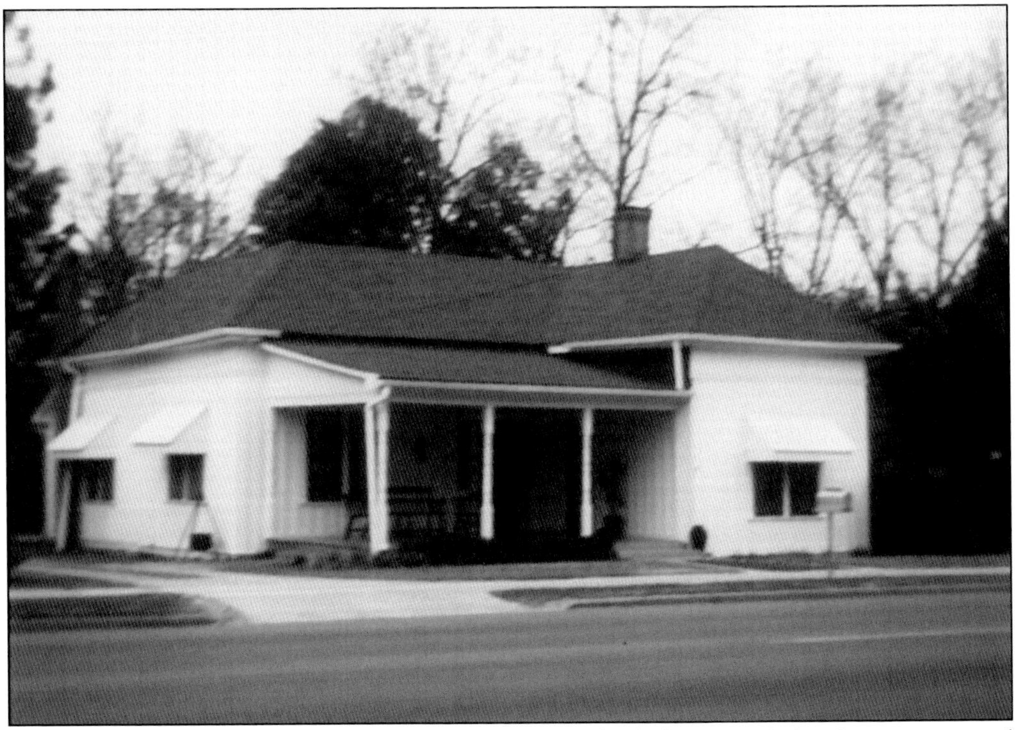

Part of the Fred S. Hendricks and Emmie Lee Lister Hendricks home on Dykes Street was rented to Jazzbo and Clara Weatherly and their three daughters, Vickie, Tina, and Rene.

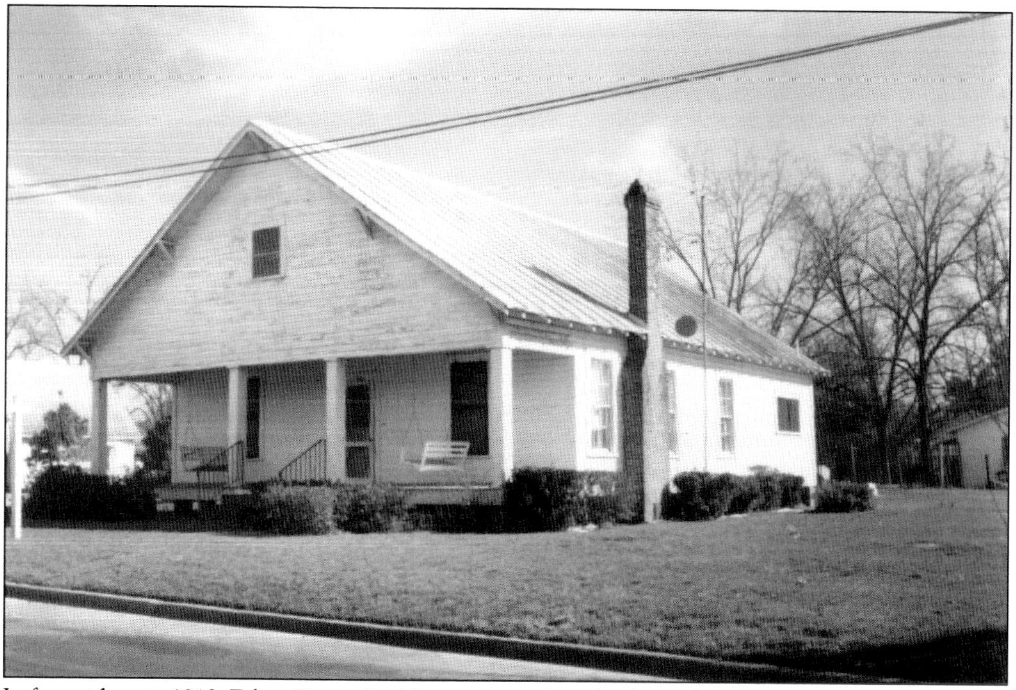

Left a widow in 1913, Edna Crumpler Horton moved to Cochran from Cary and built this house in 1919 for herself and four children, Joe, Alice, Mary, and Nettie. It was later the home of Rev. Ronnie and Susan Turner.

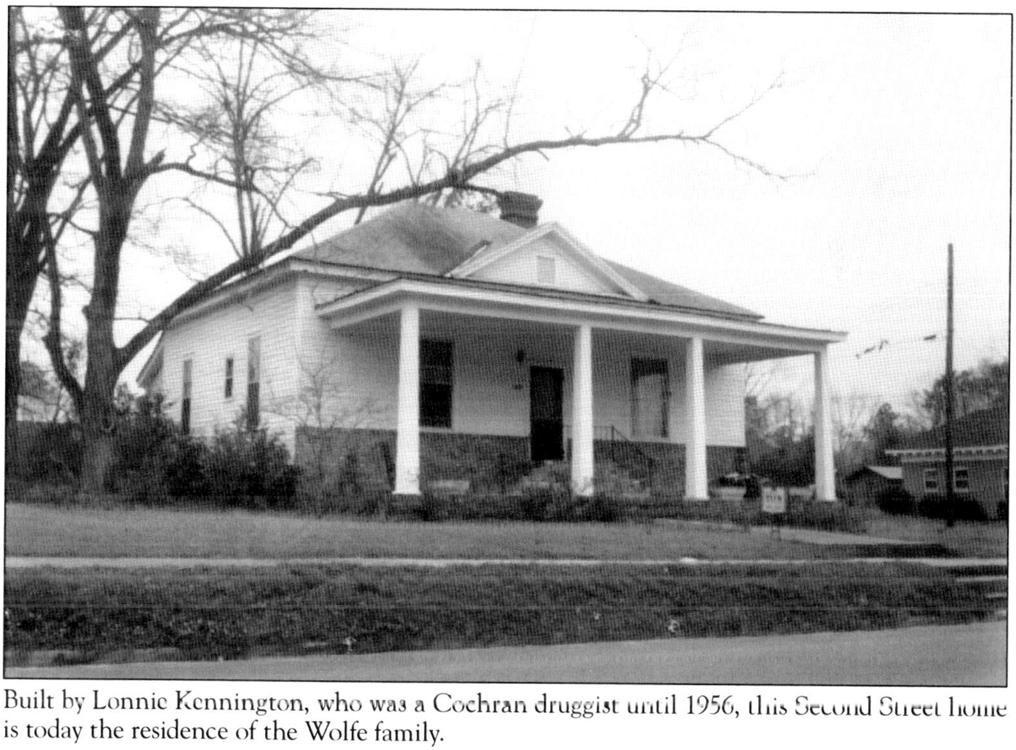

Built by Lonnie Kennington, who was a Cochran druggist until 1956, this Second Street home is today the residence of the Wolfe family.

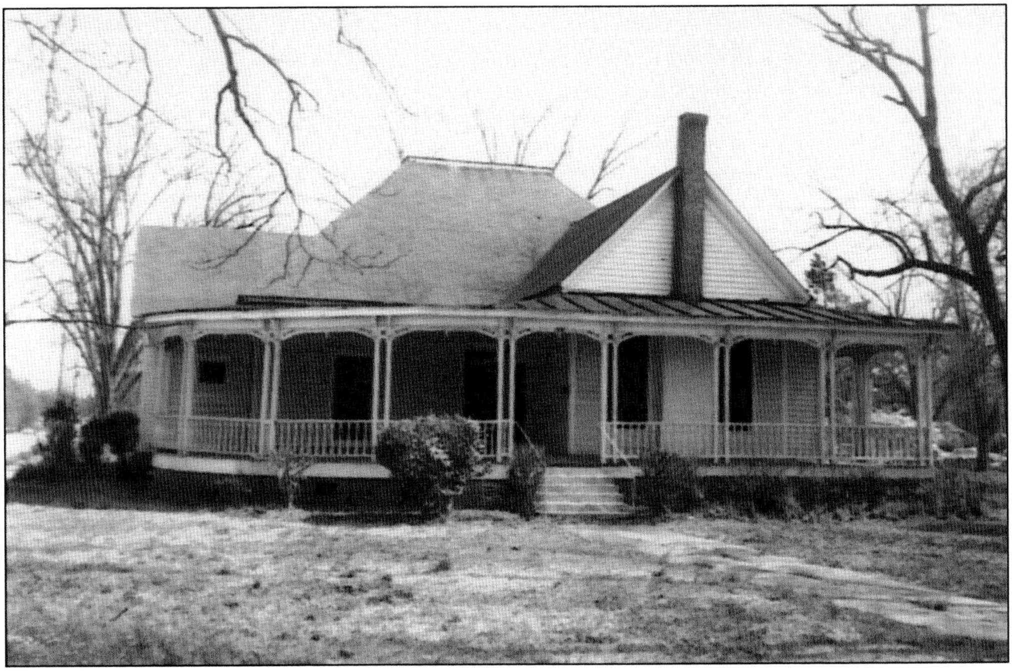

The home of Andrew Jackson Thompson and Frances Parten Thompson on Dykes Street at Third Street was a Cochran landmark for many years. Later it was the home of Kindred Allison Thompson and Mary Mullis Thompson. It was last occupied by Julia Thompson Vinson and her brother, Mac William Thompson. Today it is part of Cochran First Baptist Church.

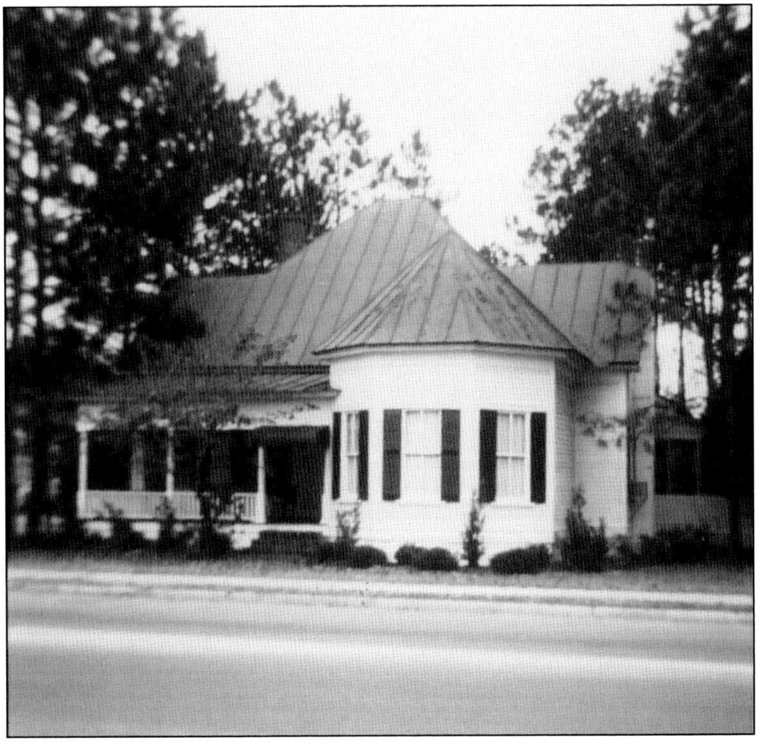

Built by Arthur T. and Mary Walton Wiggs (for whom Wiggs Hall at Middle Georgia College is named), this Third Street residence became the home of R. E. and Emily Nichols and later of Robert A. and Sallie Willis Harrell. It was moved to Knoxville, Georgia, and is today the home of Robert and Martha Carter.

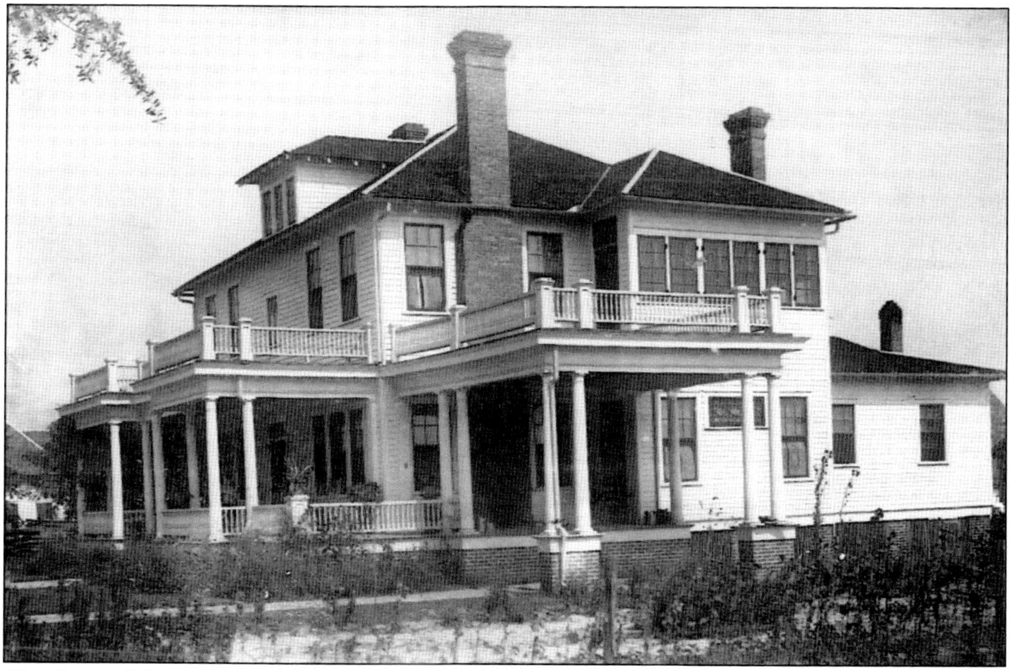

The Second Street home of Dr. Robert L. Whipple Sr. and Gladys Harvard Whipple was built in 1914. From 1955 until 1970, it was the home of Buddy M. NeSmith and Wena Hunt NeSmith. It was the home of Ken Mathews and Eleanor Usry Mathews until 2005, when it was purchased by First Baptist Church, and it is known today as the Whipple House.

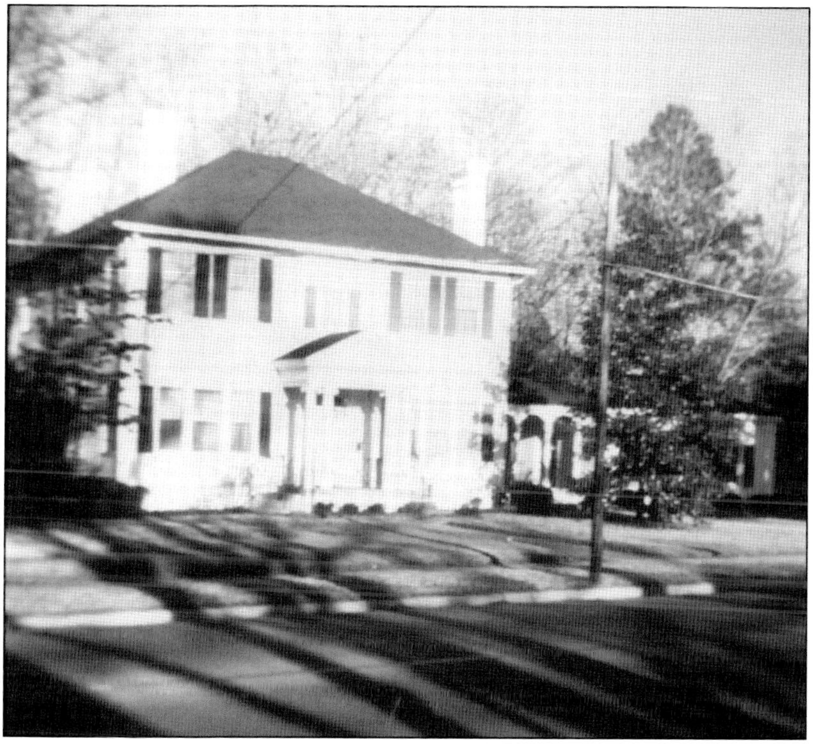

The Whipple House's exterior was remodeled by Buddy M. NeSmith and Wena H. NeSmith.

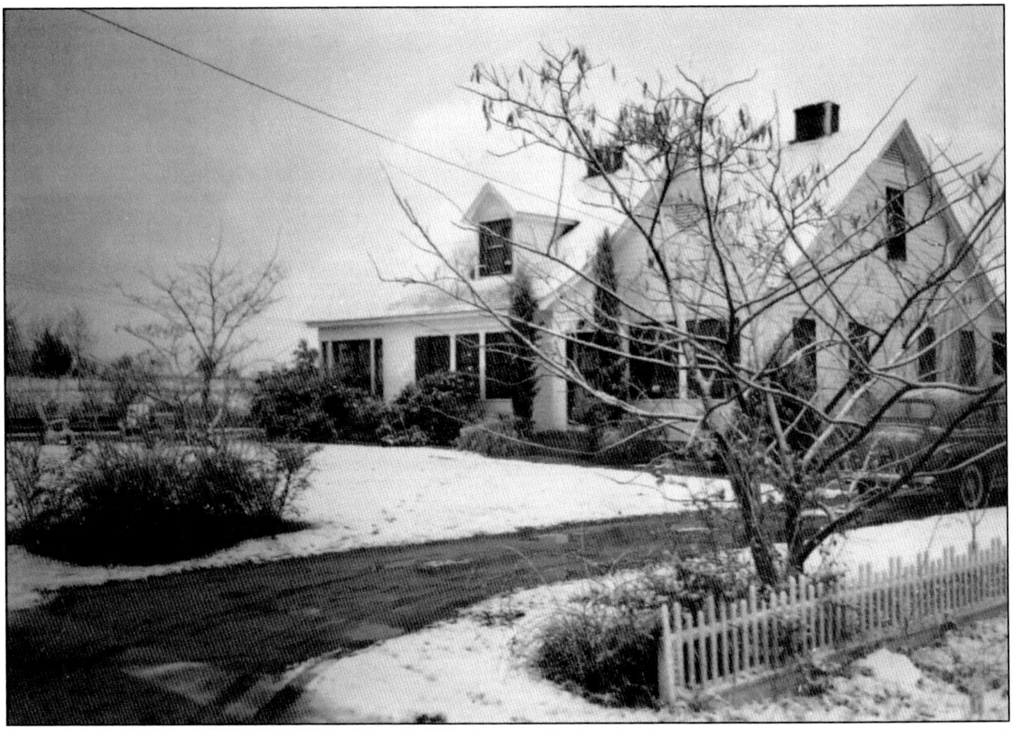

The Second Street home of Garner B. Hill became the home for 40 years of D. Kemp Garvin and Elizabeth Hill Garvin. The backyard was once the scene of the Sam and Nelda Bryant wedding. It is today the home of Barbara C. Anderson. (Photograph by Clyde Hill.)

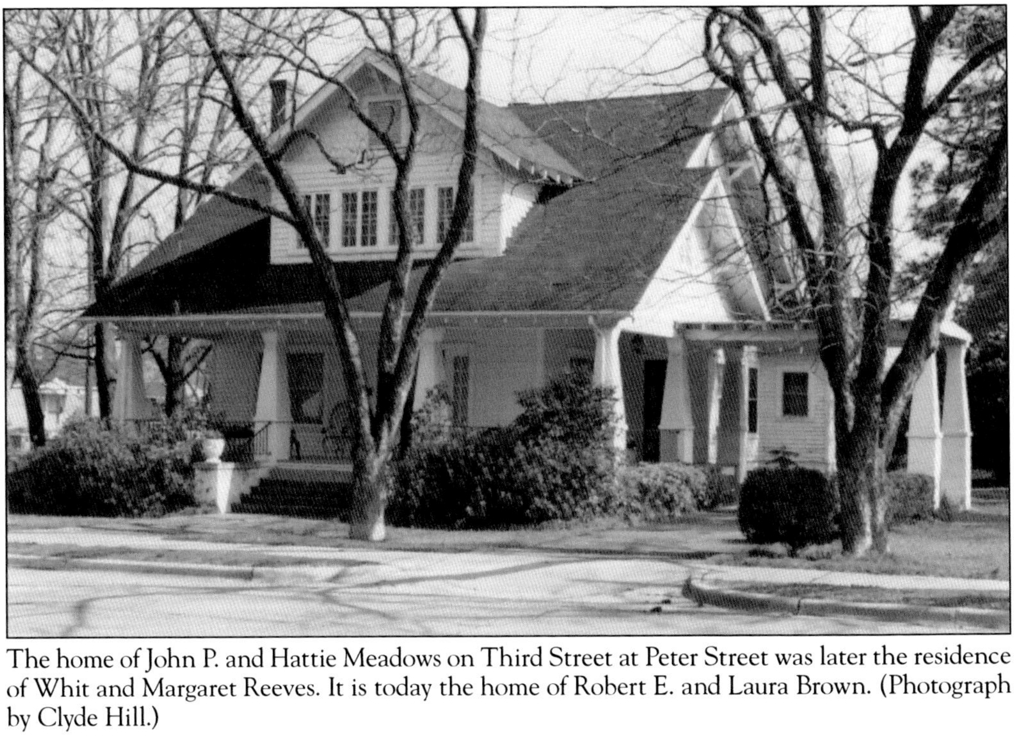

The home of John P. and Hattie Meadows on Third Street at Peter Street was later the residence of Whit and Margaret Reeves. It is today the home of Robert E. and Laura Brown. (Photograph by Clyde Hill.)

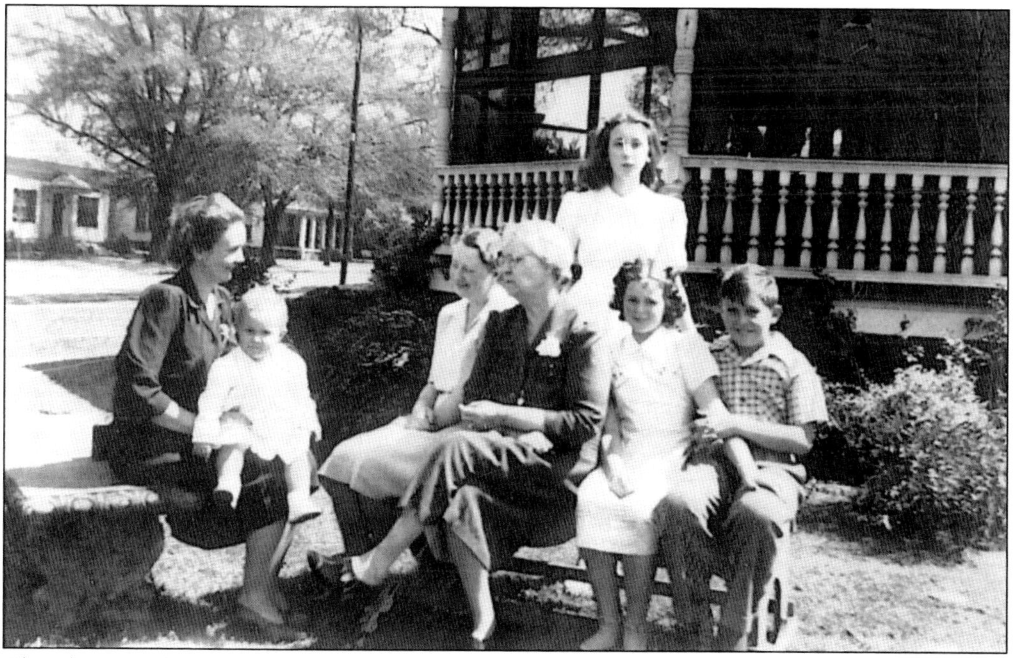

The photograph of the home of Barkwell Thompson and Willie Mullis Thompson shows the Charlie and Katherine Thompson home in background next to the original Methodist parsonage. Pictured, from left to right, are Marie Dykes Thompson (the wife of John Barkwell Thompson Jr.) holding little daughter Sue Marie Thompson (the wife of William "Bill" Turner), Sarah Lovett Thompson, Willie Mullis Thompson, Saralynn Thompson (standing), Gwendolyn Thompson Salter, and Dr. Dan Thompson. (Courtesy of Mattie Lee Mullis Baxley.)

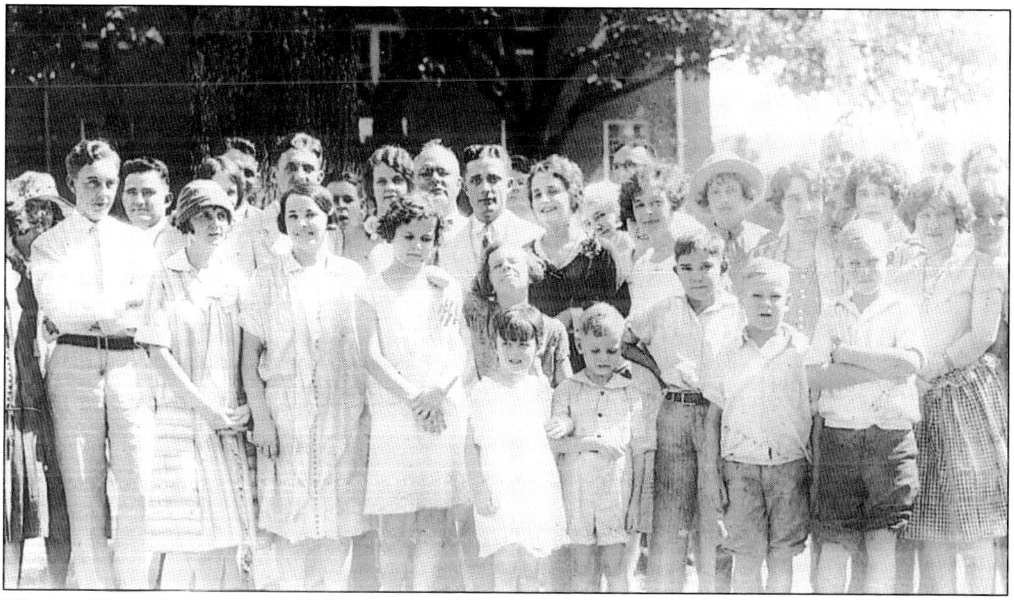

The wedding day picture of John Barkwell Thompson Jr. and Marie Dykes Thompson on the lawn of the Barkwell Thompson home on Third Street shows the guests included the Mullis, Morgan, Dykes, and Thompson families. The original Cochran High School building is in the background. (Courtesy of Mattie Lee Mullis Baxley.)

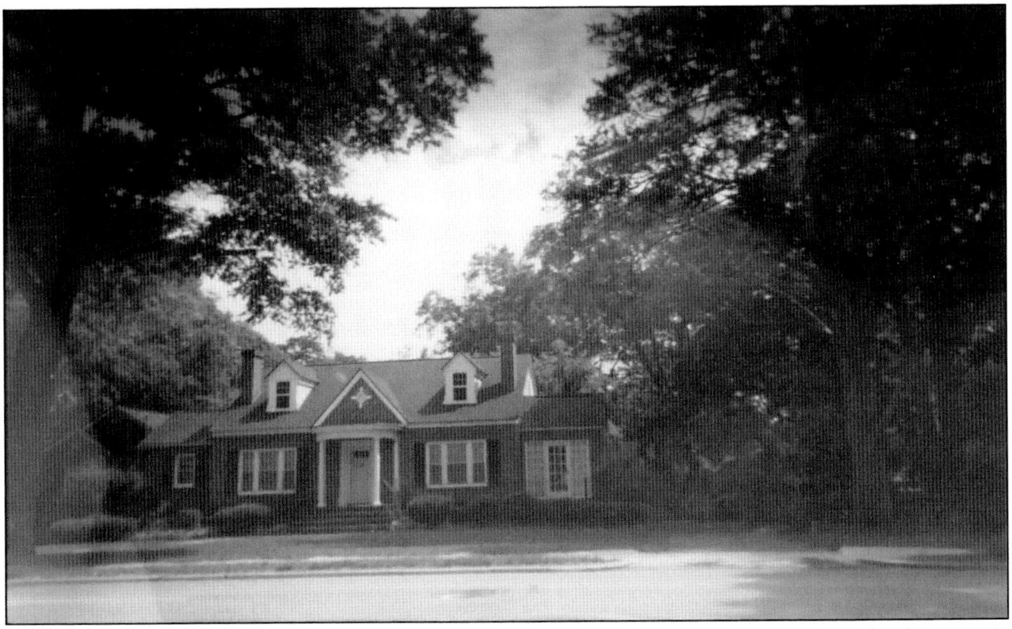

The home of Leo L. Phillips Sr. and Anne Newton Phillips on Second Street was built in 1942. It was later the home of Jason and Tracy Phillips Johnson and is today the home of Tracey A. Deavers and Shannon Deavers.

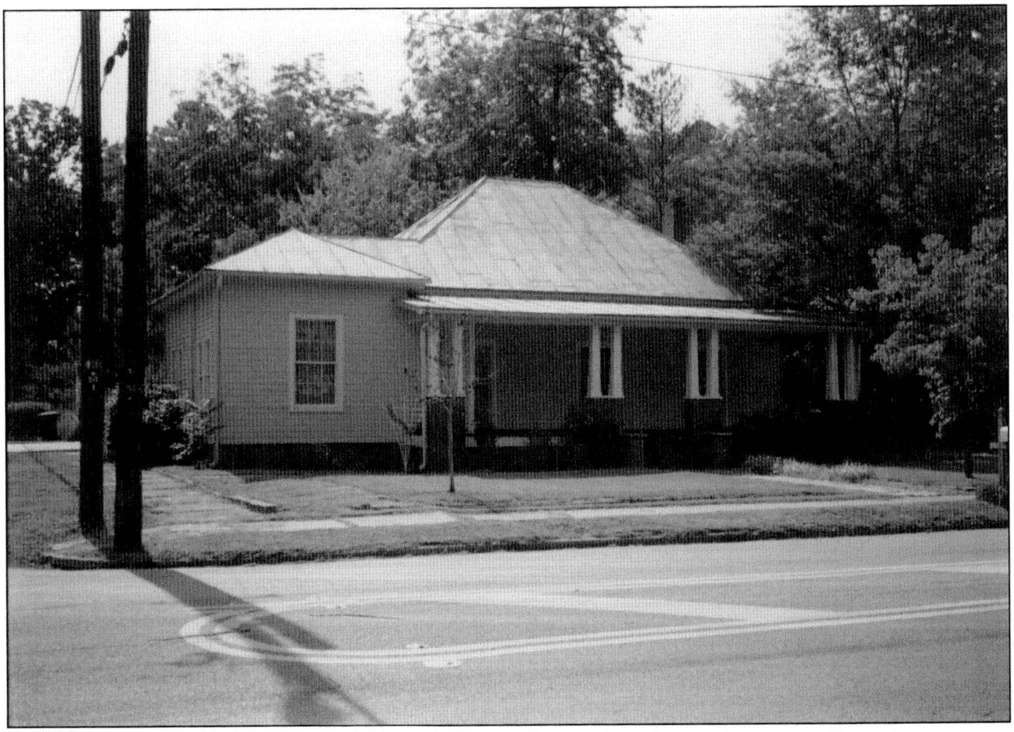

The home of Dr. L. D. and Annie Mae Rhodes is located on Second Street at Peter Street.

The Evans home on the Chester Highway was built by Gus Evans Sr. and Lou Pearl Evans. Here Gus and Marie Evans raised their family, and it remains the Evans home today.

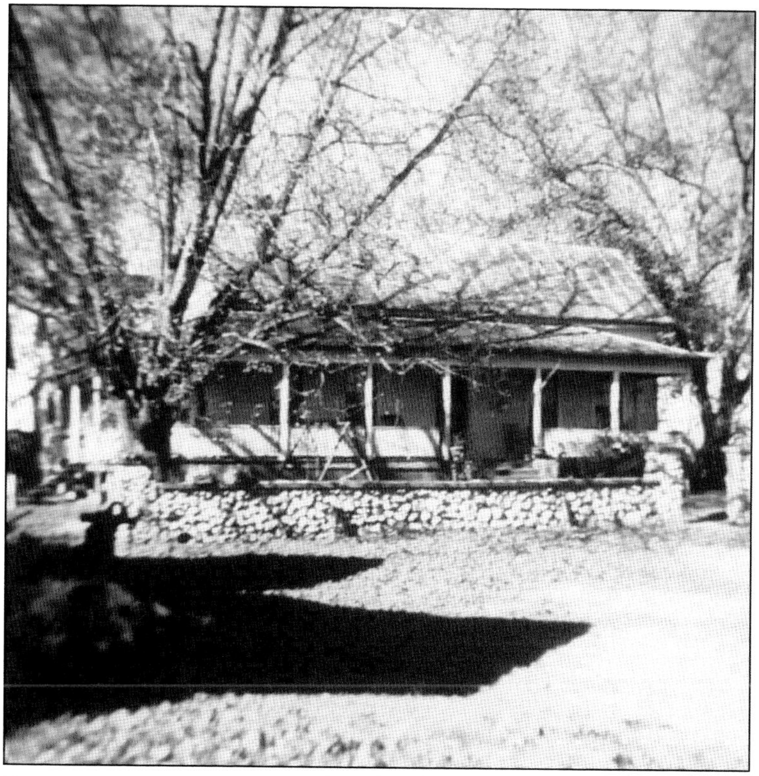

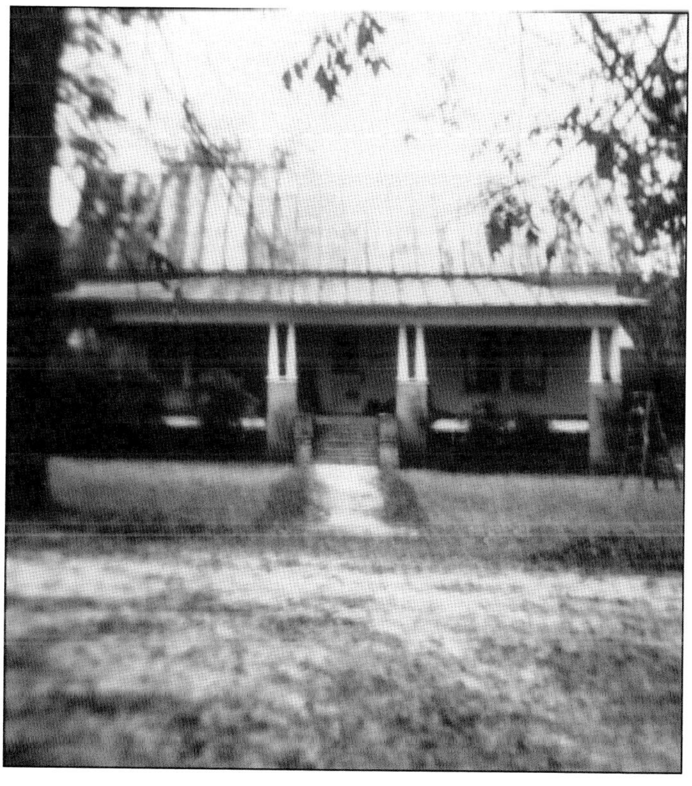

The John G. NeSmith home on the Dublin Highway is today the home of Charlie and Jerri Tuck.

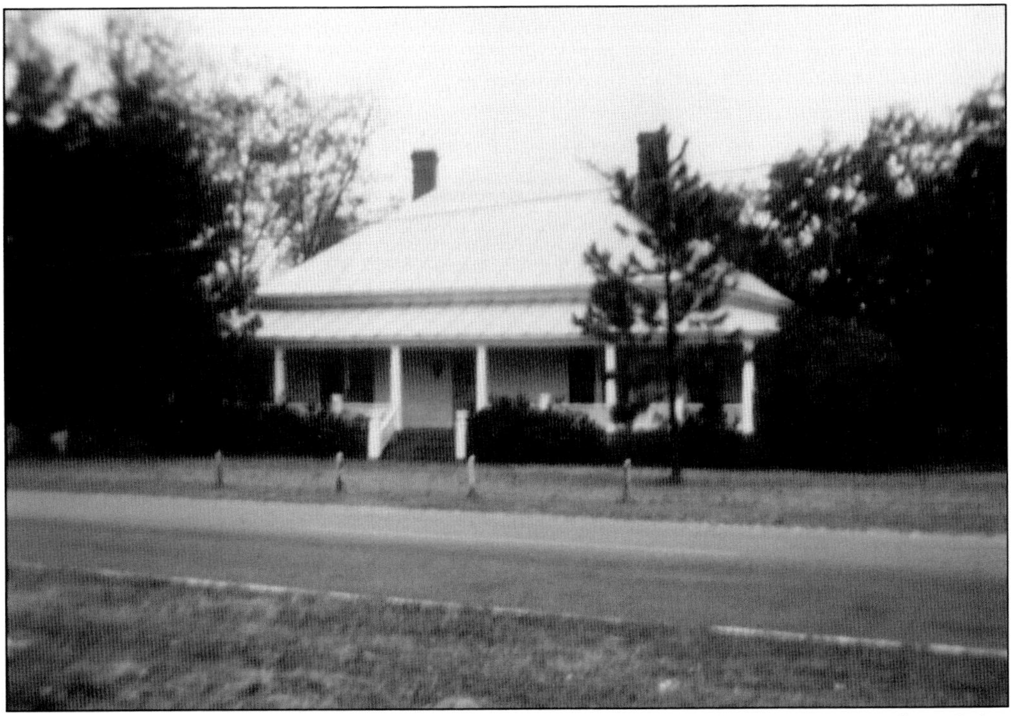

The home of Gent and Nellie Lanfair Grantham and their six children, Burney, Julian, Riley "Bud," Howard, Melton, and Nellie Mae, was located on the Dublin Highway.

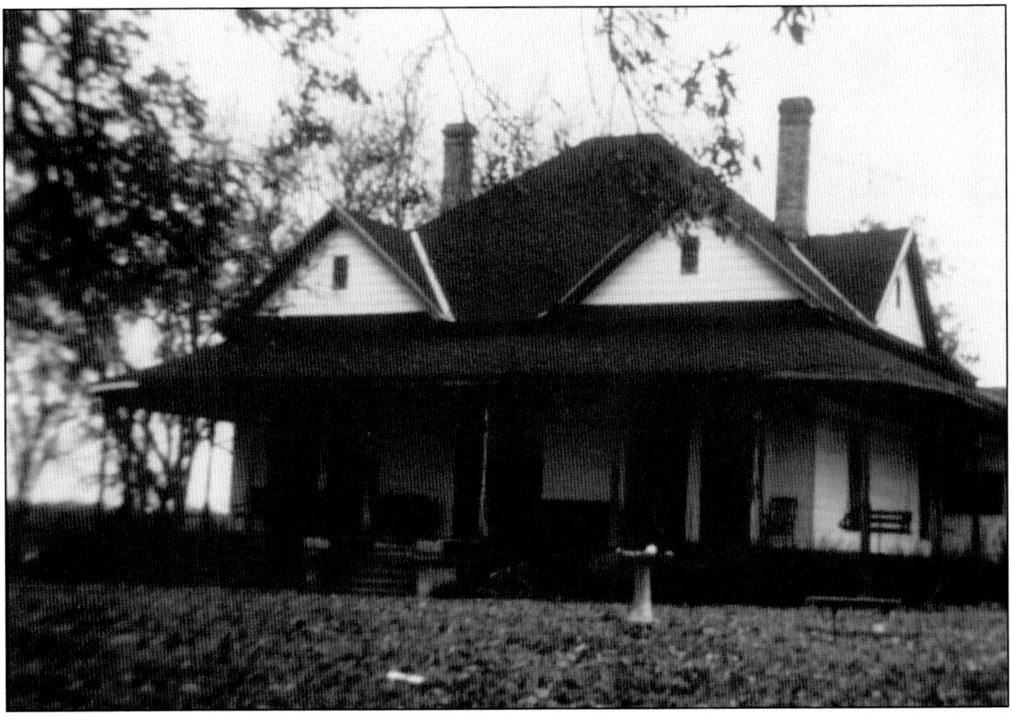

The home of the Ernest G. Sparrow family on Chicken Road is today the home of Michael and Tami Harmon McGraw.

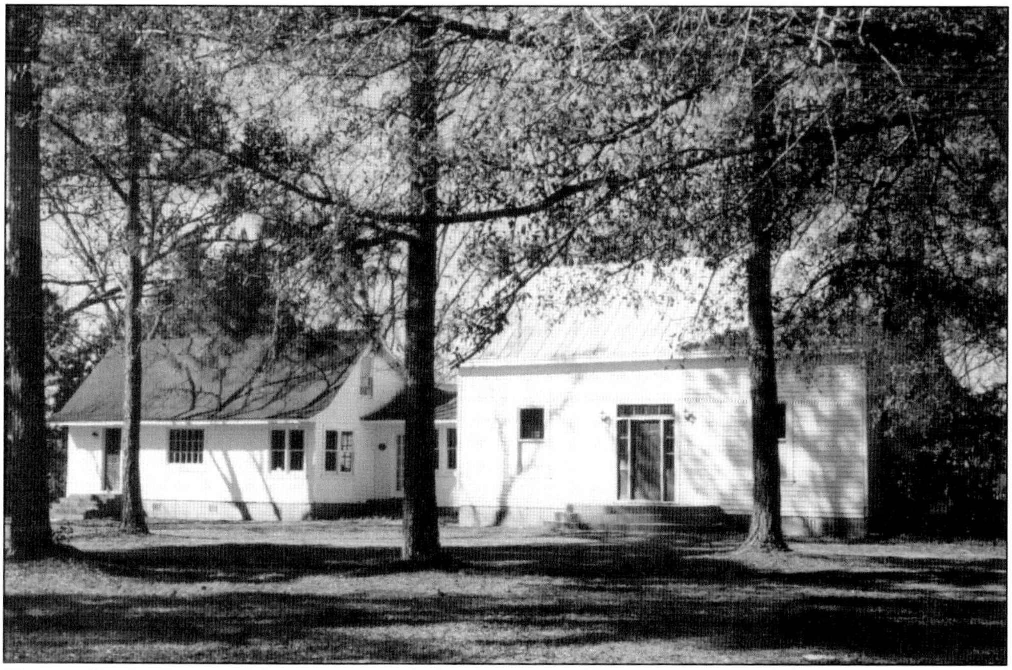

Originally the home of the W. O. Peacock overseer on the Hawkinsville Highway and later the home of Robert L. Hendricks and Mary Lou Brown Hendricks, this home is today the residence of Steve and Winter Darsey.

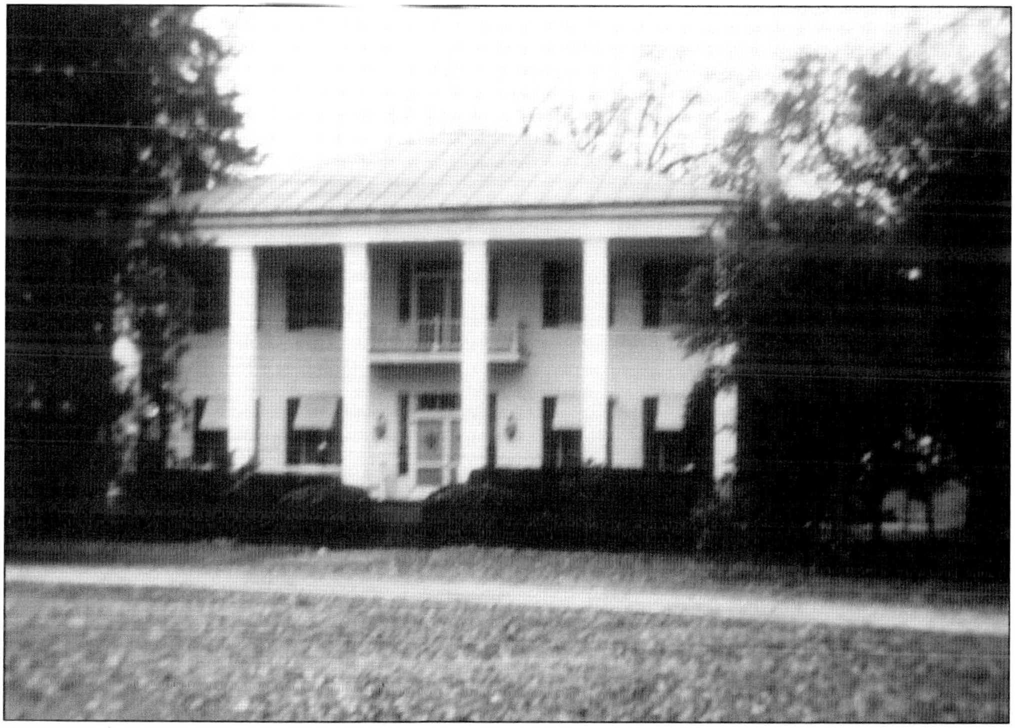

Built by Alcana Coley, this antebellum home was known as the English home on the Dublin Highway. It was home to W. B. and Mary English and later to their son, Paul English, and Ann English.

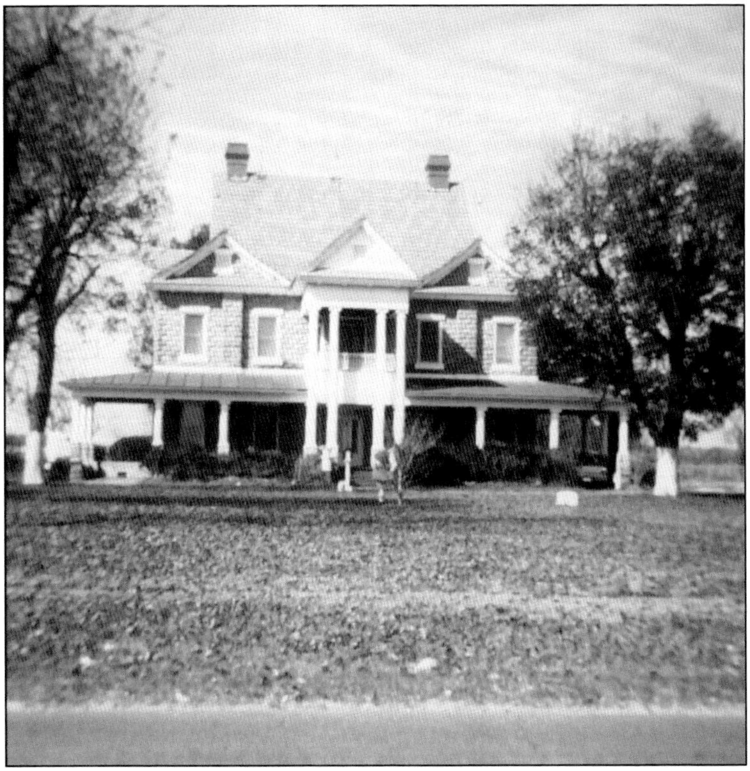

Built by F. D. Wimberly with blocks made on his plantation, this stately home was later the residence of Henry and Sara Alexander Griffin, of Cliff Dunn, and of J. D. and Alice Paulk. It is today the home of Cliff L. Paulk and Kathryn Southerland Paulk.

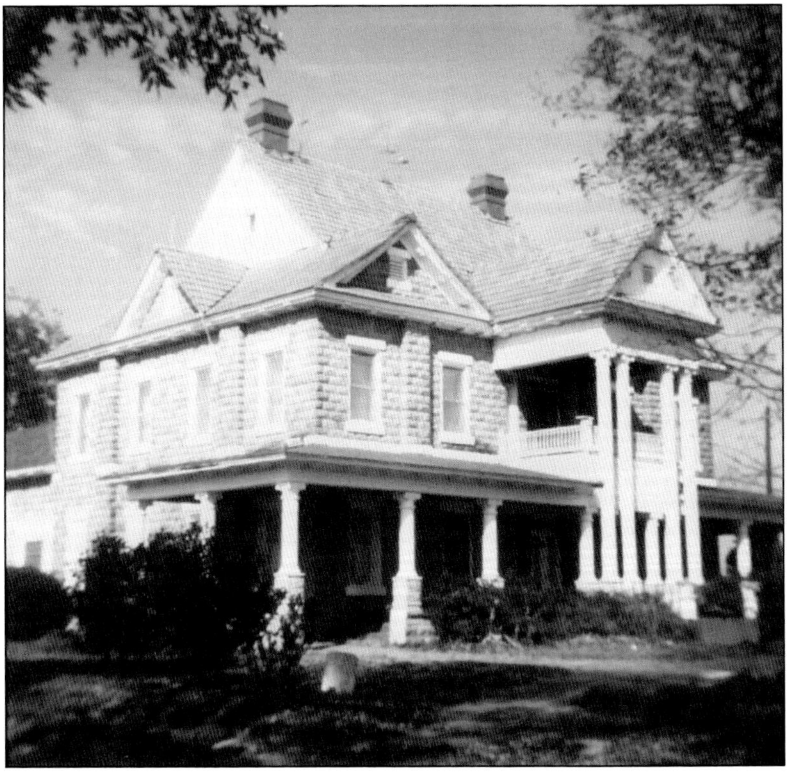

This is a side view of the home of Cliff and Kathryn Paulk.

Known as the "Big" Eli Mullis home near Rebie, this large residence was the home of Lois McDaniel and is today owned by Wendy McDaniel Allen.

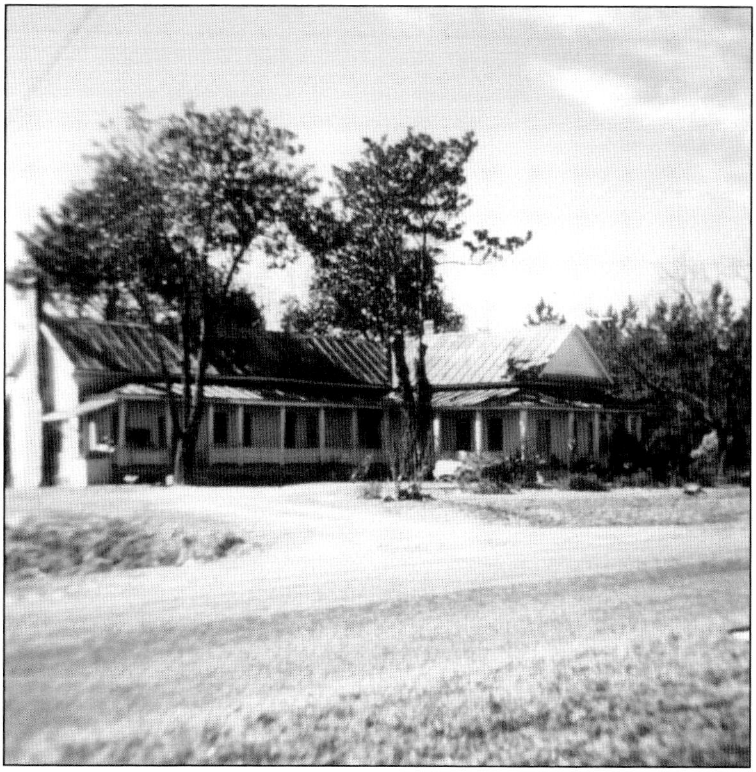

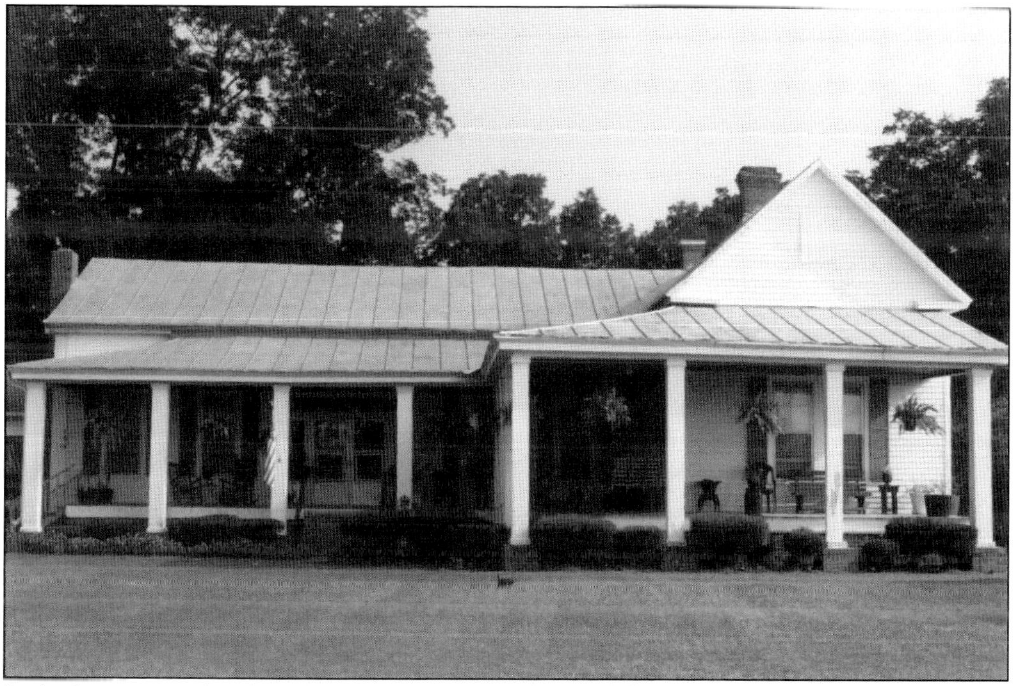

Built about 1840, the Eli Mullis place between Salem and Cary was the home of Emmie Mullis and later of Walker A. and Ruth Mullis. It is today the home of Emmie Faye Mullis. (Courtesy of Faye Mullis.)

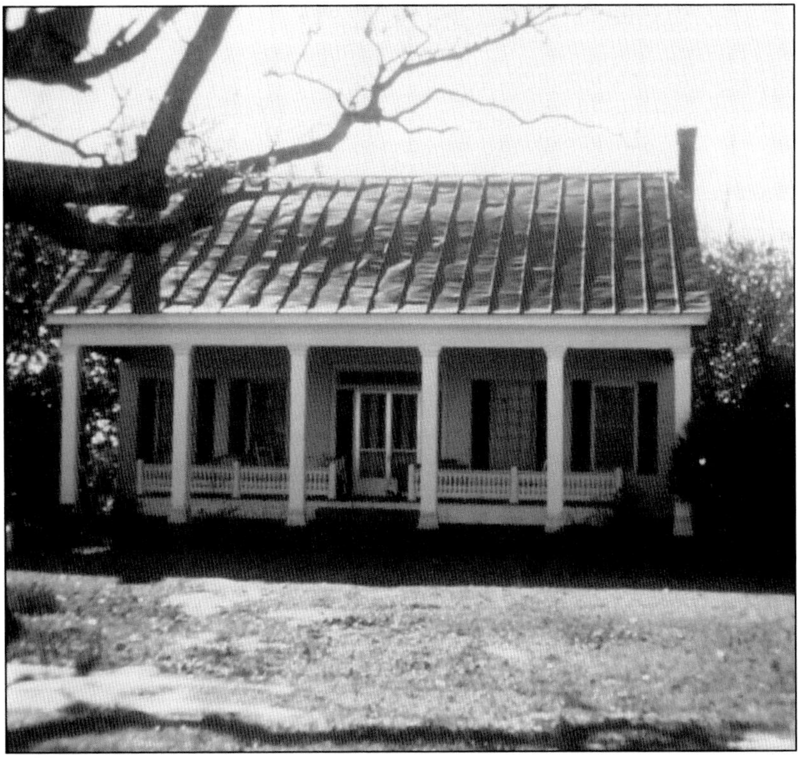

The Joseph Helms home on Centenary Road is today the residence of Charles and Nancy Parker.

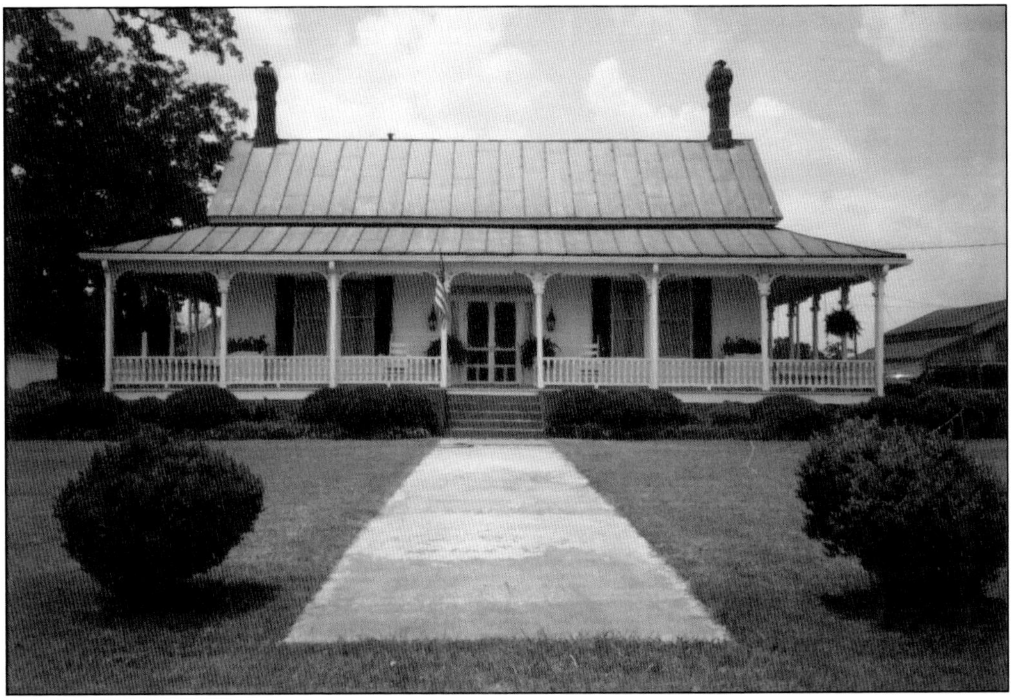

The Walker A. Meadows home on Porter Road has been home to generations: Walker and Annie Meadows; Joe Walker and Mary Ann Meadows; Joe Walker and Kemper Meadows; and Joe and Wendy Meadows.

The home of Joe Dykes Bullard and Jane Bullard on Porter Road has been in the Bullard family for several generations.

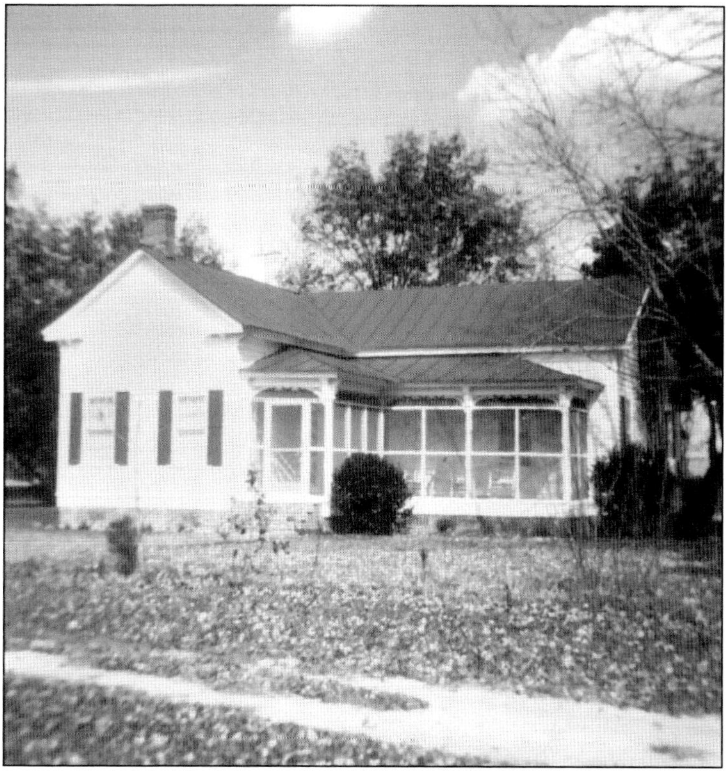

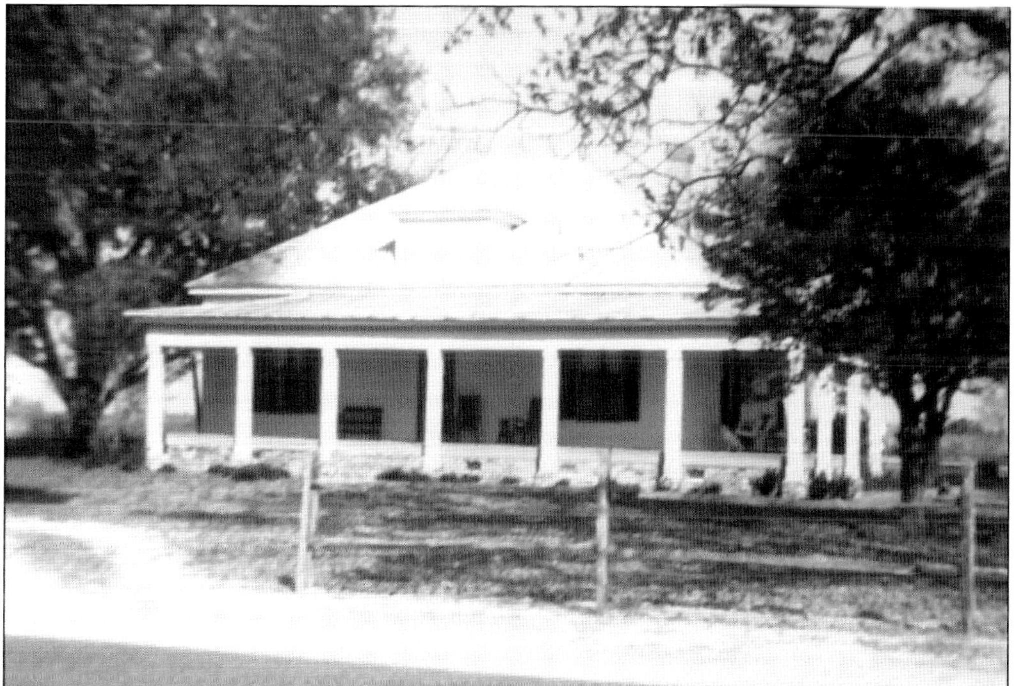

The home of Snell Coley and Druscilla Bullard Coley on Porter Road was later the home of Emory and Linda Peacock Porter. It is today the home of Hugh "Red" and Patsy Waller.

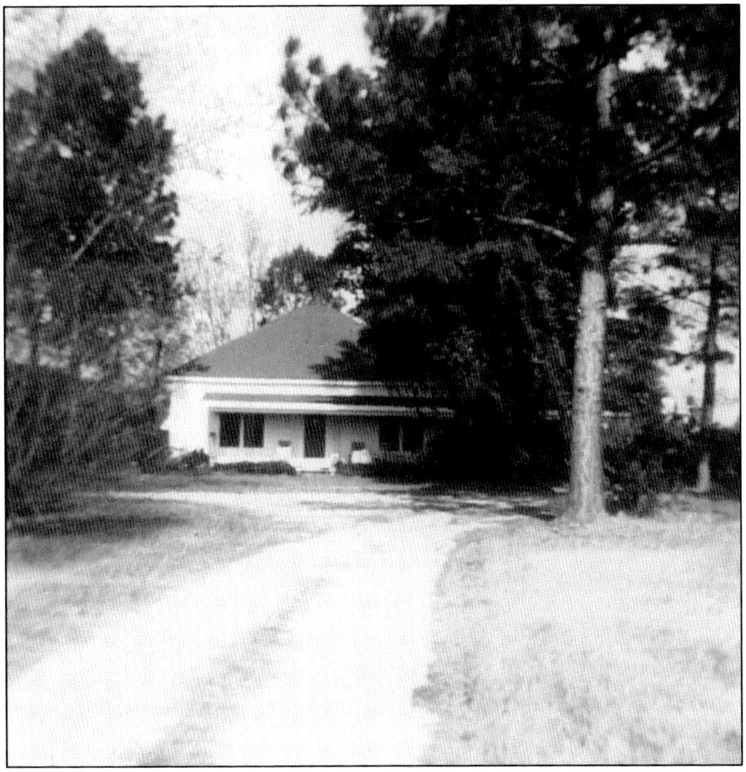

The John F. Fordham home on the Macon State Highway remains in the same family and is today owned by James W. Fordham.

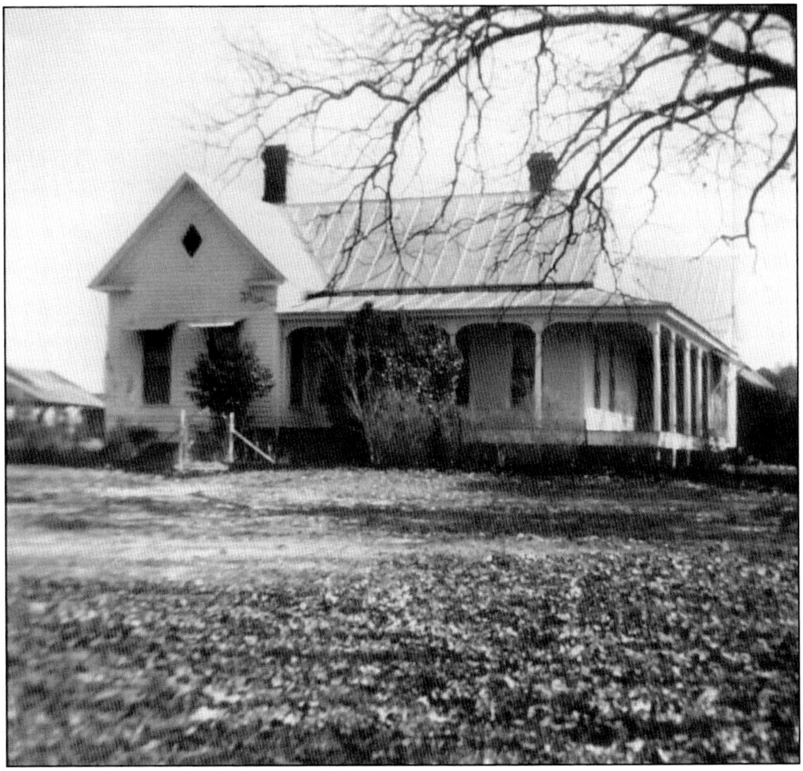

The Tobe and Ella Pusser Young home on Antioch Road is today owned by Earl and Wanda Barrs.

The James Beck home on Dykes Street at Fifth Street is the present location of Mathis Funeral Home.

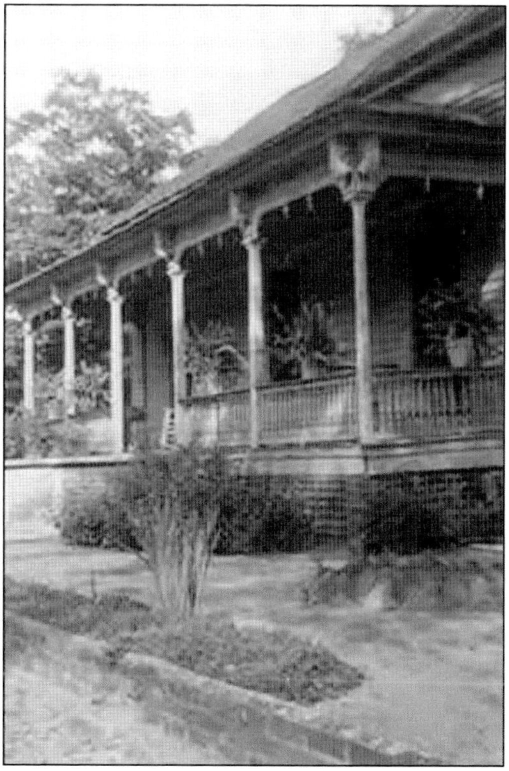

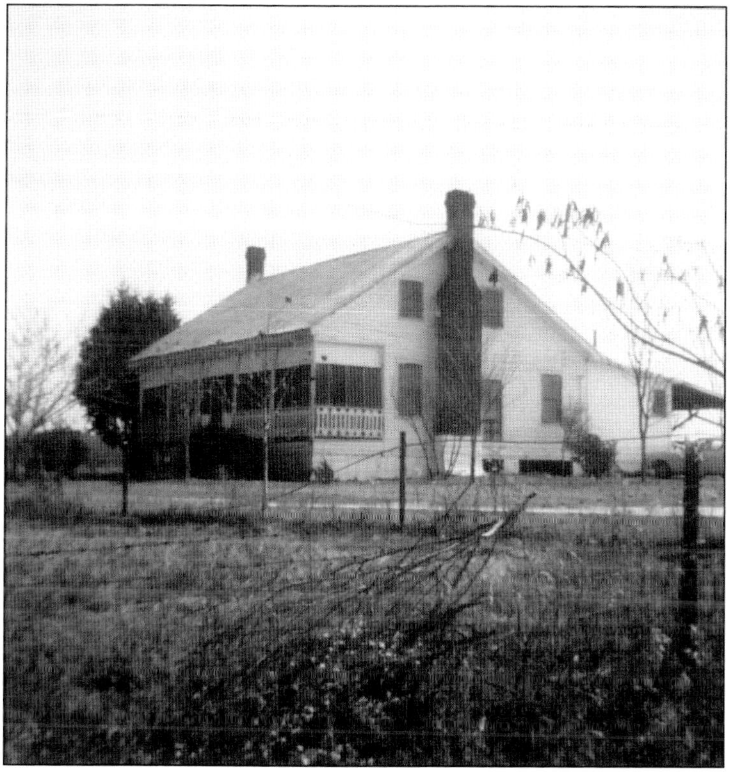

Built by John Pusser and Edith Helms Purser, this home was later the residence of I. P. and Minnie Sheffield.

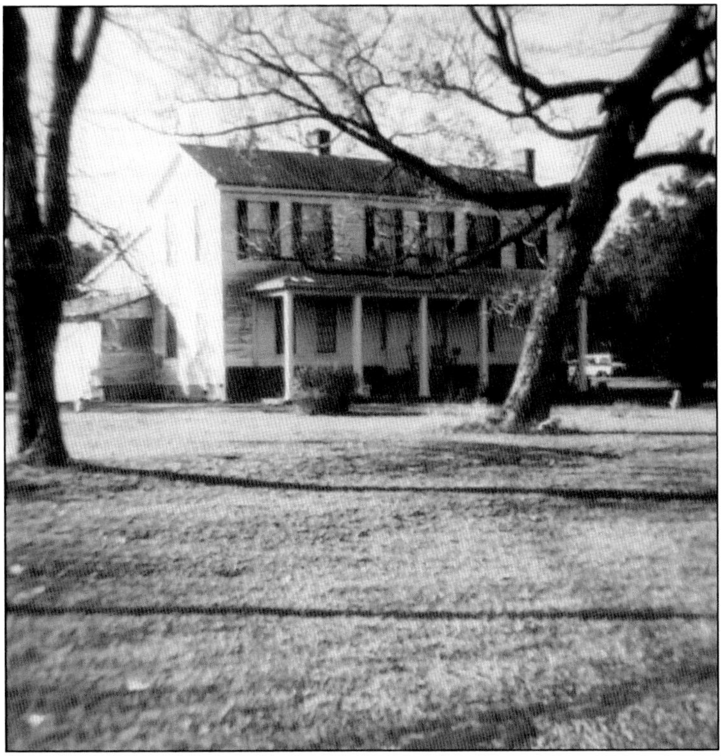

The George Walker home on Longstreet Road is the oldest home in Bleckley County. It was once the home of Joel Shedd Sr.and his wife, Inez.

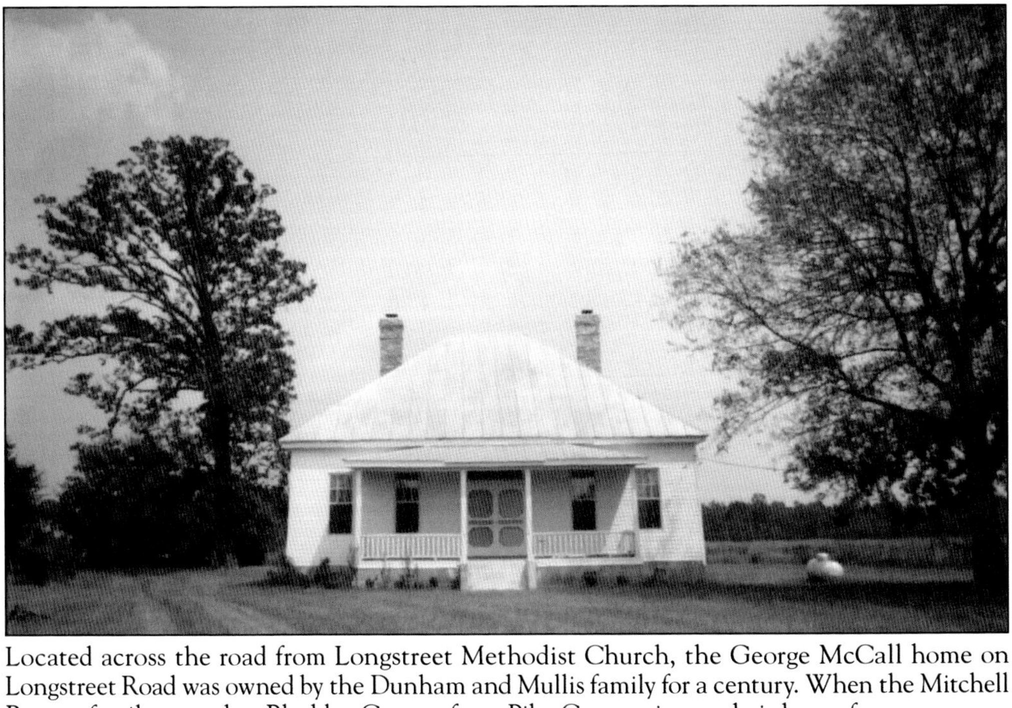

Located across the road from Longstreet Methodist Church, the George McCall home on Longstreet Road was owned by the Dunham and Mullis family for a century. When the Mitchell Barrow family moved to Bleckley County from Pike County, it was their home for many years. In the 1970s, it was renovated and restored by Mattie Lee Mullis Baxley, and today it is owned by the family of Dr. B. B. Sanders.

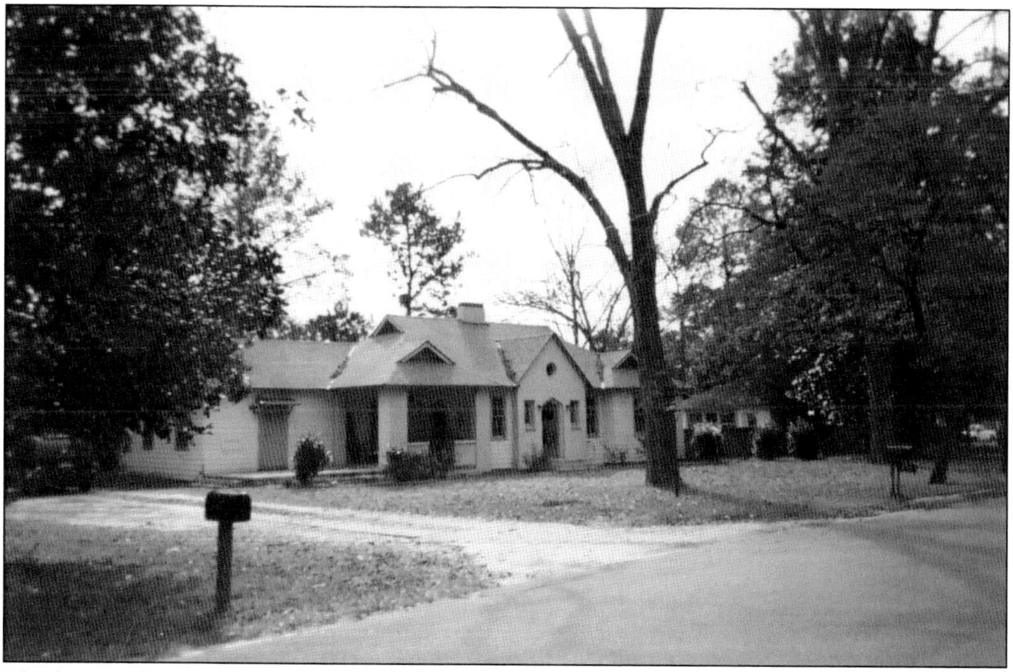

The home of J. Luther Horne and Nell Duncan Horne on Beech Street is today the home of Mayor Cliff and Allison Avant.

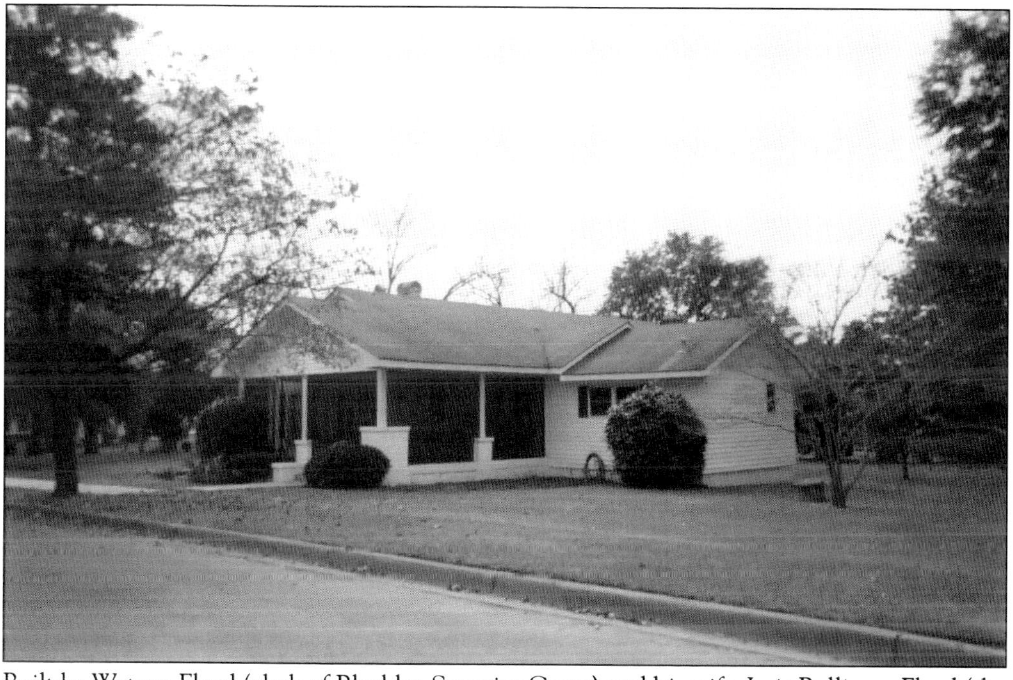

Built by Watson Floyd (clerk of Bleckley Superior Court) and his wife, Lois Bollinger Floyd (the first female clerk of Bleckley Superior Court after the death of her husband), this Rose Street home was later the home of Andrew and Dolores Peacock Kingery and of Doug and Barbara Goen. It is today the residence of James E. and Teri Coley Adams.

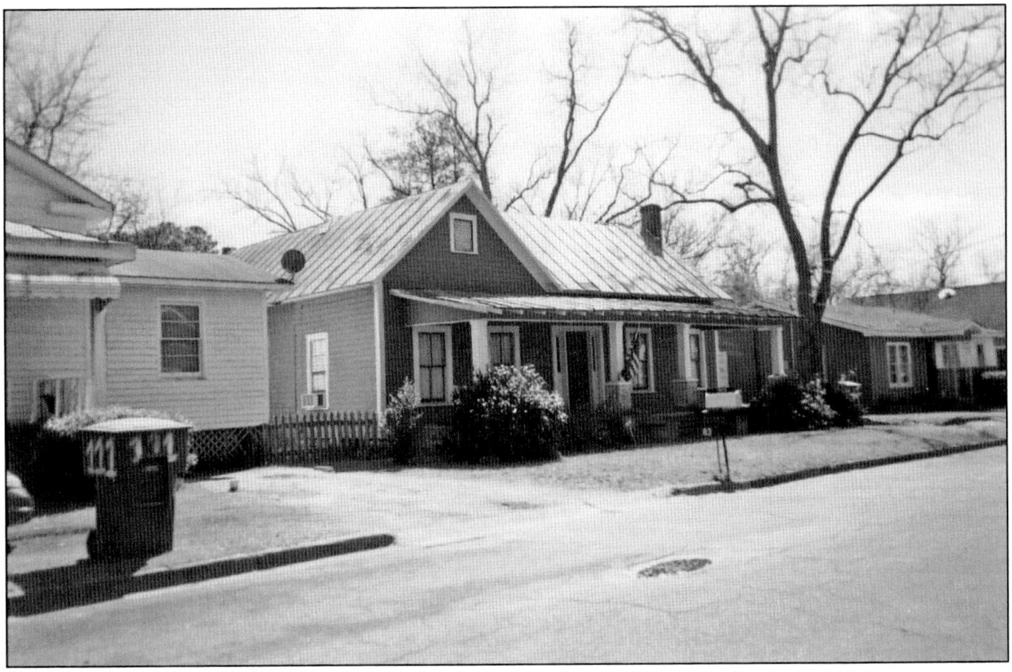

W. A. Redmond was the founder of the Cochran Hardware Store. His home on Violet Street was later the residence of Hewell E. and Susie Hammack and is today the home of George Ronnie Smith and Donna Scarborough Smith.

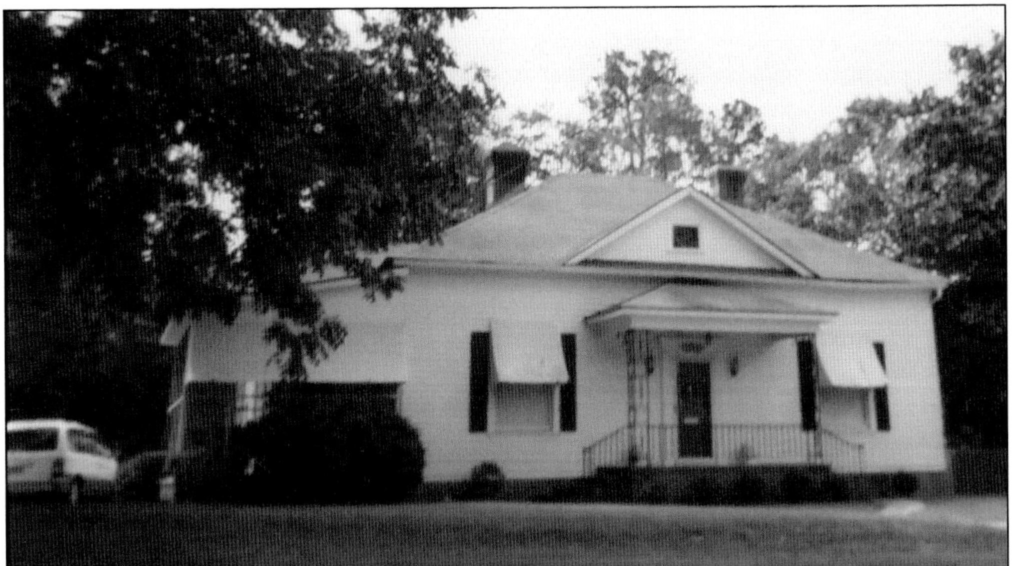

The home of J. J. Taylor and Lida Morris Taylor on Beech Street is today the home of John G. and Melanie Eubanks.

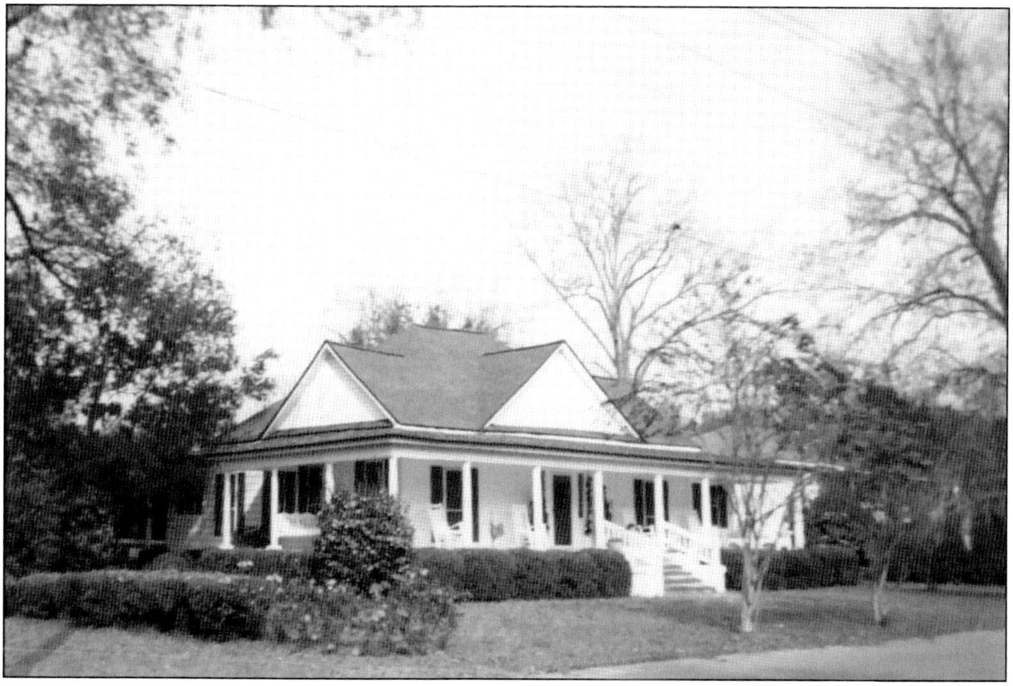

Built by Prior Greene Purser and occupied by members of the Purser family for many years, this Beech Street home is today the residence of Wyndall Ray Simmons and his wife, Sue.

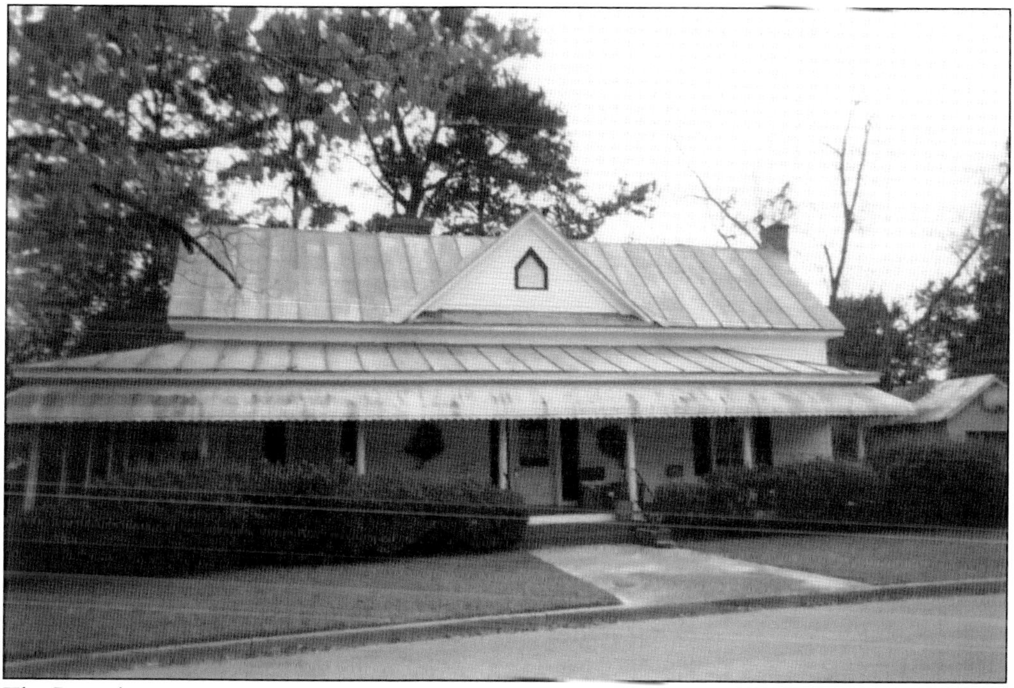

The Daniel Morgan Forehand and Rosa Jones Forehand family occupied this Violet Street home until 1977. Mr. Forehand was clerk of Bleckley Superior Court from 1948 to 1966. It is today the home of Louis and Willene Wimberly Foster.

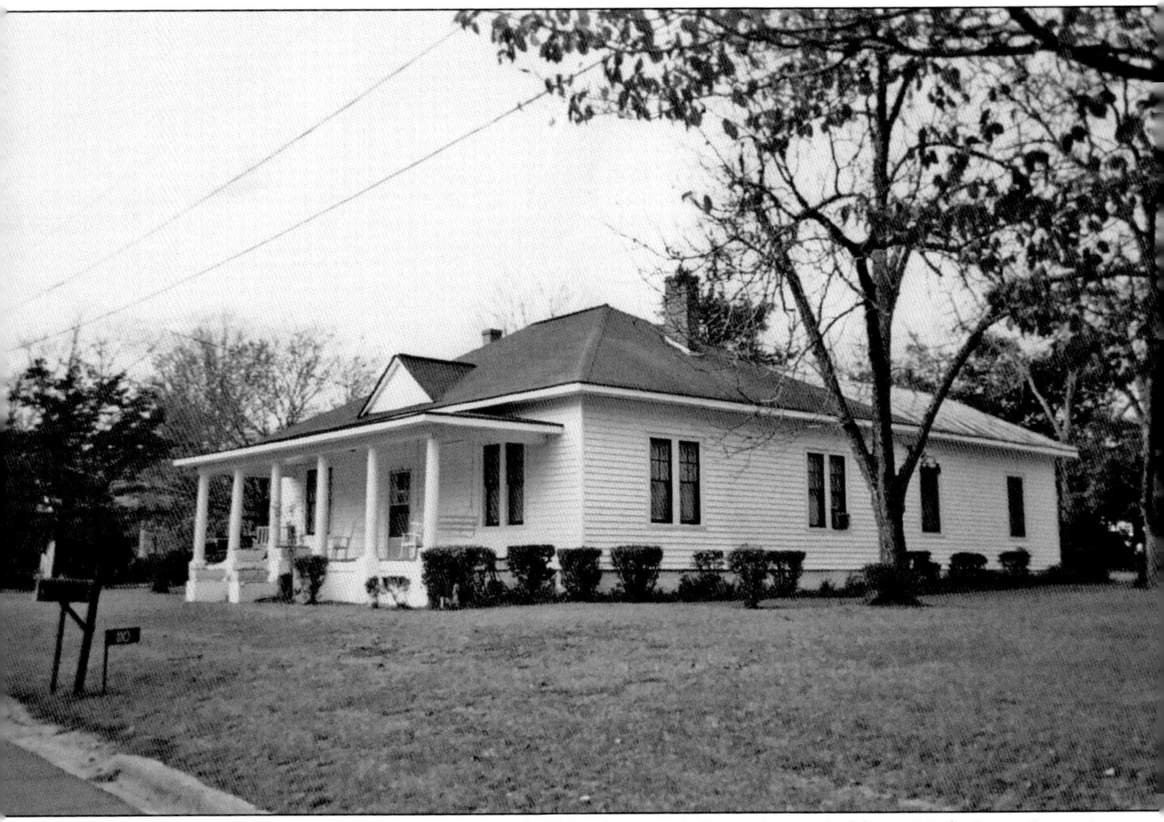

Nolan Henry Barlow and Frances Berryhill Barlow and their three children, Nola Jean, Lonnie, and Mary Anne, occupied this home at 110 Violet Street for 36 years. It is today the home of Evelyn Horne.

AFTERWORD

In the small town of Cochran and the community of Bleckley County in the heart of middle Georgia, we have known the love of so many good people through the years—parents, spouses, teachers, ministers, friends, and loved ones. In these homes, the love of a mother and father, of sisters and brothers, and of family was learned. Home is the place to remember when we were young, newly married, raising a family, or enjoying grandchildren. Home is that place where we long with all our heart to be once more. The ones who lived in these homes spent their days in service and died in the confident hope of seeing God and of seeing each other again in heaven. The 20th century was their turn to lay a foundation, to preserve, and to pass on to future generations a heritage so that those who live here today may know the values that were woven together by a thread of love in homes, schools, churches, and governments in a community we cherish so much.